BLACK PLAYS

Chameleon by Michael Ellis, *Lonely Cowboy*
Depths by Tunde Ikoli and *Basin* by Jacqueline Rudet.

Chameleon, *The Lower Depths* and *Basin* each carry a preface by the playwright; Alfred Fagon, author of *Lonely Cowboy*, died suddenly in 1986 before completing his preface and we have reproduced in its place his obituary notice from *The Times* and a poem written for his Memorial Service by T-Bone Wilson. The editor, Yvonne Brewster, opens the volume with an introduction to the plays.

YVONNE BREWSTER has worked extensively in theatre, film, television and radio both as an actress and director. In 1965 she began her career as a director by co-founding The Barn, Jamaica's first professional theatre, with Trevor Rhone. The Barn is dedicated to staging new plays from the Caribbean and Africa and celebrated its 21st anniversary in 1986. For the past fifteen years, Yvonne Brewster has lived in England working primarily as a director. Her most recent productions include: C.L.R. James's *The Black Jacobins* for Talawa Theatre Company, Dennis Scott's *Echo in the Bone* and *School's Out* by Trevor Rhone. In 1986, she became Associate Director at the Half Moon Theatre, London, where her first production was *Trash* by Barbara Gloudon.

in the same series
PEACE PLAYS
(*The Fence* by Common Ground; *The Celebration of Kokura* by Berta Freistadt;
Clam by Deborah Levy; *Keeping Body and Soul Together* by Stephen Lowe;
The Tragedy of King Real by Adrian Mitchell)
Introduced and edited by Stephen Lowe
HOW THE VOTE WAS WON: AND OTHER SUFFRAGETTE PLAYS
(*How the Vote Was Won* by Cicely Hamilton and Christopher St John; *Votes for
Women* by Elizabeth Robins; *Lady Geraldine's Speech* by Beatrice Harraden;
A Chat With Mrs Chicky and *Miss Appleyard's Awakening* by Evelyn Glover;
A Women's Influence by Gertrude Jennings; *The Apple* by Inez Bensusan) Edited
by Dale Spender and Carole Hayman with an Introduction by Dale Spender and
Notes on Performance by Carole Hayman
PLAYS BY WOMEN: VOLUME ONE
(*Vinegar Tom* by Caryl Churchill; *Dusa, Fish, Stas and Vi* by Pam Gems;
Tissue by Louise Page; *Aurora Leigh* by Michelene Wandor)
Introduced and edited by Micheline Wandor
PLAYS BY WOMEN: VOLUME TWO
(*Rites* by Maureen Duffy; *Letters Home* by Rose Leiman Goldemberg;
Trafford Tanzi by Claire Luckham; *Find Me* by Olwen Wymark)
Introduced and edited by Michelene Wandor
PLAYS BY WOMEN: VOLUME THREE
(*Aunt Mary* by Pam Gems; *Red Devils* by Debbie Horsfield; *Blood Relations* by
Sharon Pollock; *Time Pieces* by Lou Wakefield and The Women's Theatre Group)
Introduced and edited by Michelene Wandor
PLAYS BY WOMEN: VOLUME FOUR
(*Objections to Sex and Violence* by Caryl Churchill; *Rose's Story* by Grace
Dayley; *Blood and Ice* by Liz Lochhead; *Pinball* by Alison Lyssa)
Introduced and edited by Michelene Wandor
PLAYS BY WOMEN: VOLUME FIVE
(*Queen Christina* by Pam Gems; *A Raisin in the Sun* by Lorraine Hansberry;
Piper's Cave by Rona Munro; *Money to Live* by Jacqueline Rudet)
Selected and introduced by Mary Remnant
GAY PLAYS: VOLUME ONE
(*Submariners* by Tom McClenaghan; *The Green Bay Tree* by Mordaunt Shairp;
Passing By by Martin Sherman; *Accounts* by Michael Wilcox)
Introduced and edited by Michael Wilcox
GAY PLAYS: VOLUME TWO
(*Quaint Honour* by Roger Gellert; *Bearclaw* by Timothy Mason; *Cracks* by
Martin Sherman; *Lies About Vietnam* by C.P. Taylor)
Introduced and edited by Michael Wilcox

BLACK PLAYS

CHAMELEON
by
Michael Ellis

LONELY COWBOY
by
Alfred Fagon

THE LOWER DEPTHS
– an East End story –
by
Tunde Ikoli

BASIN
by
Jacqueline Rudet

Selected and introduced by
Yvonne Brewster

A Methuen Paperback

A METHUEN THEATREFILE

This volume first published in Great Britain as a paperback original in 1987 by
Methuen London Ltd., 11 New Fetter Lane, London EC4P 4EE and in the
United States of America by Methuen Inc., 29 West 35th Street, New York, NY 10001

British Library Cataloguing in Publication Data

Black Plays: an anthology containing
   Chameleon by Michael Ellis, Lonely Cowboy
   by Alfred Fagon, The Lower Depths by
   Tunde Ikoli and Basin by Jacqueline Rudet.
   — (A Methuen theatre file).
   1. English drama — Black authors 2. English
   drama — 20th century
   I. Brewster, Yvonne
   822'.914'080896   PR1246.B5

   ISBN 0-413-15710-5

Printed in Great Britain by
Richard Clay Ltd, Bungay, Suffolk

CONTENTS

INTRODUCTION

This is the first anthology ever of plays written by and about black people living in Britain. In the forties very few plays written by a black person were performed in this country, in fact only C.L.R. James's *The Black Jacobins* springs to mind. Then the trail-blazing American Negro Theatre Company brought *Anna Lucasta* to the World Theatre Festival at the Aldwych Theatre. The play, although not written by a black man was performed by an all black cast.

In the fifties Lorraine Hansberry's *A Raisin in the Sun*, and James Baldwin's *Amen Corner* (brought over from the United States, lock, stock and barrel) were both West End successes. It could well be noted here that both these plays have recently been produced again in this country in the Fringe. Then in 1956 the young Errol John won the Observer Playwrighting competition with his haunting *Moon on a Rainbow Shawl* and his play was given a main house production at the Royal Court. Barry Reckord's *Flesh to a Tiger*, *Della*, *You in your Small Corner* and *Skyvers* were all soon to be seen in Sloane Square.

These small important beginnings have led us to the eighties when some now consider Black Theatre to be one of the most vibrant areas in the cultural life of the nation. Yet most black playwrights living in this country, with the exception of Mustapha Matura, Caryl Phillips and Edgar White, have had few opportunities of seeing their work in print. This volume is an attempt to begin to put that right. The book is more than timely when one considers the emphasis which the funding bodies have recently been placing on the cultural needs and the work of the black community. The work of those who live in this country must become more accessible; if not, then the work of playwrights living in the Caribbean and Africa will continue to dominate the scene as their plays are more readily available in the Educational editions meant for the schools of the Third World. These 'source' plays establish vital links with essential cultural roots, but the indigenous voice is just as important.

Chameleon: Michael Ellis's play is totally irreverent in style and resolution. The play looks at the horizons of two black people, one female and one male. Benjamin inhabits the dungeon of a large insurance office building. He tries not to disturb those on the higher floors in case they see him and he loses his tenuous foothold on what he thinks is his ladder to success. Marcia realises Benjamin is buried and attempts to disinter him. It is a straight-talking, fast-shooting play which presents a microcosm of our society with wit and energy.

Lonely Cowboy: Alfred Fagon came to this country from Jamaica in 1955.

He began writing slowly and instinctively. There is a deceptive naïveté about his work and some may make the mistake of taking his work on face value; its narrative element is indeed beguiling, but for me *Lonely Cowboy* is more about black people's right to be tragic than it is about a newly-opened café in Brixton. The threads which weave the story together pull us downhill to the last tragic scene. Before Alfred Fagon died so suddenly in 1986, I made sure he wanted to use his original ending in this volume. The sheer wonderful madness of leaving most characters dead or dying at the end of what might have been seen as a light comedy of Brixton manners is part the magic of the piece for me. It is also interesting to hear the viewpoint of a writer nearing fifty years old on the concerns and development of a Black British population, and the subtly captured rythms and the speech eccentricities of a generation raised by immigrants makes this play rewarding.

The Lower Depths: Tunde Ikoli is virtually a growth industry in himself. These days his work is in demand in all areas of the media. He belongs to a rare school of Black British playwrights whose work is even enjoying revivals! One might rightly ask why choose an adaptation when there is so much more from which to choose? Because it's very good theatre, with wonderful parts, crackling dialogue, and because the adaptation is somehow so much the work of an alien eye on the status quo. This will be the first Ikoli play to be published and I am sure it will lead the way for a host of others.

Basin: Jacqueline Rudet writes modern, uncompromising plays. Basin sensitively portrays the world of the younger black woman in metropolitan Britain today. In dealing with lesbianism and by not falling into the trap of being modish, by taking care not to draw her conclusions predictably or too comfortably, she helps pave the way for more and more serious black women playwrights to appear.

Living as part of a 'minority' in England whose artistic voice could become subsumed in the feverish maelstrom of theatrical activity, we have to ensure that we remain truly visible and audible. We can do this in our honest plays.

Yvonne Brewster, 1987

CHAMELEON

MICHAEL ELLIS was born in the East End of London in the mid-fifties. His parents are Jamaican, his mother a nurse and his father a sheet metal worker. While still at school, Michael Ellis began writing articles, book and music reviews for the local and West Indian press. In 1981, he won the best newcomer ACER penmanship Award for Black writers. His other plays include: *A Temporary Rupture* (Lambeth Ensemble Theatre, 1983; Bridge Theatre, 1986) and *Starliner 2001, A Soap Odyssey*, (Copyright Theatre, 1984).

Author's Preface

'I read *The Chameleon* and I just wanted to take a look at you really,' said the famous Black American playwright from his leather chair. 'It most probably will never go on, of course; audiences are not really interested in relationships *between* Black people but I thought we'd have a chat anyway before I left for the States.'

What did he mean? I've never been able to decipher the strange tongues of theatre people. He went on speaking as if I was about to become a casualty. He had his finger on the button and I just wasn't clued-in. On the Hampstead bus back to Brixton I looked over the script of *Chameleon* again. It is based on comic-tragic personal experience telling the tale of Benjamin, born in Jamaica and coming to England to make it anyway, anyhow, and Marcia, born and bred in Britain whose sole priority is to make sure the indignities of her youth are not visited on her child. When Marcia joins the large insurance company that Benjamin has already worked in for seven years, Benjamin is terrified that Marcia's 'attitude' will bring him down. I'd met 'a Benjamin' while working as an accounts clerk. He wouldn't speak to me or any other Black people in the company. Fine. But when we found ourselves alone in that great leveller, the bog (the workers' bog actually, it was that sort of company) he spoke. The bolt out of the blue nearly made me miss the urinal and zap his shiny black shoes. 'You must wonder why I never speak to you at work?' I nodded dumbly trying to keep my aim true.

He explained to be seen chatting to other Blacks could ruin his prospects, he wanted to get ahead. He too spoke as if he was clued-in to the thing that would make me a casualty. He had worked in an insurance company and . . . A white face walked in and we never spoke again.

The head of Temba Theatre, Alby James, liked the script. He took time out to knock it into shape and along with Paulette Randall directed *Chameleon*'s first production at The Oval House, South East London in January 1985. The critics were lukewarm to out-and-out hostile (are these the people the playwright so dreaded?) but audiences took to it. The scheduled nine-month national tour was extended to the end of January '86, the play being re-cast three times. The sky didn't fall in as forecast; instead there were reports of *Chameleon* spawning two new drama groups in its wake – although there was another report of an audience accusing the cast of inciting the Tottenham Riots.(?)

Michael J. Ellis

Chameleon was first presented at The Oval House, South East London on 23 January 1985. The cast was as follows:

BENJAMIN HOWARD *Flashy West Indian, early thirties* — Junior Walker

MARCIA JACKSON *elegant and attractive West Indian (British Black); early twenties* — Susan Harper-Browne

Directed by Alby James and Paulette Randall
Designed by Paddy Kamara

Set: a rather bare basement office. Two desks, a filing cabinet, a rubber plant, a hatstand, desk lamps, a cupboard and a telephone.

Lights up on **BENJAMIN** *alone on stage. He addresses the audience.*

BENJAMIN: Hi! My name's Benjamin. I've come to talk to you about . . . about everything. About things slipping through your fingers. About things going rotten. About things being turned upside down and inside out. About children with snotty noses telling you to fuck off. About empty churches and dangerous streets. Na, na, I'm not talking about cruising Christians looking for bovver. Take me for example: I'm what your ethnic magazines call a Black achiever. I'm into the real world. I've got a Mercedes, a mortgage and an expensive woman. I've put a foot where few Black men have put a foot before. (*Pointing up to the heavens.*) I'm going up there baby. Up there. I've got a good position and the future looks bright if I keep my nose clean. I'm in insurance. A fascinating world. It's a little world with rules all of its own. 'Invisible earnings' they're sometimes called. And that's exactly what they are, invisible. All this money comes out of nowhere, for nothing in particular, for little or no reason. Anyway, back to the point: er . . . oh yeah, things being turned upside down and inside out just when they seemed to be going so well. Let me tell you about it. There I am minding my own business, waiting for the inevitable promotion to be thrust upon me when along comes this chick: Marcia. Straight away I had to check for my vitals in case she'd blown them clean away. Anyway, this was her first day working as my new secretary, the first of only five as it worked out for reasons you'll soon find out.

Lights up on whole office. MARCIA *enters following* BENJAMIN.

BENJAMIN: Welcome to my office said the spider to the fly. Some might call this the arsehole of the building.

MARCIA *takes offence at the word arsehole but* BENJAMIN *doesn't notice. Unhurriedly,* MARCIA *looks around the office.*

Search parties have been known to need search parties to find their way out of here.

BENJAMIN*'s all teeth and gestures as he laughs.* MARCIA *doesn't.*

It's a pity you couldn't have come a little earlier, I could have introduced you to our Managing Director, Mr Hamilton-Forsyth, himself. He doesn't often come down here. But still, another time maybe, eh? Buses always make you late, don't they? I drive to work myself. Anyway Miss Jackson, this is where you and I are going to be working. Cosy isn't it?

MARCIA: Excuse me. (*As she tries to pass him.*)

BENJAMIN: It's not a bad little office – well, as far as offices go these days. This, of course, is just a stop over for me. The office I had before was much larger than this with lots of rubber plants and leather swivel chairs and everything.

MARCIA: Excuse me, please. (*This time trying to get a word in edgeways.*)

BENJAMIN: However, I shall endeavour to show you round and make sure you meet all the right people. One thing that can be said for Warrington & Bridges Insurance is that they've never let the colour of a man's skin – or indeed a woman's – blind them to that individual's potential. Take myself for example –

MARCIA (*shouting*): I said excuse me!

BENJAMIN: Mmm? What is it child?

MARCIA: Is there anywhere I can hang my coat up?

BENJAMIN: Of course, of course. There's a hatstand just behind the door. (MARCIA *half expects* BENJAMIN *to help her off with it but he doesn't.*) That's right, the hatstand is just behind the door. Yea, this is just a stop-over for me. I want to get back to the office with the leather swivel chair and roller-coaster wheels.

MARCIA *goes to sit at the larger of the two desks.*

No honey, that's your desk over there.

She gives him a 'look' and moves over to the smaller, scruffier desk.

That's right, make yourself comfortable. Do you smoke? Have one of mine.

BENJAMIN *reaches into his pocket and produces a gold cigarette case. Offers her a cigarette and lights it with the desk lighter.*

You'll like these. You can't get them in the shops. I have them specially delivered. An articulated lorry brings them all the way from Liverpool. Well, you've got to be particular haven't you? You've only got one life, no point wasting it on second-rate rubbish is there? Some people live their whole lives never taking a chance on the best things in life, saving it all for some mythical day in the future only to find that that mythical day catches up with them on their death beds. Too late then isn't it, Miss Jackson? No second chances are there?

No response from MARCIA.

Well, I think we'll be off to a good start if I tell you a little about myself.

MARCIA: Lard God.

BENJAMIN: I've worked my way up to where I am today: Head of the Expenses and Petty Cash Department. It's a responsible job but I don't let it get to me. Oh no, I pride myself on being able to handle all situations, taking all the possibilities into account. That's how I earned my Mercedes. I don't drive it to work, you understand. I use the company car for that. There's a lot of envious eyes who wouldn't like to see a Black man on anything better than a pogo stick. Let's face it, it can never be easy being a Black executive in a company as big as this. Now, are there any questions you'd like to ask me?

MARCIA: Yes, there is one. When, if ever, do you manage to take in oxygen?

BENJAMIN: What? Oh, you mean the windows. You're wondering where the windows are? Well, we're too low down for windows. We just have that air vent there, see?

MARCIA: I can see that I'm going to have to struggle for my share of the supply.

BENJAMIN: You know what they say, Marcia . . . it's all right to call you Marcia?

MARCIA: I suppose so.

BENJAMIN: Now what were you doing before to keep body and soul together?

MARCIA: I was a typist in a bank.

BENJAMIN: A typist in a bank, eh? Put it there.

He holds out his hands to be slapped 'soul style'. She ignores the gesture.

Did you like it?

MARCIA: No.

BENJAMIN: Oh? Why?

MARCIA: Because the work was boring and trivial and the people were two-faced boring farts.

BENJAMIN: Er, right . . . right. Well, you won't find that here. Oh, no.

Straightens up as if he's going to make a speech.

The people here are straightforward and I think you'll find the world of insurance an intriguing one. All this money comes out of nowhere and sits in hallowed vaults all over the world committing perpetual incest with itself, coming and coming – if you know what I mean – and voilà, there's more of the stuff everywhere.

MARCIA (*looking around suspiciously*): Is this room bugged?

BENJAMIN: What?

MARCIA: You mean you're for real? Jesus help us all. Look, I have to call my mother, make sure she has the telephone number in case something happens.

She picks up the phone and dials.

BENJAMIN: What, is she sick?

MARCIA: No, she's looking after my son.

BENJAMIN: Oh, you're one of them.

MARCIA: What do you mean 'you're one of them'?

BENJAMIN: Oh, you've got a child, have you. How old is he/she?

MARCIA: *He's* six. I'm keeping him away from school at the moment as a sort of protest so my mum's looking after him.

BENJAMIN: Don't you know it's illegal in this country to keep children away from school?

MARCIA: All of us on the Afro-Asian Committee are doing it until they remove all the books containing black stereotypes. Would you believe it, after all these years they're still reading *Tom Sawyer* and *The Adventures of Huckleberry Finn* in primary schools?

Speaking on the phone.

Hello, Mummy, it's me ... Mummy, don't shout, it's a telephone not a megaphone. Listen, my number is 352 1111 and the extension is 118 ... No 1, 1, 8. How's Tony? ... Good ... No, we've got no idea. We're miles underground here. If a pipe was to burst you know what we'd be up to our eyes in, don't you? ... No, there's just the two of us ... No, he's Black ... I think ... All right if you're not choosey ... Look Mummy, I've got to be going. Don't forget I'll be late back. I'm going to picket outside the school as soon as I'm though here ... OK, OK ... Look, Mummy, I'll see you later. Kiss Tony for me ... Yes, bye.

She puts the telephone down.

Very sweet but you can't get a word in edgeways.

BENJAMIN: With my mother everything is 'back home'. 'Back home' this and 'Back home' that If 'back home' is such a paradise on earth I don't know why any of them bothered to come here. It would have saved us all a lot of trouble.

MARCIA: I don't know. She sounds like a lady who knows where her head is, to me.

BENJAMIN: Head in Jamaica, feet in England, spirit in Africa. How does she manage to get clothes to fit such an international physique?

MARCIA: What people like you don't understand is that home for us will always be 'back home'.

BENJAMIN: Is them the kind of character-building proteins you feeding your boy?

MARCIA: Oh Mother!

MARCIA *has noticed the portrait photograph on his desk and picks it up and speaks, amazed.*

MARCIA: Benjamin, how can you work with so much pork staring at you?

BENJAMIN: Pork?

MARCIA: You know, white people. This photograph on your desk.

BENJAMIN *gets up and grabs the photograph.*

BENJAMIN: Pork! That's most unusual phraseology. I don't think I'm familiar with it.

MARCIA: You know, we're beef? Brown, hot and juicy. Well, they're pork: white cold and clammy.

BENJAMIN (*looking hot and uneasy*): We?

MARCIA: You know, Blacks! I'd go mad if I had that staring at me from close quarters all day.

BENJAMIN: We should be getting rid of those silly racial insults, not inventing more.

MARCIA: Oh, that's not really an insult. No, that's more like a good definition. So, who is that?

BENJAMIN (*putting it into his drawer*): Miss Hamilton-Forsyth, my intended and sweetheart.

MARCIA: You mean the boss's daughter?

BENJAMIN: I don't waste my time on rubbish.

MARCIA: I don't believe it, I just don't believe he's for real.

BENJAMIN: Marcia, I hope there's nothing on your mind.

MARCIA: On my mind?

BENJAMIN: Yes. I hope there's nothing on it ... if you see what I mean. If there is I'd like to feel you could talk to me about it. These things usually feel better after they've been explained away and it would be better to talk to me than someone else in the company. You know, they're such gossips these people, things get around ... Is there anything you want to talk about?

MARCIA: No.

BENJAMIN: Oh. Good. I wouldn't like to think you were brooding about anything.

MARCIA: No, I'm fine.

BENJAMIN: Good ... Now I've got a report to be typed. All the figures and comments are there, just copy them.

He hands her some papers.

One hapless fool made the mistake of losing those figures and Mr Hamilton-Forsyth banned him from the executive dining and washrooms for one whole week. Well, that won't happen to me so be careful what you do with them. Give them straight back to me when you've finished.

MARCIA: Where's the typing paper kept.

BENJAMIN: Oh, there. Over there in the bottom drawer of the filing cabinet.

MARCIA goes over to the filing cabinet. BENJAMIN admires her figure.

MARCIA: What sort of paper shall I use: blank or letter-head?

BENJAMIN: I'd use blank if I was you. Always make it blank when it's internal.

She returns to her desk and proceeds to type efficiently. BENJAMIN continues to watch her. MARCIA looks up, he looks away. He relaxes and runs his fingers along the edge of the desk.

One thing you must remember, Marcia, is never to call our guys here salesmen. They don't like it. Financial or Investment Consultants are the titles they prefer. It stands to reason really becau- Lord God, have mercy! (*Lapsing into a broader patois accent.*) The blood clart ting jook in me rarted finger! Oh, God, the pain! Help me, Marcia.

MARCIA *stops typing.*

MARCIA: What's the matter? What's happened?

BENJAMIN: A splinter! It's gone right through to the bone.

BENJAMIN *holds the offending finger up for her to see.*

MARCIA: Hang on, I'll get it out for you.

MARCIA *collects some tweezers from her handbag.*

Hold still. I'm very good at getting splinters out.

MARCIA *concentrates. Through his sobs* BENJAMIN *takes a good look at her.*

BENJAMIN: Is it bad?

MARCIA: I don't know. Have you made your will?

BENJAMIN: Don't jest woman. That may not look much to you but to my finger that's a whole javelin.

MARCIA *removes the splinter.*

MARCIA: Look, that's all it is, you baby.

BENJAMIN: Take it away. Look, I'm bleeding. You know, I wanted so much to be a doctor. If only God hadn't invented blood. Have you got a band aid?

MARCIA: For what? Sheesh!

MARCIA *gets an oversized band aid from her handbag.*

Is this one big enough for you?

BENJAMIN: It's all right for you to laugh but bacteria can get in anywhere. They just wait for an opportunity like this to get into your system. I've known men to have lost fingers, arms, their whole lives because of something like this.

MARCIA: Benjamin, were you dropped on your head as a baby?

BENJAMIN: A man in my position can't afford the luxury of getting poisoned. Thank God you were here. Women know how to deal with these situations.

BENJAMIN *is exhausted.*

Situations are always arising: situations that need decisions, decisive decisions. Of course, they hardly ever happen down here but if they do I like to feel I'm ready.

MARCIA (*looking at her watch*): Ain't we supposed to get some coffee about now?

BENJAMIN: We are but we won't. The tea-woman says it's too far down the stairs for her to come. It gives her bunions hell!

MARCIA: I don't care about her feet. So long as she doesn't stick them in the coffee she can wear them down to the bone.

BENJAMIN: Well, she's a right battleaxe. It's best to leave her to her business.

BENJAMIN *gets out a copy of 'The Times'.*

MARCIA: Is that so. Well I ain't going

thirsty for her. I want what I'm entitled to. I'm not begging for anything; it's part of my pay. Now what floor is Mr Hamilton 'super-hyphen' on? Sixteenth, I think.

BENJAMIN (*panic*): Where are you going? You can't . . .

MARCIA: And while I'm up there I might as well see him about the ventilation down here and luncheon vouchers. I haven't had any luncheon vouchers yet.

BENJAMIN: You can't just go up there like that. You need an appointment.

MARCIA: He'll need an appointment with me. There are certain organisations that would like to know about these sweat-shop conditions.

BENJAMIN: There are procedures.

MARCIA: I'm going to starve and evaporate and you're going to tell me about red tape!

BENJAMIN: Please, Marcia; you've got to cool down. I'll sort this out for you.

Leading her back to her chair.

Please just sit down. Please. I promise I'll sort it out for you.

MARCIA *sits.* BENJAMIN *looks relieved.* BENJAMIN *goes back to 'The Times'.*

BENJAMIN: Gold is up, baggies are down.

He turns the page and soon after begins to laugh.

Black people are the only people in the world who would allow it: virginity tests. Jesus Christ, amazing.

In a mock colonial accent.

'Excuse me, madam, there is just one more formality to perform before you enter our green and pleasant land', says he pouring Dettol over his index finger. I can't remember us giving them virginity tests before they took over our land. (*He laughs.*)

MARCIA: No, you men were too busy trying to make sure the old dip stick and nuts didn't become a stuffed trophy on a Surbiton mantlepiece. Anyway, can you imagine them trying to do that to a West Indian?

BENJAMIN: What!? When a Jamaican woman go fe holler blue murder you got fe pray that the Lord has mercy on your nervous system. It's like the scream of the banshee.

MARCIA (*enjoying this joke*): Send you into a coma for days on end, bwoy.

BENJAMIN: I remember my mum's hollering. Jeeesus! Especially when she did it without warning, just outta the blue. (*Screams:*) WOWW! My dad would have to drink half a bottle of whisky to numb the pain. Bwoy, there was always something to shout about back in J.A. Man those days were hard. I swore I'd never court poverty like that again for as long as I live.

MARCIA: My parents are Jamaican, too, but I was born over here.

BENJAMIN: Well, ask them, girl, what it was like for some of us. I hear people over here saying how them is hungry, how them is starving, I just have to laugh. What they really mean is they are peckish. They want a little appetizer before the next meal. Bwoy, hunger is when you feel you have a football in your bowels, twice as heavy and three times as empty and you *know* there's no next meal that day.

MARCIA: You weren't ever like that.

BENJAMIN: What you know gal? It was like that right up till I turn twelve. That's when I joined my mother over here.

MARCIA: I thought you said your mother was in J.A.

BENJAMIN: That's my granny. My real mum was over here. She wasn't too happy to see me either. Man, she give me some hot licks the night I arrived. Bwoy! She believed in starting as she meant to go on.

MARCIA: She beat you the day you arrived?

BENJAMIN: Well, not only was I an extra unwelcome burden, I'm also the spitting image of my father, wherever he is.

MARCIA: I can't say I remember hunger. Well not that sort. I remember a hunger for friendship at school. I was very much an object of curiosity. You know, those stupid comments: 'Can I touch your hair?' 'When do you know if you're dirty?' 'Is it easier to breathe through your nostrils?' That sort of thing. What with that plus the images of us in those books – Do you realise those pictures always showed us chained up, caricatured or a diseased corpse? Well, your credentials have to be better than that to join in even the playground games.

BENJAMIN: Yeah, man, you've got to know how to handle these people or they'll be taking your fingerprints to catch a bus.

MARCIA: I know just how to handle them.

BENJAMIN: I really know how to handle them. Gentle but firm. The velvet glove in the iron hand or whatever.

MARCIA: The supervisor at my last job was always making snide remarks.

BENJAMIN: Letting them know you'll accept no nonsense.

MARCIA: Always under her breath, little creeping remarks.

BENJAMIN: No need to gwan with a lot of bad word. Just put them gently in their place. Show them you have a good command of the English language, that you can articulate yourself.

MARCIA: I knew what she was up to and she know I knew.

BENJAMIN: Ar-tic-u-late.

MARCIA: So, one day after work I waited for her under the stairs . . .

BENJAMIN: You can tell I'm different from the rest by the way I can articulate myself.

MARCIA: . . . and gave her such an almighty slap –

BENJAMIN *jumps up as if waking with shock.*

BENJAMIN: You what?!

MARCIA: I slapped her. I slapped her so hard she was the first woman to catch a glimpse of Mars with the naked eye.

BENJAMIN: You struck your supervisor? My God!

MARCIA: Why not? She asked for it.

BENJAMIN: But . . . but striking your supervisor . . . that's completely wrong. You can't go round doing that sort of thing.

MARCIA: Well, she soon polished up her act and gave me some peace and quiet into the bargain.

BENJAMIN: Well, I hope you're not planning to do that sort of thing here?

MARCIA: Why? Do I look like a bouncer to you?

BENJAMIN: Well, that's an attitude that won't go down well here.

MARCIA: As you said, 'You've got to know how to handle these people.'

BENJAMIN: Yeah, baby, but there are ways and ways.

She finishes the typing.

MARCIA: This is finished. Do you want to check it out?

BENJAMIN: Oh, just put it in a safe place. I'll look at it some other time.

Lights down focusing on BENJAMIN *alone, addressing the audience.*

Did you hear what she said? Man, I didn't like the vibes this chick was giving off. I didn't like them one little bit. She was one of those 'I bitch therefore I am' women. And all that stuff about beef and pork, have you ever heard such nonsense? It takes just one of that kind to collapse a really good scene. Today the Salvation Army, tomorrow out in the streets like the Dirty Dozen. I've seen it before. (*Cooling down.*) But I know how to handle situations like this. I pride myself on it. No matter what the colour of the skin involved. (*Confidentially.*) Did you notice the way she was looking at me? Yea, I thought you did. Well, if I can get it together with her that'll sort out the other thing at the same time. I'm quite used to women finding me attractive but I don't let it go to my head. 'Cool' is the key word. Well, if I wasn't I wouldn't be laying the Managing Director's daughter now would I? Well, you got to be nice to somebody, haven't you? It's only fair. And why not make it a bit of class at the same time? That's the trouble with girls like Marcia: no 'Je ne sais quoi'.

That's French. You know, lacking that little bit of French polish. Anyway, Tuesday. Only her second day and she was late and came in with some cock and bull story about a lunatic dentist. I just told her to sit down. Sit down, Marcia.

Lights up on the office. MARCIA *has just entered and she is getting herself organized.*

MARCIA: I forgot to tell you yesterday. I had an appointment with the dentist.

BENJAMIN: Typical! Typical! Black people can never be on time and we all get tainted with the same brush. It's a good thing Mr Hamilton-Forsyth is a reasonable man. He looks at the individual otherwise I'd have no chance with people like you around giving such a bad impression.

MARCIA: Look, my dentist is very, very old.

BENJAMIN: What the hell has age got to do with it?

MARCIA: Well, he's lost all his own teeth and with them went his self-confidence.

BENJAMIN: What?

MARCIA: So he drinks – but that's really nothing to do with his confidence – that's just 'cause he likes to.

BENJAMIN: Look, just sit down and don't be late tomorrow or you're going to see something. I know what you're thinking; you think that just because we're both Black you won't have to obey the rules, but think again. Skin colour makes no difference to me.

MARCIA: Oh get off your high horse, Benjamin. I had a reason didn't I?

BENJAMIN: Look.

MARCIA: Here, I brought some flowers to brighten up the place.

BENJAMIN: Well, put them on your desk. They might bring on my hay fever.

She puts them in a vase on her desk.

MARCIA: There, doesn't that brighten up the place? Eh, Benjamin? Doesn't that brighten up the place?

BENJAMIN: Listen, you know why

women like flowers don't you? Because the bloom is the flower's sex organ. That's right, its privates. The sight of them awakens something in the deep recesses of their mind. (*He leans forward.*) Something prehistoric. What do you think of that then?

MARCIA: I think . . .

BENJAMIN: Yes?

MARCIA: . . . it adds a whole new meaning to 'Say it with flowers'.

BENJAMIN *goes back to reading the papers.*

BENJAMIN: I didn't get a wink of sleep last night, my finger was throbbing away.

MARCIA: You poor thing. How you must have suffered.

BENJAMIN: There's a letter I want you to type up for me and circulate to all the departments. I'll dictate it to you.

MARCIA: Do you have to? I can copy what you have there.

BENJAMIN: 'Dear staff, in these times of rapidly rising material costs it has come to my notice that there is what can only be described as a wicked waste of company property. For instance, it is not unusual to see ballpoint pens purposely discarded although still half full of ink . . .

MARCIA (*mocking*): How can people sink so low?

BENJAMIN: Amazing isn't it? 'I'm sure the Managing Director, Mr Hamilton-Forsyth, will join with me in condemning such practices.' Well, what do you think?

MARCIA (*she thinks for a moment*): You know that stuff they keep having to clean out of budgie cages? Well, I think you're full of it.

BENJAMIN: Thank you. Well, I thought it'd be rather effective myself. It sort of shows that no problem is too big or too small for me to handle. I have the best interests of Warrington & Bridges at heart.

MARCIA: Brother, you're different. Ballpoint pens for Chrissakes! To think I used to think the Mad Hatter was a creep.

BENJAMIN: You laugh if you like but four, five, ten years from now you'll still be pumping that typewriter.

MARCIA: And where will you be Mr 'Man who knows no fear'?

BENJAMIN: I'll be up there, baby. Up there.

MARCIA: Well, if you've got to become a toad to get 'up there', I'd rather stay down here with my feet firmly on the ground.

BENJAMIN: What, you calling me a toad just 'cause I take pride in my work?

The telephone rings and cuts off any further conversation. BENJAMIN waits for MARCIA to answer it. She doesn't move.

Now is that the telephone ringing or are we just on fire?

Neither of them moves.

No, don't move. I'll just wait for it to jump into my hands.

MARCIA *answers the phone.*

MARCIA: Hello? . . . Yes, he's here.

MARCIA *hands the phone to* BENJAMIN.

It's for you.

BENJAMIN: Who is it?

MARCIA: I didn't ask.

BENJAMIN: Cha. What kind a secretary are you anyway?

He takes hold of the receiver and speaks into it in his best voice and diction.

Benjamin Howard here, can I be of assistance? . . . Ah, Mr Hamilton-Forsyth, how are you this fine spring morning, sir? . . . I'm glad to hear it. And how is the little lady not to mention the wife. (*He laughs loudly.*) Well . . . (*Looking at* MARCIA.) She's settling in, sir . . . Yes, yes . . . Well, there is room for improvement . . . Well, you know how they are . . . Yes, yes . . . Well, I'll do that and of course I'll . . . Oh . . .

MR HAMILTON-FORSYTH *has hung up.* BENJAMIN *replaces the receiver.*

That was Mr Hamilton-Forsyth. A great guy, great.

MARCIA: Well, thanks for giving me such a glowing report . . . I don't think.

BENJAMIN: What's the matter with you girl, don't you recognize strategy when you see it?

MARCIA: Oh, you mean the 'let me oil your arse' strategy. I recognized that one.

BENJAMIN: Hold your mouth a minute. You got to be cool. If I get on that telephone and start enthusing about how wonderful you are he's only going to think, 'Well, that's just typical: Blacks sticking together.' It's better to sound as if I have my doubts. You know what I mean?

MARCIA: Oh, come on, Benjamin. Better for you, you mean.

BENJAMIN: I tell you I know how to handle these people.

MARCIA (*really not sure whether he's being sincere*): I don't know about you, Benjamin. You're a funny sort of guy.

BENJAMIN: Funny? How?

MARCIA: I don't know. Funny. Just different.

BENJAMIN (*to the audience*): You hear that? Different eh? Women, man. Women. I don't know what this power is I have over them. It's going to be interesting watching her do her manoeuvres. I mean, you guys think it's you that capture chicks. You always hear guys saying how they captured this one and how they captured that one but you're wrong. Oh, so wrong. Women are the real predators, and they know it. If you want to find out about them, read their magazines. Yea, you may laugh but believe me, read them in their thousands and a whole new world will open up to you.

MARCIA: Would you like some coffee? I decided to bring some in today.

BENJAMIN (*being snapped back to the moment at hand*): Uh?

MARCIA: I borrowed the flask from my mum. Coffee?

BENJAMIN: You mean you brought coffee in for me? Well, well, well.

To the audience.

See what I mean?

MARCIA: It's for both of us actually.

BENJAMIN: Of course, of course.

MARCIA: A cup for you and a cup for me.

BENJAMIN: A right little mum you are.

To the audience.

Well, I might as well give her a little bit of encouragement.

To MARCIA.

Only one sugar, I'm sweet enough already.

MARCIA: So me notice.

BENJAMIN *lifts his eyebrows to the millions gathered to witness this masterpiece.*

BENJAMIN: Mmmm, just the way I like it, strong and boiling hot. Man, we don't know what good coffee is over here. It's got to be so strong it burns the hairs up your nostrils. Have you ever taken a good look at the Americans, not one of them have hairy nostrils. I swear it!

MARCIA *laughs.*

MARCIA: Last night on my way out of here I met the tea-lady.

BENJAMIN: Right old boot. Can turn milk sour jus' by looking at it.

MARCIA: Well, she call me over and ask me if I'm new here and my name and where I came from, all that sort of thing. Then she start on about how she have a son in South Africa – a plumber's mate or something – and she went out there for a holiday.

BENJAMIN: She talks about nothing else.

MARCIA: Then she pull out these photographs and show me how her scrawny looking offspring has got this big house and swimming pool with five black servants that wait on him hand and foot at all times day and night. 'Such wonderful people. A bit simple, you know, but so loyal and cheerful and hardworking.'

BENJAMIN: Don't worry about her. The bitch is just geeing you up.

MARCIA: But she wasn't, though, Benjamin. She thought I was genuinely interested; glad that our brothers and sisters are sweating and starving their lives away to make them live in luxury. That's a bigger insult than trying to gee me up.

BENJAMIN: Besides, they're not your brothers and sisters; they're African.

MARCIA *looks at him for a moment, astonished.*

MARCIA: Benjamin, I want you to tell her she's got to come down here and give us our coffee and no bullshit about the stairs. Tell her you want coffee hot and strong and with cream, not milk.

BENJAMIN *gets up.*

Are you going now?

BENJAMIN: No. I just want to get something.

He goes over to the cupboard and starts rummaging.

MARCIA: Why should we be left out just because she doesn't feel she has to put herself out for a couple of Blacks?

BENJAMIN: Well, you know how some of them are; unless you're licking their arses they ain't playing anymore.

MARCIA: Well, she's met her Waterloo. You're a Head of Department and you're going to show her. You know how to handle them.

BENJAMIN: I certainly do, honey. (*Coming out of the cupboard.*) But I'll handle this in my own way. Make waves and that old bag will go straight to Mr Hamilton-Forsyth.

MARCIA: So what? You tell her what to do. If she don't like it she can sling her fucking hook.

BENJAMIN (*going back to the cupboard*): There's a lot you don't understand.

MARCIA: Seems pretty simple to me. She either gets the coffee in here or her arse into another job.

BENJAMIN: Leave it, Marcia.

MARCIA: But –

BENJAMIN: LEAVE IT! (*He comes out of the cupboard with a golf club and ball.*) Now I want to practise my putting.

MARCIA: Your whatting?!

BENJAMIN: My putting.

MARCIA: Oh, your ... er ... putting.

It's a small practice set.

Black men don't play golf, do they?

BENJAMIN: This Black man does.

MARCIA: Cha, only white people play games like that and enjoy it.

BENJAMIN: In America lots of Black guys play. It's only in Britain that Black people are too paralyzed with self-consciousness to do anything but slide into a blues on a Saturday night. Well, I do as I please.

MARCIA: So you keep saying. Well, I think it's boring. That and show-jumping. It's enough to drive you to see a play.

BENJAMIN: Oh, it's not that bad. It's a game requiring stamina, intellect, co-ordination and a high level of concentration.

MARCIA: But you're going to play it anyway.

BENJAMIN: You know how I got into this game? The company was doing this sales drive into all them African countries like Nigeria and Zambia. They made me into their African Sales Advisor. Bwoy, did I live. An office with thick pile carpet, the works. And did I travel or did I travel? All over. That's when I got the Mercedes and when I learnt to play golf.

MARCIA (*sucks her teeth*): Give me that stick. Anyone can do that.

BENJAMIN: I used to even have my picture on the advertising posters, the lot.

MARCIA *takes the club off him and starts to swing it wildly.*

I was somebody.

MARCIA: See, there's nothing to it.

BENJAMIN: Look, stop swinging it like that before you kill somebody. Now hold it like this. You have to control it.

MARCIA *can't get the knack.*

He takes hold of her and demonstrates putting his hands over hers.

Hold the club firmly but not too tight as to give it no play at all. Now, what happens before and after you strike the ball is just as important as the rest of it. Now come up in a nice curve but remember to keep your body as straight as possible. Now go on, feet slightly apart.

MARCIA: OK, here goes.

This time he has to duck to avoid being struck.

BENJAMIN: Lard God! Is kill me ya wan' kill me?!

MARCIA: Sorry. I think you're going to have to show me again. I don't think I've quite got it yet.

BENJAMIN: You're not joking! Maybe hand-to-hand combat is your real forte.

BENJAMIN *takes the club from her and shows her again.*

Here. Watch.

He demonstrates.

See. Cool ...

MARCIA: I still can't see what's so wonderful about hitting a little white ball around a field.

BENJAMIN: What's wonderful about it? I'll tell you what's wonderful about it. Getting it into that hole.

He holds the club up in the air.

Getting it into that hole, driving it into that little gap in the grass. Nothing in life could seem so straightforward yet so fraught with such complex frustrations, high aspirations and low realisations and sometimes terrible, terrible let downs. But that doesn't put you off. Oh no, stand there with your iron warm and ready in your hands, thinking 'relax, this could be the biggest, the best moment in your life, the hole-in-one. If only you can keep it up.' For a man not in his prime it can be quite difficult but the objective is crystal clear in your mind, despite the strain; getting it into that hole! For those few moments it's all a man lives for. Getting it into that hole. The rest is just window dressing, ploys and counterploys to conceal the real motive. Concentration and single mindedness is essential. Without it your balls could come loose and end up in the rough. You might find yourself wedged inside there for day. But keep your iron straight and respect the unpredictability of your balls and you can't go wrong . . . You know what I mean?

Long silence.

MARCIA: I know what you mean all right.

Lights down to focus on BENJAMIN.

BENJAMIN: Well, as you can see, me pull no punches in the engagement of chicks. And don't they love it? You see the glaze over their eyes? She's standing there thinking is this really happening to me or is it a dream? She reminds me of me sister you know. Same eyes and fingers. You know, just like my sister. But that ain't no big thing. Half the girls in Brixton are my relatives. My dad sure made good use of his Red Rover . . . I don't think Marcia's my type. There's a missing ingredient. Anyway, come Wednesday she seemed to have cooled down but it didn't matter because I was excited anyway. On the way in I'd caught wind of some information that could have been beneficial to me in my shooting-star ethnic achiever career . . .

Lights down. Lights up on the office. MARCIA *is already there listening to loud reggae music on a portable cassette.* BENJAMIN *enters singing.* MARCIA *tries to turn the cassette off before* BENJAMIN *comes in but she doesn't manage it.*

BENJAMIN: Marcia, Marcia, my own sweet baby!

He rushes in and gives her a kiss on the forehead.

MARCIA: What was that for, may I ask?

MARCIA (*he grabs her out of her seat*): Sweet music this. Let's you and me rock to it.

MARCIA *resists. He dances on his own.*

MARCIA: Has somebody been spiking your cornflakes, Benjamin?

BENJAMIN: Quiet. Listen to the tune.

MARCIA: Benjamin?

BENJAMIN: You believe in good omens?

MARCIA: You mean obea?

BENJAMIN: If you like, but you only been here two days and they have promoted me already.

MARCIA: What to?

BENJAMIN: It'll mean a bigger office, leather chair, rubber plants, too . . .

MARCIA: What to, Benjamin!

BENJAMIN: I don't know yet.

MARCIA: Ahh.

BENJAMIN: Ahh, nothing. (*He stops dancing.*) It's almost as good as mine. There's only Huddlesmore and Henderson and they're both drips.

He slaps his desk.

There's no competition for I, the royal ruler.

MARCIA: You all right, Benjamin?

BENJAMIN: All right? Of course I'm all right. I've never felt better . . . Put it there. (*He holds out his palm to be slapped.* MARCIA *refuses.*) Can anyone stop a tiger on the rampage? A runaway train?

MARCIA: Oh my dear, is that what you are now?

BENJAMIN: I need something, a ruse to show these people my po-ten-tial!

MARCIA: You keep your potential to yourself, nasty boy.

BENJAMIN: Stop farting about, woman! This is important. You'll always be just where you are. Think everything is a joke.

MARCIA: You said the job is yours so what you getting worried about.

BENJAMIN: One step ahead. That's what you got to remember. You always got to be one step ahead when you're Black in a company like this. They're too eager to forget you exist.

MARCIA: You said you had it all sown up.

BENJAMIN: Shut up, I got to think. Whenever I need my brain most that's the time it chooses to seize up on me. Jesus Christ! Maybe I should remind them of the great job I did for them in Africa. I sure made a killing for them there.

MARCIA: Maybe you should mug Mr Hamilton-Forsyth in the corridor. They always remember Black people then, have nightmares about them even.

BENJAMIN: Seven bloody years in this basement. He won't forget, he won't forget, he won't. I ain't asking for anything that's not mine. I won't be passed over again. I can cope and I'm ready. I'm ready. What they waiting for? I'm ready I tell you. I'm ready. (*He takes out his handkerchief and mops his brow.*) Come on, I'm waiting for the call. (*To* MARCIA.) Turn that damn thing off! Didn't you hear? I said I can't think! My mind's all seized up!

MARCIA turns the cassette off.

MARCIA: Cool down for God's sake, man. Don't get so worked up. You'll either get the job or you won't.

BENJAMIN: Typical! Typical of you people. 'You'll either get the job or you won't.' Meanwhile these people are walking all over you. Well, not me, baby, not me. I got good brains and I intend to use them. 'You'll either get it or you won't.' What is it with this dumb arse women, eh? Seven shitting years in this basement and she's come along to tell me that I'll either get it or I won't.

MARCIA quickly pours a cup of coffee.

Seven bloody years. The woman's crazy. If Miss Lutus was here she'd know what to do.

MARCIA (*going up to him with the mug of coffee in one hand and the flask in the other*): Here, Benjamin, drink this. Nice and hot. The way you like it. Burn the hair out of your nostrils.

BENJAMIN: Seven years of cold manoeuvring. I ain't staying in this shit hole anymore.

MARCIA is pushing the drink under his nose.

MARCIA: Come on, Benjamin, drink it. You'll feel better.

BENJAMIN: What? I don't want your fucking coffee. Take it away.

He slaps the flask out of her hands. It shatters as it crashes onto the floor.

That's it. Take it away you silly bitch. I can't think.

MARCIA: You bastard, you've broken it. My mum's best and you've broken it.

She gets down on the floor and picks up the pieces.

All I said was 'Do you want some coffee'? That's all.

BENJAMIN: No eye-water, please. Didn't you hear me say I can't think.

MARCIA: This is civilization. If you didn't want the coffee all you got to say is 'Marcia, I don't want the coffee, thank you'. See? That's all.

BENJAMIN: It's no good, my mind's gone a complete blank.

MARCIA: My mum's going to kill me.

BENJAMIN reaches into his pocket and offers MARCIA a fiver.

BENJAMIN: Here, take this and buy her another one.

MARCIA: It's not that easy. This was the last present my dad gave her before he moved in with Auntie Hortense.

BENJAMIN: It may have sentimental value but it still looked very old.

MARCIA: It's nothing to do with sentiment. She just wanted it to hit him with if he ever comes back.

BENJAMIN: Well, it's a good thing he didn't buy her a cocktail cabinet. Here, don't you want the money?

MARCIA: Put it away and stop waving it about like a flag.

BENJAMIN: Huh? . . . Oh, you mean the money?

MARCIA: Oh, very funny. Always full of jokes, aren't we?

BENJAMIN puts his money away.

BENJAMIN: Well, it's up to you.

MARCIA: You must be hell to live with, Benjamin. One minute you're as calm as a cucumber, the next you're like a wild animal.

BENJAMIN: Go and sit down. I'll do that.

MARCIA goes to sit down while BENJAMIN finishes clearing up the mess.

Now, Miss Lutus would have known what to do. She was never stuck for ideas.

MARCIA: Who the hell is Miss Lutus?

BENJAMIN: She was my secretary before you.

MARCIA: Oh, you mean that one they were all telling me about in the canteen.

BENJAMIN: Not one word of it is true, you hear? I was just trying to remove a piece of fluff from her skirt when she tripped and fell over dragging me down on top of her. And then she started getting all up-tight and shouting and then when the lost typist walked in the whole thing jus' got outta hand.

MARCIA: Out of whose hand?

Lights go down to focus on BENJAMIN addressing the audience directly.

BENJAMIN: I swear I'm telling the truth! I was just trying to be friendly, that's all. Next thing I know this bitch is screaming out 'Help, help, I'm being raped by the big Black man from the basement'. Well, bwoy, the ground could have opened and swallowed me. In a matter of minutes it was all round the company. Then they come to me and tell me about they feel it necessary to move her 'for my own good'. They just took her away. Shit! Who do they think they are anyway? Sometimes I could just . . . But only sometimes . . . But back to Marcia: Thursday morning. I went in with a mind ready to forgive the unforgivable excesses of the day before . . .

Lights come up on the office. MARCIA and he are shouting at one another across their desks.

BENJAMIN: You did what! I can't believe my ears. Jesus, tell me this is part of some awful joke on your part. I know she can't be serious. (*To* MARCIA.) Are you trying to destroy me? You know my promotion is coming up any minute now! I told you I'd handle it in my own way. When I need help from little girls I'll ask for it. You've ruined me!

MARCIA: Seeing you had no intention of telling her, I just told her myself.

BENJAMIN: You must be mad. Clean off your head. Making waves at the worst possible time.

MARCIA: Making waves?! Asking the tea-lady to bring me tea is making waves.

BENJAMIN: You realize, of course, she'll take a complaint straight to Mr Hamilton-Forsyth. Thanks to you I'm going to have a black mark against my Black name.

BENJAMIN *looking to the heavens again.*

Lord, look what this girl has done. Why? Oh, why?

MARCIA: It's as if you don't understand anything.

BENJAMIN: No. It's you who don't understand. And only time and experience will explain it to you: explain the delicate balance I have to maintain here. The right non-decisions at the right time; the over-extravagant expenses discreetly overlooked at the right time; the right smile; balance! If I'm going to marry this woman (*Takes out the photograph of Miss Hamilton-Forsyth and puts it back on his desk.*) then I must have position, title. She doesn't want a Black without one and her father can whip the rug from under my feet any time the whim takes him. So I have to be cool. One step ahead of these bastards.

MARCIA: Benjamin, you're a fool. He's never going to let you marry his daughter. He knows your place and he'll make damn certain you'll stay there licking his boots and oiling his arse. You don't seem to know who you are. You're just like a chameleon changing your colour for whatever seems most appropriate. You're in such a mess. Face up to it!

BENJAMIN: If I'm in a mess it's because you've put me there. How am I going to smooth this over? Everything was so peaceful before you came along; now my whole world is in turmoil.

MARCIA: Do you know what's put your world in turmoil? A tea-lady! A bloody tea-lady that won't bring tea!

BENJAMIN: I need to think. I need some peace and quiet to think.

MARCIA: You're not joking! It's as if you've got everything inside out. You're driving in reverse and sitting the wrong way round at the same time.

BENJAMIN: There's one thing I'm sure of; you're trouble and you've got to go before I'm standing in the dole queue counting the holes in my shoes. You give off nothing but bad vibes and I've learnt never to ignore my feelings. No, baby, something's got to give and it's going to be you.

MARCIA: Benjamin, the woman wouldn't bring us our tea because she's a racist bitch. Why can't you see? It's as if you've wrapped your head in an impregnable force-shield and ripped out the connections but one day, Benjamin, there's going to be a re-connection and all those waves you didn't make will suddenly fuse a sonic boom. What you going to do with all this shit then?

BENJAMIN: What's your hang up, eh? You trying to punish me? Is that what you doing? What did I ever do to you girl? I never seen you before you walk in this building on Monday morning. Get off my back before I lick you down, you hear?

He takes the flowers out of the vase.

Maybe if I take her these? Maybe if I caught her up and apologized before she got to Hamilton-Forsyth. 'It was all a terrible mistake. Let's make it like it was before.'

MARCIA: You could sing the praises of South Africa, too.

BENJAMIN: Do you think it would work?

MARCIA: Do what you want, Benjamin. Blame it on me if you like. As far as I'm concerned, a job's a job. When it becomes any more than that the walls become bars and the windows become TV cameras and we become prisoners.

BENJAMIN *puts the flowers back in the vase.*

BENJAMIN: It's no good, I'll never catch up with her in time. She'll be long gone to Hamilton-Forsyth. She can move like lightning when she's got a grouse.

MARCIA: I said you can blame it on me if you like. I don't mind.

BENJAMIN: Now what good will that

do? You're just a fly. They're going to want a big head for this; they're going to want mine. But don't you worry. You're going to get yours. You're going to get yours yet.

MARCIA: What are you going to do, Benjamin? What has your little devious mind thought up now?

BENJAMIN: Don't you worry, Marcia, you'll find out soon enough.

Lights down on the office focusing on BENJAMIN *addressing the audience.*

BENJAMIN: What else could I do? What right had that bitch to come charging through here upsetting everything? She had no right! I told her I'd handle it in my own way. You'll bear witness to that! And it wasn't just that bloody tea woman, it was everything, her whole bloody attitude. She was poison. Hamilton-Forsyth's secretary bumped into her in the hall or something. Would Marcia let this incident pass? Oh, no. She told her, 'If you don't keep your rarse-clart chinky eyes open I'm going to tump yer down.' It's just as well she didn't understand a word Marcia said. It doesn't do any harm to turn a blind eye every now and then. We all have to. Anyway, she'd have to go and that would be the end of it. That's when I got this brainwave: a petition! It was a master stroke; two birds with one stone; her gone and my credibility back; show them that as far as colour was concerned it held no sway with me; I could make a decisive move regardless. That's right, isn't it? That *is* right! I know that's right . . . Shit . . . What the hell are you staring at?

Lights up on office. MARCIA *is sitting at her desk, typing,* BENJAMIN *is watching her and tapping a pencil on his desk top.*

MARCIA: It was really funny on the picket line yesterday.

BENJAMIN: Oh, really?

MARCIA: To pass the time away my friends and I started to swap bits of useless information. You know, stuff like we human beings are nine-tenths water and if we tried to sell the basic ingredients of our bodies to a chemist he wouldn't give us more than thirty pence. Isn't that a kick right up the ego? Anyway, Pamela, who's a real useless information enthusiast – she even knows the number of the C.R.E. – says that if you were to put a goldfish in a pond it may grow to six or seven inches long, but if you were to take that same goldfish as an infant goldfish and put it in your average goldfish bowl it may only grow a couple of inches or so. Isn't that amazing Benjamin . . . Benjamin?

BENJAMIN: Riveting.

MARCIA: You see the goldfish's size is not preset by its chromosomes but the size of its environment will allow it to grow. I couldn't stop thinking about that, even as my tomato hit the nice councillor's window.

BENJAMIN *gets up and strolls around.* MARCIA *stops typing.*

MARCIA: I brought some cake in today. And I'd just like to say that I won't be talking to that woman again seeing it means so much to you. So let's call it quits, eh? It's not that I agree with you but why should we be at one another's throats all the time, eh Benjamin?

He looks at her but doesn't say anything.

I've seen this before, you know. Black people who in normal circumstances would get on so well, fighting like cat and dog once they're at work or in a situation where they're under the close scrutiny of white people. Why do you think that is, Benjamin?

He shrugs.

I was thinking about it all last night. There must be a reason. If you look hard enough there's a reason for everything.

BENJAMIN *picks up the photograph from his desk and looks at it.*

BENJAMIN: Listen, girl, I'm not interested in your opinions.

MARCIA (*to audience*): Can you believe this jerk? If ever there was anyone living in cloud cuckooland it's him. No political awareness, no understanding of history; totally out for number one . . . himself. Well, before I leave this is one Black man who's gonna know he's a Black man.

(*to* BENJAMIN:) I remember in my last job there were these two Nigerian girls. I always used to think of African people as much more united than us West Indians or the Americans but they'd come in in the morning and by ten o'clock they'd be at one another's throats. No matter how far you sat them apart their Black skins would draw them together and their Black skins would rip them apart. First there'd be the vocal friction and then the physical ignition. The white girl's positively glowed at the flying insults about the other's natty hair, the Blackest skin or the men they'd been having and you know what I thought as I watched them, Benjamin?

BENJAMIN: No, what did you think Marcia?

MARCIA: I thought they knew what they were doing, exactly what they were doing. They were aware of their entertainment value and they played it up. Each fight would, predictably, reveal a few more sordid details about their private lives, a little more hair would be torn out, a little more clothing would be ripped. They were only doing what was expected of them. If once they got together and chatted among themselves it was seen as conspiracy, the whites were excluded, we had to be planning some kind of plot to bring down the white power structure, we had to be talking revolution. No, it is not healthy! To this day I think those girls knew what they were doing as they spat in one another's eyes. And it worked, too. As far as I know they're still there getting regular wage rises with the supervisor . . . God, I hated that bitch: claiming there was equal opportunity for everyone in that office. I suppose she had a point, though. I've never met a white person yet who didn't show that integration meant whites policing Blacks as Blacks try to cut one another's throats. That's the real reason I hit her. I'd been planning to for a long time.

BENJAMIN: Oh, yes, the infamous slapping of your long-suffering supervisor.

MARCIA: She deserved it and worse.

BENJAMIN (*to the audience*): She knows. She bloody well knows about the petition. What else was all that in aid of. Oh, my God, she knows.

MARCIA: What's the matter, Benjamin?

BENJAMIN: Nothing's the matter. Why should there be?

MARCIA: Oh, it just seems you're very quiet today. Have you something on your mind? Like a bad conscience, maybe.

BENJAMIN: There's nothing on my mind. My mind's blank. It's . . . it's the heat.

MARCIA: It's not hot. In fact, it's chilly.

BENJAMIN: Then it's the cold. Stop asking me questions. What are you trying to catch me out for?

MARCIA: Why are you so touchy? I haven't done you anything today.

BENJAMIN: I'm not touchy . . . I'm touchy because you keep asking me questions, trying to get to me.

MARCIA: No one's trying to get to you, Benjamin. I hope this is not a build up to one of your attacks.

BENJAMIN: Attacks?! What are you talking about? When have you ever seen me have any sort of attack?

MARCIA: Wednesday. I thought I'd have to throw a bucket of cold water over you.

BENJAMIN: You lying bitch. Don't go putting it around that I have attacks. That's no way to get your own back.

MARCIA: Get my own back? Get my own back for what, Benjamin? But, if I wanted to I'm sure they would believe me after that episode of yours with Miss Lutus.

BENJAMIN: Go away. You're trying to make my mouth run away with me but –

MARCIA: What are you up to, Benjamin? What's going on inside that little devious bean in your head?

The phone rings. BENJAMIN *grabs it.*

BENJAMIN: Hello, Benjamin Howard here . . . Oh, how are you, sir? . . . Glad to hear it . . . Yes, I have them right here. I just got them out this minute to bring them to you . . . Yes, sir, right away. Bye.

He puts the telephone down and straightens his tie.

Give me that report, would you.

MARCIA: What report?

BENJAMIN: The report I asked you to type on Monday.

MARCIA: I gave it to you already.

BENJAMIN: No you didn't. I told you to put it in a safe place till I wanted it. Look in your drawers.

MARCIA: No, I remember distinctly giving it to you and you saying 'thank you' for giving them to you.

BENJAMIN: What!?

MARCIA: Clear as a bell, that's what you said.

BENJAMIN: Oh, my God.

MARCIA: You said 'thanks'. Just like that.

BENJAMIN: The rarse clart woman has gone and lost it.

MARCIA: Well, not quite like that. You were standing a little to your left at the time.

BENJAMIN *frantically goes through the drawers of his desk, throwing papers into the air as he goes.*
MARCIA *secretly gets out the report from her drawer and tucks it into the back of her skirt.*

BENJAMIN: She's gone and lost it! It must be here somewhere!

MARCIA: Seek and you will find.

BENJAMIN: Oh, Lord God, have mercy on one Benjamin Howard. He's only a poor guy trying to make his way, trying to keep his nose clean, trying.

MARCIA: Trying, he's certainly trying.

BENJAMIN (*going to search in her drawers*): It must be here, it must be!

MARCIA: Well, think of all the places you used to hide with Miss Lutus.

BENJAMIN: Maybe the cleaner took them away by mistake.

MARCIA: I heard you were always searching Miss Lutus, her and her greeny eyes.

BENJAMIN: Maybe if I went home and came in again everything would be better, everything would be nice.

MARCIA: I'll give you greeny eyes!

BENJAMIN: An industrial spy! That's it! We've been the victim of an inter-company plot. Maybe he'll believe that?!

MARCIA: I know, the cupboard.

He opens the cupboard door quickly and his golf equipment and his porno books fall out.

MARCIA: Ah ha! I suppose you used to read these to Miss Lutus, too?

BENJAMIN: I've never seen them before in my – I'm looking after them for a friend . . . I am! Oh, piss off. They must be here somewhere. Just one more chance, Lord. Just one.

He goes to the filing cabinet. MARCIA picks up a golf club.

Gimme me things!

He grabs it back.

What do you know bout classy stuff like this. It's beyond you. You're just a back-a-yard girl. Go back to where you belong!

MARCIA is deeply wounded.

MARCIA: Right! Right, you slimy, toady bastard! I'm going to show you who's from the back-a-yard! I'm . . . I'm going to make you fall so hard, so fast, you're going to wish your arse was a parachute made of leather.

She takes the documents from her skirt.

BENJAMIN: Those are the – You bitch, you had them all the time!

He goes to grab them.

MARCIA: Not so fast. I think it's time for me to call the shots. I've had one week of this. I've taken all that I can take.

BENJAMIN: Give me those papers!

She moves away and starts to circle him as he watches her.

MARCIA: Well, well. Look how important I've become all of a sudden and all without the aid of greeny eyes. (*She puts on an American accent.*) Um, um. I sure am making progress here.

BENJAMIN: You're crushing them!

MARCIA: Crushed, eh? Well, that's the least of your worries.

She takes the desk lighter from his desk.

Ashes to ashes, dust to dust.

He tries to catch her. She evades him, keeping the two desks between them.

BENJAMIN: Don't be stupid!

MARCIA *ignites the lighter.*

MARCIA: London Bridge is burning down, burning down –

BENJAMIN: Please don't!

MARCIA: Sorry? Didn't catch that.

He tries to grab her again and misses.

BENJAMIN: I . . . I said please don't.

MARCIA: That's right, Benjamin, I want to see you crawl. Crawl to me a Black woman – like you crawl to all those white bastards out there. How dare you sit there, all far away in your dreams, singing the praises of one piece of white arse after the other. I'm a Black woman, Benjamin. We're the most beautiful women on the earth. You've got a lot to learn, Benjamin. Why do you think all dem white women torture themselves under sun lamps and risk sun burn on expensive holidays? So they can be Black like me. Why do you think they do all sorts of mischief to themselves in discos? So they can be Black like me. Why do you think they spend a fortune to have their hair put in beads, the so-called 'Bo Derek'? So they can be like me: Black!

BENJAMIN: Give me those papers!

MARCIA: They want to know the secret. Don't come any closer or I swear I'll burn them. When you're in bed with your precious, does she ask you how she matched, how she compared? Come on Benjamin, tell me. I bet she does.

BENJAMIN: How dare you, woman! What goes on in my bedroom is no business of yours!

MARCIA: You're the one who brought it up. If not the actual words, then by implication.

BENJAMIN: Your imagination's working overtime!

MARCIA: Well, there's one woman in your life who you won't be able to make white. Your mother!

BENJAMIN: Look, Mr Hamilton-Forsyth is waiting for those papers and he is not a man who likes to be held up!

MARCIA: He can go to hell! Let him wait! You belong to us not to them!

BENJAMIN: I'm me, myself! I don't belong to anyone. I belong to myself!

MARCIA: You know that's not true. In your heart of hearts you know that's not true. You've handed yourself over to them body and soul.

BENJAMIN: I think I know best what to do with my life and I won't have much of one if I get booted out of here on my arse.

MARCIA: It could be just the beginning for you. You could go somewhere else where you don't have to act like a clown to earn your bread.

BENJAMIN: I could also go somewhere where you have to sing and dance to earn your bread . . . Now fuck all this. What is it I have to say to make you give me those papers. Just tell me and I'll say anything you want to hear, anything that will make you feel better!

MARCIA: And that sums up your whole formula to life.

BENJAMIN: Stop all this talk about 'life' as if you were some kind of guru or something. You're not a guru, you're just a pain in the arsehole, that's all. Look, if you don't give me those papers –

MARCIA: What will you do? Come down heavy on me like you did the tea-lady?

BENJAMIN: I'm going to –

MARCIA: Or will you 'sir' me to death as you do with what's-his-name? Hamilton.

BENJAMIN: Forsyth. I'll call the police for wilful damage to company property.

MARCIA: You'd do that would you, Benjamin? You'd do that to me?

BENJAMIN: I'd do that to anyone who was being a bastard.

MARCIA: You'd let the police come in here and accuse me and manhandle me for these bits of paper?

BENJAMIN: I'd like to see them handle you onto a stretcher. Has anyone ever told you before? You're mad. Completely out of your tiny IQ. Listen, you got to understand. I have a position to maintain. Where else am I going to get a job paying this sort of money with my own office and everything? Look, I don't know what's eating you. You seem to want me to confess to something I don't feel guilty of, some sense of shame, remorse that I don't have. Times have changed! People have moved on. There are no anti-Black laws now. I can do what I want and go where I please. I can marry any woman I want to. You're out of date. You've been left behind. I'm the modern space-age Black man and you're the old-fashioned Black woman still beating her washing as well as her cross down by the river.

MARCIA (*shouting*): You're full of shit!

BENJAMIN: You can throw insults all you like, baby, but I'll lay bets on one thing: you'll be out while I'm still in. Just like you were with those Nigerians.

BENJAMIN *goes to put his jacket on.*

MARCIA: One day soon they're going to eat you alive. Do you know that? And you won't even have your self-respect to fall back on.

BENJAMIN: One day we all get eaten alive, honey. that's the law of the jungle. You should know that better than me. But, you see, the difference is I might stand a chance 'cause I'll be driving a fast Mercedes and you'll be walking . . . Now, I'm either on my way to Mr Hamilton-Forsyth with those papers or to the police. Which is it to be?

MARCIA (*thinks for a moment*): You asked me what I wanted to hear. You said you'd say it.

He reaches for the papers. She pulls them away.

I want to hear you say you're sorry. Sorry that you, a Black man, have manoeuvred yourself into such a tight stranglehold that you can't even feel the pain anymore. You might even enjoy it if you could. Sorry that your balls are so sedated that they stand to attention when they're kicked. Sorry that you're so addicted to this way of life that if I took the drug away I might not recognise the remains.

He looks at her, puzzled, as if she's talking Hebrew.

Take a look in the mirror, Benjamin. Be what you see!

He reaches for the papers, slowly. She allows him to take them. BENJAMIN *goes to the door, hesitates, and then leaves.* MARCIA *bows her head, gets together her things and leaves, too. Lights down on the office and then up on* BENJAMIN, *alone. He addresses the audience.*

BENJAMIN: I'm going to have the last word. When I got back she'd already gone which was a pity really as I wanted to hand her the petition saying 'we've all decided here that you're a trouble-maker' . . . Still, you can't have all the little pleasures in life, can you? Strange girl. Confused . . . I must admit she crosses my mind, though. She crosses my mind quite a lot. Maybe under different circumstances things could have been . . . well, they could have been different. Might have taken her out as a treat. But that's not what I came to talk to you about, is it? I came to talk to you about . . . about Jesus Christ! Who did she think she was anyway coming in here turning everything upside down. Order! Order! Take away order and what are you left with? Nothing. A vacuum. She was turning everything upside down in her tiny mind. No wonder you're all having nervous breakdowns . . .
Anyway, you can think what you like . . . You all make me sick. I've got what I want! I've got something to show for all this shit!

He walks off singing.

'Learning to love yourself is the greatest love of all . . .'

Lights out.

LONELY COWBOY

LFRED FAGON was born in Clarendon, Jamaica in 1937. His work included: *Josephine House* (Almost Free Theatre, 1972); *Shakespeare Country* (BBC 2, 974); *No Soldiers in St Paul's* (Metro Club, 1974); *Death of a Black Man* (Foco ovo and Hampstead Theatre, 1975); *Bristol Air-Raid Shelter* (reading by Black heatre Co-op., Royal Court Theatre Upstairs, 1982); *Four Hundred Pounds* (Foco ovo and Royal Court, 1983) and *Lonely Cowboy* (Tricycle Theatre, 1985). A series poems entitled *Waterwell* were completed just prior to his death in 1986.

Foreword

Alfred Fagon died suddenly in 1986. At the time, this volume was still in its early stages and he had yet to write a preface to *Lonely Cowboy*. In its place, we are reproducing Alfred Fagon's obituary notice from *The Times* and a poem composed by T-Bone Wilson and read out at the Memorial Service.

The Times, September 20 1986:

Alfred Fagon, who died of a heart attack on August 29, at the age of 49, was a remarkable actor and, in his work as a playwright, an influential exponent of black writing in this country.

His plays take as their theme the relationship between the cultures of the English and Caribbean peoples, their friendships and conflicts.

He was born in Clarendon, Jamaica, on June 25, 1937, into a large and close family of eight brothers and two sisters. He left school at 13 and worked with his father as a cultivator on their orange plantation.

In 1955 he came to England, where he worked on the railways in Nottingham. He joined the Army in 1958, serving for four years and becoming a middleweight boxing champion in the Royal Corps of Signals.

On leaving the Army he travelled around England, singing calypso and taking extra work in television prior to researching, writing and performing in *John Bull* for HTV in 1969.

In 1970 he made his first professional stage appearance in Mustapha Matura's *Black Pieces* at the Institute of Contemporary Arts. Thereafter he appeared in many television, film, radio and theatre roles, most recently in BBC television's five-part drama series, *Fighting Back*.

His plays include *11 Josephine House* at the Almost Free Theatre 1972; *Shakespeare Country*, BBC2; *No Soldiers in St Pauls*, Metro Club, 1974; *Death of a Black Man*, Foco Novo Theatre Company and Hampstead Theatre 1975; *Four Hundred Pounds*, Foco Novo and The Royal Court, 1983; *Lonely Cowboy*, The Tricycle, 1985.

At the time of his death he had completed a series of poems called *Waterwell*.

He lived a simple and spartan life, dedicated to his work and writing; but to his close friends revealed great exuberance and energy.

Though never married, he had a daughter of whom he was very fond.

TELL THE TRUTH

A Tribute to Alfie

The number of nights I battle
with my friend for letting go
the struggle, and he would
disappear for months – unfound
to work upon some model.
Then out of the hazy grey he
would appear and into my eyes
he would pry – how goes
the movement? And I would say
the movement is you, and he
would say – a true! a portion
of my contribution is on its way
– a play.

Yes I know him, yes I do, well
Not as a woman would but
as a friend should – for
when happiness strikes, God
Almighty and all the angels
would come down, and your
eardrums would bleed the hardest
fun from the hallelujah! hallelujah!
say it brother move it sound.

And the sweat from Clarendon
would exude and the tears from
Shakespeare's country would intrude
with wails, hails, like a monstrous
whale, and memories pass into
future would start the torture,
pressure, pressure, seems forever.
And God becomes lip-bound, caught
as it were in a loaded fire-passion
of persecution, an insane madness
of truth, compound philosophy that would
tire a marathon runner.
Everything in totality. Those who
are around have to beg for peace
for that captured soul must free it self – at least.

Pause

(*To be sung:*)

By the rivers of Babylon
Where we sat down
And there we wept
When we remembered Zion.

No man I know has called on
God's name so – with every statement
God's reference was the preference, in
happiness or in sadness same was the

name, private, public, always the same.
Plot entered plot, development created
broken straight lines carved into
luminous loneliness, love, loneliness,
lonesomeness, from Bristol to Nottingham,
to London he galloped. He ran with the
British Army in his head, the gloves,
the boots, the bed. He never wrote about
them but they were there! there! there!

So he ran from Silverburn House, all
around this neighbourhood, often like
a lonely cowboy, trying to dig deep
into the atrocities of this wet society,
sometimes misinterpreting, sometimes
misjudging but always trying –
you see he was searching for that self.
He wanted the people to know that
He cared; that he was worth something
not just a number and a name . . .
Watch the army brother! It can toy
with your brain, the war you
fight does not always belong to you
and the gun you carry could
back-fire too – remember, there're
no soldiers in St Paul's
He was a searcher, searching, searching man.

Pause Yeah.

Yeah, I argued with the police so fucking what!
So you scattered my bones among
the rose bushes . . . whats the
matter with you? I am not a baron!
Look, don't bother talk to me about
moral ethics, who good and what bad,
Jesus was a compassionate man,
so don't tell me, tell the people . . .
and stop telling them that I die from
heart attack. Tell the truth!
Stop being dishonest and lawless –
Tell dem the truth – yes!
This is death of a Blackman . . .

For the wicked dem carried
us away captivity, required
from us a song, how can we
sing King Alpha song in a strange land

T-Bone Wilson

Lonely Cowboy was first presented at the Tricycle Theatre, London, on May 13 1985 with the following cast:

FLIGHT, *5ft. 11ins-6ft. tall, dressed in overall, jeans, pullover, shoes*   Jim Findley

GINA, *5ft. 4ins, aged 24-26, Afro hairstyle, bangles, necklace, overall, flower dress, flat shoes*   Angela Wynter

THELMA, *5ft. 5ins – 24-26 years, Afro hairstyle, short furry winter coat, jeans, blouse, earrings, bracelet, bangles, necklace, watch, handbag, rings, high-heel shoes*   Beverley Michaels

CANDY, *18-19 years, Rasta hairstyle, dressed Army fatigues, tall boots*   Joy Richardson

WALLY, *5ft. 6ins, 24-26 years, jeans, pullover, lumber jacket, ring, watch, necklace, bracelet*   Chris Tummings

DALTON, *5ft. 10ins, 21-23 years, Rasta hairstyle, army fatigues, training shoes, shoulder bag with papers*   Sylvester Williams

JACK, *5ft. 11ins-6ft., 25-27 years, dressed in police constable uniform*   Calvin Simpson

STANLEY, *23-25 years, dressed in suit, tie, briefcase, watch, shoes, bracelet etc.*   Trevor Butler

Directed by Nicholas Kent
Designed by Jan McClelland

ACT ONE

Scene One
Lights up. Autumn 1984.
Brixton, London.

All characters are English second-generation blacks.

FLIGHT *and* GINA *lifting bag of cement. Paint cans, step ladder, tool box open on floor, mirror on wall 5ft by 14ins, 4 tables, 4 chairs for each table, fridge, micro-oven, cash register, shelf 4ft high, glass cup, saucer, electric kettle.*
    All furniture is covered with plastic.
FLIGHT *takes sign brush and writes in last letter for 'Lonely Cowboy'.*
    GINA *takes plastic cover off furniture.*
GINA *exits to kitchen and comes back with apron and small hat, towel, face basin with water.*
    FLIGHT *smiles, rubbing his hands, flicks switch on and light comes up on 'Lonely Cowboy', holster with two revolvers.* GINA *and* FLIGHT *take off overalls,* GINA *puts on small hat and apron. She is looking at herself in mirror.* GINA *and* FLIGHT *washing hands in face basin.*

FLIGHT: This is it we are now open for business all roads in the world lead to Brixton's Lonely Cowboy.

He turns sign from closed to open.

God, I wonder when we are going to get the first customer, should I go around the back and do a War Dance.

He picks up face basin.

GINA: No man, stay here and pray for both of us, before the tide comes in.

GINA *takes the basin off him, exits to kitchen and comes back whilst* FLIGHT *is holding his hands in front of him as if praying.*

FLIGHT: Yes all good ships shall sail this way. We must show the rest of England that Brixton disciplines us with some heavy manners, from now on when we sleep our eyes shall become our ears. (*He relaxes.*) Gina my Princess I feeling funny and nothing aint wrong with me.

GINA: Yes my stomach is unsettle as well.

FLIGHT: A lot of the old time pressure is going to come down on us, now that we have open our base to Brixton.

GINA: We are going to need some kind of music to keep the pressure down.

FLIGHT: No man we will only harbour the wrong kind of youths.

GINA: Why are you making yourself so old, so what happen if a customer bring them own music?

FLIGHT: You understand no music or back to Africa politics. Never inside the Lonely Cowboy and hear me again as I tell you before no body popping contest.

GINA: Look people are only young once. I am not going to be happy staying here with no music.

FLIGHT: Princess you is a 26 year old woman, I is a 28 year old man.

GINA: So why are you behaving like 42.

FLIGHT: Because it is the right way to behave. We will just have to make our own music in bed. Wait you're pregnant? A stop at no red light recently.

GINA: Look at me when you are talking to me.

GINA *puts one hand on her hips.*

FLIGHT: A looking.

GINA: You think you man enough to give me a baby.

FLIGHT: So tell me something, why you hotting up the place?

GINA: Because you've not landed at my base line for a month to rass.

FLIGHT: Stop the sex talk and think about what kind of vibes you going to give off when you walking away from the customers. A selling everything in the caf except you.

GINA: Just clear off from me and don't start watching me.

She walks away.

FLIGHT: You is a joker.

FLIGHT *gets revolvers from holster, starts playing with them.* GINA *opens fridge, pours herself a glass of milk, humming a little tune to herself.*

THELMA *enters.*

THELMA: Woo waa we, it open at last.

GINA: Wha happened Thelma?

THELMA: So is when you open.

GINA: You's the first customer.

THELMA: Well sell me something.

GINA: What you want?

THELMA: Anything, just sell me something.

FLIGHT: You hungry. The soup not quite ready.

FLIGHT *puts revolvers back in holsters.*

THELMA: I want a drink.

GINA: You can have one of Flight's root drinks. So is where you coming from so early in the morning?

THELMA: Yes give me a pint of the punch. I coming from every pub in Brixton. I trying to get a job as a barmaid.

FLIGHT: You always trying to be a barmaid, but that can't hold you.

THELMA: So is what can hold me?

FLIGHT: You's too sexy to be a barmaid. Look how many men running after you and I don't see you running.

GINA: Flight shut your mouth.

THELMA: You giving me joke early in the morning. Anyway the place nice, nice, nice. Give me my drink man.

FLIGHT *gets two half pint glasses with milky liquid from fridge. Pours them into pint glass.*

FLIGHT: Be careful my juice don't make you call. Your man better be good or you will mash up in back.

THELMA: Man I have no man, just a little side line.

WALLY *enters with bicycle, big boxes on front and back, loaded with socks, shirts, hats and caps, shoes and boots, shirts.*

WALLY: You open and never a day early, nice, nice.

FLIGHT: Don't lean your bicycle on me table Wally.

WALLY: That's all right. I hear on the news in the market Jack join the police.

FLIGHT: That is old news.

WALLY: Did you get the job Thelma?

THELMA: I don't know yet.

CANDY *enters with tape recorder and music magazine, loud poetry coming from tape recorder.*

TAPE RECORDER: Bang, bang, hold corn, hold corn. Bullet, bullet, bullet. Bang, bang. Hold corn, hold corn. My mind is made up, my soul will find peace when Brixton free the slaves.

FLIGHT (*shouting*): Turn it off. Wally your bicycle, the place just open.

CANDY *switches tape off.*

CANDY: You see Dalton?

GINA: No love.

WALLY: I want to see him.

CANDY: I must find him (*She exits.*)

GINA: They are in love.

THELMA: Dalton tried it on me more than once.

GINA: Is what you telling me?

WALLY: So Jack get posted back to Brixton. Still I have no business with no policeman whether I know him or not and on top of it Jack never throw a brick in the riot. The place look nice man. I could have been a successful businessman myself if I did not get caught up in the riot. And now Jack is a policeman. One of our own blood.

THELMA: Stop worrying yourself about Jack.

WALLY: No I can't. In days gone by we used to sleep and eat in the same house. Our parents was friends when they were alive.

GINA: Buy something in the place. We just open, give us some luck.

WALLY: Give me a juice. You make the juice you promise you was going to make, Flight?

FLIGHT: Yes, man.

WALLY: Yes, yes, give it to me.

THELMA: I will serve him.

GINA: Sure.

FLIGHT: Wally keep hold of your bicycle the same way a man keep hold of his Alsatian dog in the street.

THELMA *gets one juice from fridge, gives it to* WALLY. WALLY *empties glass in one swig.*

GINA: That's £1.50.

WALLY *pays.*

WALLY: His rass join the police, so he could become the biggest man in Brixton. I glad it's not me alone hate him. I going to stand and watch them boy beat him. Rass. When he come to harrass one of them. Boy oh boy, the inspector want to post him up to the West End, and make one of them big time criminal fire a real gun after him. All I have got on me, except the goods that I am selling is me money and me knife. Jack can never harrass me.

FLIGHT: I said watch the bicycle on the table man.

WALLY: All right, all right.

Enter CANDY *and* DALTON *holding hands.* CANDY *with cassette tape magazine.*

WALLY: Boy you two is coming as I am going.

DALTON: One love.

CANDY: This is the start of the new liberated roots scene.

WALLY: So what happened Dalton?

DALTON: Nothing. Boy I just see something a while ago that I did not like. I am a youth but sometime I am ashamed of my own kind. This mugging business must stop.

WALLY: Boy, is so life go. Well I must hit the road. Rass clath Dalton. You don't hear that Jack join the police?

DALTON: Yes man, everybody knows.

CANDY: Give me two cups of tea, Gina.

WALLY *and* DALTON *shaking hands in different positions.* GINA *switches on electric kettle, puts tea bag into cup,* CANDY *pays* GINA *40p.* CANDY *sits at table reading music magazine.* DALTON *joins her.*

FLIGHT: Wally come out of the place with the bicycle and don't let me an you have anything.

WALLY: Don't lose your cool, I going. You cook yet?

FLIGHT: You not going to eat in here with your bicycle.

WALLY: Right, I going. So Thelma we can't meet up tonight for a drink?

THELMA: Not tonight.

WALLY: All right, some other time.

WALLY *exits.*

FLIGHT: I am very sad on the most important day of my life. I can't seem to find me foot. I feeling ever so funny.

GINA: If you feeling funny, go and lay down around the back.

THELMA: I could do with a little job until I start my barmaid.

FLIGHT: You mean in case we get busy?

THELMA: Yes.

FLIGHT: Talk to Gina about it.

GINA: Well since he's not well – I hope it's not too much trouble Thelma.

THELMA: Gina come on man, say yes.

GINA: All right, how much?

THELMA: A fiver for a couple of hours at a time.

GINA: O.K. Flight go and lay down before you drop dead in the place.

FLIGHT: I going to take a walk on the front line.

GINA: What front line? For God's sake stay in the place, we only just opened.

FLIGHT: Yes, yes, but I overexcited. I must go for a walk.

GINA: Excited, what? Laziness is creeping back into your head. Don't think I'm going to do all the work while you piss off all over the place.

FLIGHT: I got my business to take care of.

GINA: What business? Shut your wicked mouth. Are you selling ganja and running woman on the front line?

FLIGHT: Thelma, you see how much my woman love me?

GINA: You are lying, nothing is wrong with you. You should apply to Equity for membership card and go on to the stage.

THELMA: Well you must remember you are not a cowboy anymore – is the caf is the Lonely Cowboy.

FLIGHT: So which side are you on Thelma?

THELMA: I am on the right side.

GINA: Before the man stay here, and knead the flour for the fried dumpling. Christ Thelma, him know I can't knead the flour, my wrist is too weak.

FLIGHT: I am only going for a few minutes to spread the good news about 'Lonely Cowboy'. Yes, I now got my own base.

GINA *serves tea to* CANDY *and* DALTON.

GINA: Don't bring no ganja come back here.

FLIGHT: Thanks for reminding me, now I am a business man I stop all those foolishness.

He dances quickly, feet moving fast, twist and turn. THELMA *looks frisky as if she wants to join him.*

THELMA: Why the place so dead? Put on some music.

GINA: We haven't got any. Flight say no music.

THELMA: You mad.

FLIGHT: Mind is not you that is mad.

THELMA: All right, all right, what about the music?

FLIGHT: We will review the situation when I get back.

THELMA: What Black people is sweetly bossy when they have a few pounds in their pocket. You going to show me what to do?

FLIGHT: Gina will show you, I am going, bye babes.

FLIGHT *exits quickly.*

GINA (*shouting out to* FLIGHT): Remember the fried dumpling them. So you want to start now Thelma?

THELMA: Yes, right now.

GINA: I don't know what to do myself, we will learn together. Check the soup in the kitchen while I write the price list.

THELMA *exits to kitchen.* GINA *writes price list at table.*

THELMA: It ready, I turned the gas off.

GINA: Come back out here.

Enter THELMA *and sits next to* GINA *at table.*

GINA: Right, this is the price list. Try and remember it in your head. We have to charge some of them different prices.

THELMA: Something like service charge?

GINA: Yes.

THELMA *and* GINA *deep in thought studying price list. Police siren, car driving past.* DALTON *reading poem.* CANDY *stops reading magazine and listens to* DALTON.

DALTON: I feel the pain
My hungry belly
Not wanting white sliced bread
So ease my pain with justice for all
For the blacker if he is
The pain will disappear.

I trying to dig a poem out of my belly, you like it Candy?

CANDY: It's wonderful. I wish I could write like that. Everytime I listen to your poems I want to sing. You should try and get them published.

DALTON: No man. I just want to read my poems to the youth of Brixton and put some knowledge and wisdom in their heads. After the great success of the riots that leave us ten times worse off and poorer, we need a change which should give us a new lease in life.

CANDY: Brixton to you is like some earthly heaven. You refuse to notice the heavy pressure that is going on all day.

DALTON: We shall make progress in Brixton towards the Kingdom of Ja. And when that happens no one shall have more knowledge about Brixton than myself. The freedom train shall arrive and I want to be a consultant along the journey.

CANDY: We need to rent our own flat. Do you expect us to live in our parents' homes for ever? When do you expect the train to arrive?

DALTON: I don't know, but the more poems I write, the quicker it will come.

CANDY: Have it your own way.

DALTON *continues writing poem.*

CANDY: Excuse me.

She walks over to THELMA *and* GINA. *Sits.* GINA *takes price list and exits to kitchen.*

CANDY: Well I must say, I never believed they would even open the caf after all the trouble they've been through since they buy the place.

THELMA: It look nice.

CANDY: Yes, very modern. Maybe we could start a little women group since the place is so nice.

THELMA: Well I am busy at the moment, I got a job.

CANDY: Nice – doing what?

THELMA: Barmaid.

CANDY: That's all right. I must talk to Gina, we should have a women group.

THELMA: No man, give it a rest for a while, they just opened.

CANDY: I really miss the old group that we was in. I have never seen or heard of any of those men since the police take some of them to the hospital.

THELMA: Yes we all did went into hiding for a few months. It was the men who started the fight. That sailor was a bad man. He's probably all right anywhere he is. He wasn't any good. He was a bad man. He had no conscience or mercy how he gets his money. I know him, I used to sleep with him.

CANDY: If the group did still keep going he and his friends would have had us all in jail by now.

Police siren. Car driving past.

THELMA: What, them busy today.

Enter GINA.

CANDY: Let me personally congratulate you Gina. Your place feel nice man.

GINA: Thanks.

She sits at table with THELMA *and* CANDY.
    JACK *enters, dressed in police constable uniform.*

JACK: Morning all.

GINA: What are we supposed to do – laugh?

CANDY: Jack, you now cross Jordan river?

THELMA (*laughing*): Jack, your helmet is too big.

DALTON, *gathering his papers together.*

DALTON: No, no no it's not funny. Come on Candy, let's get out of here. Not another minute. Come on, let's go.

CANDY: All right, all right, I am coming.

Moving quickly. Picking up magazine and tape recorder.

CANDY: You must admit, it is funny.

DALTON: Shut up and come on.

DALTON *and* CANDY *exit.*

JACK: That wasn't a nice reception from Dalton. I hope things will improve around here.

GINA: Are we allowed to talk to you?

THELMA: Not me.

JACK: No, just sell me a cup of tea.

THELMA: Tea what. Drink some punch and put some strength in your back.

GINA: You don't see, he's not a human being any more.

JACK: I am a policeman, I'm not going to lose my temper.

GINA: I glad to see you know your place.

JACK: Is trying, the two of you trying to insult me?

GINA: What? No man, insult the God of Brixton. Thelma, Jack can have the punch on the house.

JACK: Is bribing? You bribing me now or what?

THELMA: Why should we do that?

GINA: What are we doing wrong?

JACK: I don't know, you tell me.

GINA: Look, you want the punch or not?

JACK: Yes, but I would like to pay for it.

GINA: It is not for sale to you.

JACK: In that case, thank you very much for your hospitality.

THELMA *gives* JACK *milky punch from fridge.*

THELMA: This is no flat-foot hustling. This is a legitimate caf.

JACK *puts his helmet on the counter and starts sipping his drink.*

GINA: And not to forget how many different pieces of paper we had to sign before we could open. The name of the caf, 'Lonely Cowboy'. So we don't want too many policemen for company.

JACK: I am a citizen, I have the same right as any person in Brixton.

GINA: You have plenty more right than most of us.

THELMA: What about those on the front line?

JACK: Some of them could turn into good citizens.

GINA: With a little help from the likes of you.

JACK: We are not as bad as you might think.

GINA: I don't have to think nothing. Every individual are a group of people, don't matter who they are, think they are best for Brixton once they live here. Christ himself is the only saviour for Brixton.

THELMA: And he's not coming back.

STANLEY *enters, with carton box measuring 18" x 18" x 12".*
STANLEY *looking at* JACK – *frozen. Police siren. Car driving past.*
STANLEY *trembling.*

STANLEY: Morning, excuse me, sorry. I don't know what to say. I am only passing through. I going.

THELMA: No wait, you look like a real good customer.

STANLEY: What?

GINA: Man, grow up, is only Jack, born and bred Brixton blackman.

STANLEY: No, well listen to me. I don't know what to say. I mean one love to the brothers and sisters, but a black policeman is no rejoicement.

JACK: What is this? Who are you?

STANLEY: A visitor.

JACK: Typical.

THELMA: Leave Jack alone, his bread is well buttered.

GINA: We only open today for the first time.

STANLEY: So what are you doing? Hosting the annual police ball?

JACK (*laughs*): I wish it was.

STANLEY *puts down briefcase and carton box.*

STANLEY: You see me, I is a real black man. Me, Stanley. That's my name. Sell me a piece of salt-fish and two dumpling.

GINA: We have salt-fish, but no dumpling. But what a man wicked like Flight, take up him backside say him gone on frontline on the first day we open. Before him stay here and make the dumpling them.

STANLEY: Well let me have some bread.

THELMA: Take a seat, I'll bring it to you.

GINA: So Jack, what kind of police work are you doing? You are too rude to be community policeman.

STANLEY (*sits at table*): Boy them give community work a bad name in Brixton. Every policeman is a anti-community person, twenty-four hours a day. They control everything and them mash up every little hustling us black people invented.

JACK: Oh my oh my. He does rabbit a bit. What are you? An undercover politician?

STANLEY: Yes, and I was born in Brixton and I just reached back.

GINA: What – our first black M.P.?

THELMA: With a Brixton credential.

GINA: Every time you talk in the House of Parliament all the other M.P.'s them would tremble.

GINA *gives* STANLEY *two slices of bread with piece of salt fish.*

STANLEY: Thanks. Well yes, could I have something to drink. Yes, give me a cup of tea.

GINA: The tea's not ready.

STANLEY: That's all right, I can wait a few minutes.

GINA: It's not going to be ready for hours.

STANLEY: Since when tea take hours to make?

GINA: Since I say so.

THELMA: Have a punch, I mean roots drink.

STANLEY: Oh yeh. Give it to me.

THELMA: Right, it's very nice.

STANLEY: You are the roots.

THELMA: Both of us.

STANLEY: That's nice, I like that.

THELMA *sits at* STANLEY's *table.* GINA *gets punch from fridge.*

GINA: So Jack, you're under attack.

JACK: No, not at all. I going.

STANLEY: That's the best thing you could do.

THELMA: Don't worry yourself about the police man.

JACK: Lucky man. (*Putting on his helmet.*)

STANLEY: You jealous?

JACK: No. (*Laughs.*) Morning all.

THELMA: You stand there and think you is going to joke me into jail.

JACK: It's not me you got to worry about.

STANLEY: Every policeman is the same, whether they are black or white. You sell your birthright to the Englishman.

JACK: I am an Englishman. Boy oh boy you have got chips, mountains and pressure on your shoulders.

STANLEY: Yes I know, while you is as free as a bird.

JACK: One . . . two . . . three . . . four . . . (JACK *walks away.*) five . . . six . . . seven . . . eight . . . nine . . . ten (*Exits.*)

THELMA: Ah der you are, he's gone, relax.

STANLEY: What's your name.

THELMA: Thelma – and that's Gina. I am just helping out for a while.

STANLEY: So Gina, how comes you harbour uniform policemen in here?

GINA: It is not my business who comes in here, as long as they behave themselves. That's £2.50 you owe me.

STANLEY: Sure (*Gets £20 note from pocket –* GINA *collects.*)

GINA: Thank you. (*Gives* STANLEY *change.*)

THELMA: You're nice when you're calm.

GINA: Thelma, I'm going round the back, if you get busy call me.

THELMA: Sure. (GINA *exits.*)

STANLEY: This could be my lucky day. I know about the caf. Where is Flight?

THELMA: He is on the front line.

STANLEY: What is he doing on the front line?

THELMA: I don't know.

STANLEY: Does he have many friends on the front line?

THELMA: I don't know very much about his business except what Gina tells me.

STANLEY: What does she tell you?

THELMA: Come on man, what is this?

STANLEY: OK. OK. I should not question a pretty woman.

THELMA: What's that supposed to mean?

STANLEY: It means you is very nice man.

THELMA: You're funny as well.

STANLEY: You make me feel nice man. You giving me a kind of homely welcome.

THELMA: That's a nice thing to say to a stranger that is close to you.

STANLEY: Oh what a way I am so slow. I now just notice how beautiful you are.

THELMA: I operate at a faster pace. I notice how handsome you was minutes ago.

STANLEY: You making me taste sweetness inside my stomach.

THELMA: The bubbly stuff?

STANLEY: Yes we can have plenty of that.

THELMA: You making me glow in the early part of the day.

STANLEY: I don't know the runnings in Brixton at the moment. Where can we get a drink and a smoke? I don't want to go on the front line.

THELMA: Later. I want to hear some more about the bubbly drink.

STANLEY: Your glowing have overpowered me.

STANLEY *holds her hand. They stand and kiss.*

THELMA: Do you like me?

STANLEY: Like you? You's the best thing I ever seen.

THELMA: Don't be stupid.

STANLEY: Stupid? I'm willing to put my money where my mouth is.

THELMA: Oh yeh?

STANLEY: Let's go up the West End and do some shopping.

THELMA: You don't even know me.

They kiss.

THELMA: What can I say?

STANLEY: Nothing, let's go.

THELMA: Let me talk to Gina.

They kiss.
   THELMA *exits.* STANLEY *lights big cigar. Lights going down.*

Scene Two
Lights up. Three days later.
   FLIGHT *sits alone at table with ingredients to make punch. Lots of unlabelled bottles – Nestlés condensed milk, plastic bucket and half pint glasses.* GINA *in kitchen.*

FLIGHT: Gina keep your eye on the soup, don't let it burn, you know how easy it is to burn peas soup.

GINA: You don't see is only one dumpling in the glass case. Come and knead the flour, I can't knead the flour.

FLIGHT: Later, I haven't stopped working since I get back.

GINA: Next time you disappear you must make sure you play a game with the traffic.

FLIGHT: Oh lord have mercy. Pressure, pressure.
(Singing):
One bright morning
When this life is over
I shall fly away home
Me say fly away home to Master Jesus
Fly away home.
(Repeat.)

STANLEY *enters with suit, tie, overcoat, carton box, brief-case.*

STANLEY: You happy man?

FLIGHT: No, not really.

STANLEY: Well you sound happy to me.

FLIGHT: No man, business is very bad. Is rock, me rocking me head to get some money to go and insure me car.

STANLEY *(puts briefcase and carton box on table – sits at table with FLIGHT)*: Well, I will come straight to the point. We both need each other.

FLIGHT: What man, no kidding? Gina, come serve the gentleman. I got problems.

GINA *(from kitchen)*: What's happening, somebody trying to rape you?

FLIGHT: Stop your chatting and come serve the man.

GINA: I busy.

FLIGHT: You're not as busy as me.

GINA: I work my backside off yesterday, and last night while you was farting about.

STANLEY: No hurry, I can wait till you finish man.

FLIGHT: Boy, these women.

Enter GINA.

FLIGHT: Is why you so miserable?

GINA *(kissing her teeth)*: I tired. Oh, it's you.

STANLEY: Yes, hello again.

GINA: There is nothing in the caf to sell you at the moment – go away and come back.

STANLEY: What?

GINA: Yes, leave, I want to talk to Flight.

FLIGHT: The man come to talk business with me – what's your name?

GINA: Him name Stanley, he's not going to talk to you until I do.

FLIGHT: No kidding?

GINA: No kidding.

FLIGHT: All right man, I see you later.

STANLEY: OK. OK. I see you spar.

GINA: Flight is not your spar, you'is just another freak who comes back to Brixton to cause trouble and mash up the caf.

STANLEY: I'm not going to mash up your caf, and I am not a freak.

GINA: I don't care what you are.

FLIGHT: All right Stanley, I'll see you later.

STANLEY: OK OK have it your own way. I will be back.

STANLEY *exits*. GINA *sits at table with* FLIGHT.

FLIGHT: And what was that about?

GINA: One thing at a time. I feel like killing you.

FLIGHT: Why, what have I done now?

GINA: For what you done to me since we opened the caf. How could you be so wicked? The very day we open the caf you disappear instantly and never come back for days until late last night.

FLIGHT: Princess, I was trying to collect my money that I lend the man. The car need insurance. We only just open, we need a good cash flow.

GINA: If you didn't lend it in the first place, you wouldn't have to go back to collect it.

FLIGHT: You know I make a little profit on the money I lend the boys.

GINA: I don't know nothing. All I know is that you lend money to ganja sellers and you're not selling ganja.

FLIGHT: Oh God Man, don't cold me up so early in the morning.

GINA: No ganja money did not help us to open Lonely Cowboy.

FLIGHT: I don't know, sometime is only ganja money that is going around in Brixton.

Police siren. Car driving past.

GINA: When are you going to take life serious?

FLIGHT: You don't believe I'm serious.

GINA: No stay here and help me run the caf and stop driving up and down the place like a madman.

FLIGHT: I will stop when I finish collecting me money.

GINA: You know when you didn't come back the first night when we open, I think you was dead. I call the police station and I expect Jack to answer the phone but he didn't.

FLIGHT: Oh God, cool it man.

GINA: And no more regular Soho night out, we can't afford it.

FLIGHT: All right, all right, what about Stanley?

GINA: And another thing again, Thelma did not spend half an hour in the caf after you left.

FLIGHT: Pressure, pressure, what about Stanley?

GINA: I coming to that, he's no good. I don't like him. He looks like a killer.

FLIGHT: Leave people business alone. I warning you. Leave Brixton people business alone and don't let me lose my temper. What else you have against him?

GINA: Let me start at the beginning.

FLIGHT: Out with it man.

GINA: Don't shout at me.

FLIGHT: All right, all right, don't torture me.

GINA: Jesus Christ, what a big stupid bastard you is.

FLIGHT: Stop hitting my balls and tell me about Stanley.

GINA: Well as soon as you left, him walk in and give Jack one piece of cussing.

FLIGHT (*stands up*): I going for a drive.

GINA: No, no, sit down. Sit down.

FLIGHT: I almost got a headache. (*He sits.*)

GINA: Him just sweeped Thelma off her feet, take her up the West End, buy her three spanking new dresses, one helluva overcoat and shoes, a right here so, me sit down, 9 o'clock the other night when they come back with cartonbox upon carton box and show me everything. What is he? Shakespeare – Romeo and Juliet?

FLIGHT: I see.

FLIGHT *begins stirring punch with wooden spoon energetically.*

FLIGHT: He's that kind of man. So where is Thelma?

GINA: Me don't know, they left together last night.

FLIGHT: Wally get burned again.

GINA: He didn't stand a chance in the first place. Wally's not a fool – he knows her.

FLIGHT: So Stanley's a millionaire.

GINA: Don't get mixed up with him, that's all.

FLIGHT: Poor me, how can I get mixed up with him? I don't know him.

GINA: As soon as Thelma take one of the carton boxes back to the car he was giving me the eye.

FLIGHT: That's interesting. Maybe he wants to give you the same things that he gives Thelma.

GINA: Make him clear off from me.

FLIGHT: Anyway, my cowboy days are over – I don't want no trouble.
So Stanley think him can kidnap my woman.

GINA: Make him think what him want – I don't care nothing bout him.

FLIGHT: I wonder what him want to see me about.

GINA: Whatever it is it spell trouble.

JACK *enters, short leather jacket, open-neck shirt, two gold necklaces, bracelet, watch, three rings on each hand.*

GINA: Jack, is it your day off? Are you join the drug squad?

JACK: I am not answering no question and I am not asking any. I just want a cup of tea and a chat.

GINA: You and your tea.

FLIGHT: Jack, taste this and tell me if it wants anything.

FLIGHT *uses cup to pour drink into glass.* JACK *tastes drink.*

GINA: Boy oh boy. Policemen are really lucky.

JACK: Yes, it's not bad. Good – but it could do with a touch more rum.

FLIGHT: Why rum? And not nutmeg? The man choose the most expensive ingredient. All right – I have a little left. (*He pours rum into punch, stirs and gives* JACK *full glass.*) How it taste?

JACK: Yes it is full of goodness. How much is it?

FLIGHT: No man, you catch me making it, next time you pay. Gina, you want a glass?

GINA: No sir, me no want no punch.

FLIGHT *drinks punch.*

JACK: Give me a dumpling and a piece of salt-fish.

GINA: Flight, go and make the blasted dumpling them.

FLIGHT: I haven't finish yet.

GINA *serves him.* JACK *pays with £1 note* GINA *gives* JACK *30p change. Police siren. Car driving past.*

GINA: So Jack you know where the police cars them a drive to now.

JACK: I am here, how must I know that?

FLIGHT: Good answer.

He begins clearing table. Puts plastic bucket in fridge, unlabelled bottles under counter.

GINA: I hope you don't expect us to give you information.

FLIGHT: But Gina, what is the matter with you this morning? Did Jack ask you for any information?

GINA: Well he might.

FLIGHT: Tell me something, you don't have anything to do? You have any information to give to Jack?

GINA: No, but I was thinking about Stanley.

FLIGHT: But oh God in heaven, what am I listening to in my base?

JACK: What about Stanley?

GINA: Well he was arguing with you yesterday again when he came in here looking for Flight.

FLIGHT: I feeling pain to rass.

JACK: Well I am used to black people trying to get at me.

FLIGHT: I feel stupid listening to the both of you.

JACK: Where is Stanley?

GINA: He is with Thelma.

FLIGHT: How do you know that?

GINA: That's no secret, everybody see them together.

JACK: So what about Wally?

GINA: Wally can't keep up with him, he's a big shot. Buy her carton box upon carton box of clothes.

JACK: He only met her recently.

GINA: It was like grease lightning. They just zoom off up to the West End.

FLIGHT: Gina, leave Brixton people and police business alone before people start calling you police informer.

GINA: This is no informing. This is domestic talk.

FLIGHT: So suppose people come in the cafe bar and hear you talking to Jack.

GINA: That is not one God thing, because Jack is going to come in here every day.

JACK: I might.

FLIGHT: You see you, you want to kill me.

GINA: Lonely Cowboy must have protection.

FLIGHT: Any protection that is going to get done around here, I will do it.

GINA: You are not going to be here. You will be gallivanting all over the place, collecting money that people borrow from you.

FLIGHT: So you're telling Jack everything?

JACK: Come on now, you're losing me.

FLIGHT: Jack, stop the police talk man.

JACK: So because I is a policeman you think I is not a black man.

FLIGHT: What does black have to do with it? Murder is murder and police work is murder to me.

JACK: What murder?

FLIGHT: Murder, plain and simple that. Lonely Cowboy is no place for controversy.

JACK: But murder man, what you talking about? You making me body jump.

FLIGHT: Everyman is free, so the law say.

GINA: I feel like Job with the amount of patience that I have got.

FLIGHT: Shut up man. You see, a black policeman must have his differences with black people.

JACK: So our parents didn't have black policemen where they come from?

FLIGHT: Brixton is different. Everything is jail here, even murder.

JACK: But why murder?

GINA: Yes and some of them will murder you in here for a penny.

Enter STANLEY *with carton box.*

FLIGHT: Oh my God! Pressure brings on a thousand mountains to climb. I say how far are we away from new year? I must make a resolution.

JACK: Well, time to move on.

GINA: That was quick. (*Looking at* STANLEY, *she exits to the back.*)

STANLEY *comes close to* FLIGHT.

STANLEY: I want to talk to you.

FLIGHT: Yeh.

JACK *and* STANLEY *catch each other's eye, very tense. Police siren. Car driving past.* JACK *exits.*

FLIGHT: So here we are then. You want to talk.

STANLEY: Yes, everybody seems to be giving me the cold shoulder around here.

FLIGHT: Nothing to do with me.

STANLEY: I know that. I was born in Brixton. Went to the East End to grow up and travel the world. And now I come back to Brixton to rest.

FLIGHT: You look well off man.

STANLEY: Why because of the suit and the briefcase?

FLIGHT: You seem sure of yourself and you got money as well.

STANLEY: Let's get down to business. I can supply Brixton with a lot of ganja.

FLIGHT: Listen man, come out of my place and don't make me angry.

STANLEY: Oh, so you're afraid of big money.

FLIGHT: What money?

STANLEY: Big money if you become my partner.

FLIGHT: I have got a partner, she's around the back.

STANLEY: Look man, you've got a nice place. This is where we can make a good start of something big. Brother, my ship have come in. It is your lucky day.

FLIGHT: How – and for what?

STANLEY: Let's work the front line with some good ganja.

FLIGHT: I don't know the front line.

STANLEY: Yes you do.

Enter GINA.

GINA: I'm going to the market to get some vegetables.

FLIGHT: Yes, all right.

GINA *exits.*

STANLEY: Right, back to what we were saying. I'm willing to get rid of the briefcase and suit any minute now.

FLIGHT: I don't know what you're talking about.

STANLEY: Ganja man, ganja.

FLIGHT: What about it?

STANLEY: We could supply all the boys in Brixton with them stuff.

FLIGHT: How?

STANLEY: First, we will just run through the front line.

FLIGHT: You is a farmer? Are you talking about home-grown stuff?

STANLEY: No man, the real macoy.

FLIGHT: Listen Stanley, I don't know

you and I don't know if you are mad or not.

STANLEY: Mad? But what the rass you talking about?

FLIGHT: How can any one man supply all of Brixton with ganja?

STANLEY: Boy is you mad.

FLIGHT: Is who you calling boy?

STANLEY: You – I is a big man, boy. My ship have come in.

FLIGHT: Don't call me boy.

STANLEY: Boy to me, right now, because I am big.

FLIGHT *punches* STANLEY *with his fist.* STANLEY *punches* FLIGHT *with his fist. Punch for punch – fighting.* STANLEY*'s carton box gets knocked over, ganja spills on the floor, table, chairs falling over, both of them groaning.*

FLIGHT: Fighting me in my own place, I kill you blood cloth.

STANLEY: Is who you think you punch? I broke up you blood cloth.

Enter WALLY.

WALLY: Flight, stop the fighting in your place. Come on man, violence is no good.

FLIGHT: I tell you not to call me a boy.

WALLY: Man stop the violence in the place.

They stop fighting each other. Holding each other's chest with one hand.

STANLEY: I is a big man, why can't I call you a boy?

FLIGHT: Stop it, I tell you.

FLIGHT *pulls* STANLEY *closer to him.* WALLY *moves quickly in between them.*

STANLEY: Why take it so serious?

WALLY: Yes, done with it.

WALLY *pulls* STANLEY *and* FLIGHT*'s hands from each other.*

FLIGHT: Wally take the rass cloth bicycle off my table.

WALLY *quickly holds on to bicycle.*

STANLEY: All right, I done.

FLIGHT: Don't do it again.

WALLY: Boy, black people is really serious.

FLIGHT: Boy. I hope is not me you talking to Wally.

STANLEY: Jesus Christ, look what the man done to me weed.

STANLEY *shovels up ganja with his hands.*

WALLY: Is herbs that? Lord, what a lot of ganja.

WALLY *quickly shovelling with his hands into the carton box.*

STANLEY: Move away from my things.

WALLY: All right. (*He stands up, quickly holds on to bicycle.*)

FLIGHT: This bloodcloth bicycle.

FLIGHT *is picking up knife, fork, generally tidying up.* WALLY *looking at ganja.* STANLEY *puts carton box on table.*

WALLY (*shaking hands with STANLEY*): You're bleeding man, go wash your face in the toilet.

STANLEY: I'm bleeding?

WALLY: Yes, man.

FLIGHT: Wally, take the bicycle out of the place.

WALLY: All right, I hitting the road again.

STANLEY: Thanks. (*Exits to back.*)

WALLY: Brother Flight, this is your base, no violence. This is where you take off and land. If you mash it up you will have nowhere to land when you finish flying.

FLIGHT: I know. Go now with the rass cloth bicycle out of the Lonely Cowboy.

WALLY: I is also a cowboy. The only thing is, my horse is a bicycle. Right, I going.

He starts to leave, stops dead at door, turns about, FLIGHT *busy, don't see him,* WALLY *gently leans bicycle on table, tip-toe. Grabs carton box.* FLIGHT *looks at him.* WALLY *at door. Looks at bicycle. Police siren. Car driving past. He runs away leaving bicycle.* STANLEY *comes*

running in. He sees the back of WALLY *with box.*

STANLEY: Where him gone?

FLIGHT: You don't see I am cleaning up.

STANLEY: Where him live?

FLIGHT: I cleaning the place up.

STANLEY *exits very quickly and comes back.*

STANLEY: Him gone, where him live?

FLIGHT: I don't know.

STANLEY: All right. (*Looking at bicycle.*) Him bicycle will lead me to him. All I have to do is ask the right questions.

STANLEY *exits with bicycle and briefcase.* FLIGHT *stands still for a few seconds, puts his hand on his head.*

FLIGHT: I am sure they are trying to mad me. Where is the respect from these people?

He removes his hands from his head.

FLIGHT: Look how the man want to mash up my pretty, pretty cafe bar. The first man him pick on when him come back to Brixton is me. Christ the prison troubles have now begun. I bet I kill one of these monkey rass cloth idiots.

He removes the holsters and buckles the belt around his waist.

FLIGHT: Yes I must prepare my head to fight these people. (*He plays with revolvers for 6-10 seconds.*) Is going to be rass to play between me and them.

He sits on table and put his hands on his head.

I shall not fall under the pressure.

Lights going down.

Scene Three
Lights up. Later that day.
CANDY *and* DALTON *sit eating steak, rice and peas.*

CANDY: I must get a job, or some good volunteer work to keep me on the straight and narrow road to find my roots. Maybe my roots are not in Brixton.

DALTON: You are with Mr Roots himself! And Brixton is my number one.

CANDY: I wasn't talking about you. I like your poems and so does a lot of other people. Listen. What about asking Flight to let us have this place and we could charge people to listen to you reading your poems.

DALTON: That sounds good, but this place is too small.

CANDY: Oh, I forget about your friends.

DALTON: What about the club?

CANDY: Yes, we will do it, on Tuesday night.

DALTON: It will be a great night.

CANDY: And we will be giving the youth them some good culture at the same time.

DALTON: You think he will let us have the place?

CANDY: Yes man, its empty on a Tuesday night.

DALTON: We will go and see him when we leave here.

CANDY: Good idea. He's a nice guy. He will let us have the club every Tuesday night if there is no trouble.

DALTON: Yes, and with you working with me he might let us do our thing. Dalton rise again. My youth them always behave themselves.

CANDY: As soon as there is a fight, I don't want to know no more.

DALTON: Keep away from the violence before we get started. This is the good book telling us what to do.

CANDY: Well tell your friends them to behave themselves.

DALTON: Yes I will. I am going to do a great reading.

CANDY: Oh I would love to hear you read your poetry in the club.

DALTON: Right, we will do it.

CANDY: I think my mum wants to get married again.

DALTON: So she wants you to leave home.

CANDY: Well sort of, but she's worried about me.

DALTON: She doesn't like me, does she.

CANDY: Well you never have any money.

DALTON: I am doing Ja work. Where I man must get money from?

CANDY: Well even in church they have collection boxes.

Enter FLIGHT *collecting empty cups, saucers and plates from table. He puts them on counter.*

DALTON: Brother Flight, the steak tastes good man.

FLIGHT: Yes, it was well seasoned.

CANDY: The smell is fantastic.

DALTON: Let we have two root juice.

FLIGHT *gets drinks from fridge.*

FLIGHT: Is what win the 2.30?

DALTON: Running Wind.

FLIGHT: Jesus Christ, I knew the horse would win.

DALTON: Yes I lose in the same race myself.

FLIGHT: Why don't I follow my mind, the bookies sting me again.

DALTON: Don't make them mad you.

FLIGHT *puts drinks on table and takes empties away.*

FLIGHT: No sir, I don't have much to do with them these days.

CANDY: Wise man. The bookie is the only winner.

DALTON: I only have one bet today.

CANDY: Bookie and ganja, mash up the older black people in Brixton.

FLIGHT: Is joke you making? The church have a lot of them as customer.

DALTON: Boy, I have nothing against the church as long as black people can find peace in them. So Flight I hear you discipline a stranger.

FLIGHT: The man cheeky calling me boy.

GINA *enters from outside.*

GINA: So Flight, you have a fight in the cafe with that Stanley and tell me nothing about it.

FLIGHT: That was no fight, nobody didn't get hurt.

GINA *takes empties to kitchen. He gets 'Sporting Life' and sits at table.*

DALTON: How much is that Brother Flight?

GINA *enters.*

FLIGHT: Let me see – £8 – pay Gina man.

DALTON *pays* GINA.

CANDY: You ready?

DALTON: Yes.

They exit. GINA *sits at table with* FLIGHT.

GINA: What happen? I told you he was a bad one.

FLIGHT: He's not all that bad.

GINA: What is he – a ganja man?

FLIGHT: I don't know.

GINA: Come on, tell me what happened

FLIGHT: He called me a boy.

GINA: Well that's not too bad, you are a little boy most of the time.

FLIGHT: Oh yeh!

GINA: What did he want to see you about?

FLIGHT: He wants us to make some big money together.

GINA: Doing what? Not selling ganja I hope.

FLIGHT: What have you got against ganja?

GINA: I can't stand the smell – is he a ganja man?

FLIGHT: No.

Enter JACK. *Police constable uniform.*

JACK: Hello, hello. This is official.

FLIGHT: One policeman cannot carry out a raid.

JACK: This is no raid, just a few questions.

GINA: You all right Jack?

JACK: Yes, yes.

GINA: You want something to drink?

JACK: No, I just want to ask a few questions about Wally's bicycle.

GINA: Wally bicycle? What bicycle?

JACK: Well Flight might know something about it.

FLIGHT: What about Wally bicycle?

JACK: We got Stanley at the station.

FLIGHT: Yeh – what for?

JACK: Wally claims Stanley steal his bicycle from here.

GINA: What, Stanley's got a car.

JACK: Well he was joyriding around the front line with the bicycle.

FLIGHT: I don't know, he and Wally leave here together, but again I am not sure. I was cleaning up.

GINA: Stanley's no good, but I don't believe he would thief Wally bicycle.

JACK: Wally claims he's afraid of Stanley.

FLIGHT: Wally is a coward, he's afraid of everybody.

GINA: I wonder if Thelma have anything to do with it.

JACK: Could be.

THELMA *enters.*

THELMA: Jack you have a lot of guts to come here so often in uniform.

JACK: No, not really.

THELMA: Gina I am worried. I want to talk to you.

JACK: Oh yes? What are you worried about?

THELMA: This is no police work. I am worried about the man in my life.

JACK: You mean men don't you?

THELMA: No, I mean a man.

JACK: You know that Wally want to lock up Stanley for stealing his bicycle.

THELMA: I never hear so much rubbish – what does a big man like Stanley want with Wally bicycle?

JACK: Revenge I suppose. Are you sleeping with both of them at the same time?

THELMA: You've got a dirty mind for a policeman.

JACK: No, not really, I just trying to sort things out.

THELMA: Where is Stanley?

JACK: At the station with Wally.

THELMA: What?

JACK: Flight have you got anything to tell me about this?

FLIGHT: Jesus, no sir, nothing at all.

JACK: Something fishy is going on.

GINA: Yes, I think so.

FLIGHT: Shut up.

GINA: Stop barking at me like some dog.

FLIGHT: Is who you calling dog?

JACK (*commandingly*): She did not call you a dog!

THELMA: What about Stanley and Wally?

JACK: Would you like to come with me to the station?

THELMA: No thank you.

JACK: Oh well, I must get back.

JACK *is walking away.*

GINA: Good luck Jack.

JACK: Thanks. (*Exits.*)

FLIGHT: You like policemen?

GINA: I like Jack.

THELMA: Why Wally so wicked? Why he wants to lock up Stanley?

GINA: Jealousy I suppose.

FLIGHT: I am going to sell the caf. Oh my God the pressure is too much for me.

GINA: Quiet your backside. I own half of it.

FLIGHT: Would you like to buy me out?

GINA: I might.

THELMA: I want to talk to you. Christ, I am so worried about Stanley. He is too much for me.

FLIGHT: Since when you own half of my caf?

GINA: Since the government change the law.

THELMA: What are you two carrying on about?

FLIGHT: Gina, who owns the caf?

GINA: You do, but I want half of it.

THELMA *lights a cigarette.*

FLIGHT: It is my caf, and I will do what I want to do with it.

GINA: Ok. Ok don't take everything so serious.

THELMA: Can I get a word in.

GINA: Sure.

THELMA: What should I do about Stanley?

FLIGHT: He's probably a nice guy.

GINA: If he is, what is he doing in the police station?

THELMA: That's nothing. He's playing a game with Wally. He can buy himself out of anything.

GINA: How rich is he?

THELMA: Oh, I don't know. He said I am the first woman he had a relationship with for over a year.

GINA: Where was he, prison?

THELMA: No, he was working abroad. Something like travelling representative.

GINA: So what are you worried about? He's a nice guy.

FLIGHT: I will be back in a minute. I'm going to the betting shop.

FLIGHT *exits.*

GINA: So tell me about Stanley. He never look like no representative to me – but he dress nicely.

THELMA: That's one of the things I am worried about. And he's too aggressive for that kind of work.

GINA: The way he was going on, I thought he wanted to put you in a bed of roses.

THELMA: No, he is serious with life.

GINA: A working man eh. They are very rare these days.

THELMA: Yes, but I feel something is wrong.

GINA: Maybe he's only kinky that's all.

THELMA: No man, what was he doing with Wally bicycle?

GINA: Yes. That's weird and he fight Flight.

THELMA: Is what you telling me?
I didn't know he had a fight with
Flight. Is one of my little friend call me
just now and tell me that Stanley is
riding Wally bicycle up and down like
a madman.

GINA: Did you tell Stanley about Wally?

THELMA: What is there to tell him. I
have never slept with Wally.

GINA: What? And I thought it was him
who was blowing breath in your face at
night.

THELMA: When I want to go on the
front line I always go with Wally that's
all.

GINA: Oh I see.

THELMA: Listen man, help me. I don't
understand what's going on. Stanley
park his car and ride Wally bicycle all
over Brixton until he get arrested.

GINA: What Stanley tell you?

THELMA: Nothing, I haven't seen him.

GINA: Flight got the answer.

THELMA: Him like Flight. He said they
would make great partners.

GINA: But how does Wally bicycle get in
the act? Did he ever tell you anything
about Wally bicycle?

THELMA: No, not a thing.

GINA: He just come to Brixton, pick you
up, fight Flight and now he is in jail for
thiefing Wally bicycle. I don't believe
he's a working man.

THELMA: Yes I'm having my doubts.

GINA: Anyway, let's have couple glasses
of punch.

THELMA: Good. The punch will make
you mash up Flight back in bed tonight.

GINA: You see how life is sweet Thelma.

THELMA: Just make sure he tell you all
his secret that's all.

GINA: Yes I will.

*They begin laughing. Lights going
down.*

ACT TWO

Scene One
Lights up. Four days later.
Night. Cafe closed. Curtains drawn.
Everything is clean and ready for the next
day. FLIGHT enters from kitchen. He is
very tired, hasn't slept for days. He is
walking around the cafe. As he speaks his
hands are in and out of his pocket.
Sometimes his hands move gently,
sometimes vigorously.

FLIGHT: My entire world have changed
since I opened the caf. Things that I
think was impossible is now happening
to me. Blood cloth. Like tons of bricks
they all coming down on me. Something
can only be described as a miracle.
What will happen to Lonely Cowboy if
I let these people tear me apart. It is all
hustling and killing in Brixton. As soon
as you try to do anything legal. Nothing
can change me mind. I'm not carrying
no news about nobody. All I want is to
run a good, honest business in Brixton,
but no, every ball head is running to me
with their troubles as if I am Ja. Can
all these things be true? Haven't I work
hard enough to promote myself above
police station and courthouse? But what
the rass is this? What is plain clothes
policemen doing in my caf as my back
turned to do a little mini-cab
work and one trip to Birmingham?
What will happen to Lonely Cowboy if
I let these people drag me into police
station and courthouse to give evidence
against one black man for another black
man. None of it doesn't have anything
to do with me. I am not a news carrier,
so I've got nothing to tell anybody. So
I have got to stop do everything and
just sit down and watch me cafe bar.
The place haven't been open for two
weeks and already plain clothes
policemen coming here and write down
my name. Tulse Hill will have to fall
down in Babylon Brixton before I let
the pressure kill me. Bloodclath, the
end will have to justify the means. Yes
let the stamping carry on all over the
place and I myself is going to do a lot
of stamping if anybody come in here to
rugby tackle me again. Every living
person must realise that it was a lot of
hard work to open Lonely Cowboy.
People on earth I work hard for the
little I've got. Why should I let those
bastards take it away from me.

He sits. Enter GINA from kitchen.
THELMA behind. They are tired, they
haven't slept for days. THELMA
smoking cigarette nervously.
THELMA sits at FLIGHT's table.
GINA standing.

GINA: I am getting tired of your mouth.
All you said was that you was going to
the betting shop. What do you expect?
You left the place for days again, lying
bastard. You run away because you
know the police was coming to ask you
question about Stanley and Wally.

FLIGHT: Wake up to all the pressure
that is going on.

GINA: Wake up? I haven't been to sleep
again for days and it's your fault.

THELMA: All the lightning and thunder
that is clapping doesn't have anything
to do with me. I am involved with
Stanley. He is in jail, and I want to
help.

GINA sits at THELMA and
FLIGHT's table.

GINA: For God's sake, I am your woman
and Thelma is my friend. Tell us what
happened. Look, if it is big trouble it is
better to get it over with now than later.

THELMA: I thought it was a joke until he
punched Wally in the police station and
that is the only reason why they
remanded him in custody.

Police siren. Car driving past.

GINA: Listen, I was the one who disliked
Stanley in the first place, but this is
more than anyone can bear.

THELMA: You see me, if I am going to
die, I want to know why. Yes I want to
do everything with my eye wide open.

FLIGHT: Look I am not Barabas or
Judas. This is Flight who is always
flying. The name Flight is a mark of
respect for the things that I have done.
I fly away from everybody's business.
This is the only business I have got.

GINA: What about the betting shop? If I
did not threaten to leave you, the
betting shop would have continued to
mash up everything and there would
have never been any Lonely Cowboy
for you to brag about.

FLIGHT: Who's bragging?

GINA: Everything is you, you. No respect or love for me. I want to be loved since I am slugging my guts out.

FLIGHT: Are you saying I don't love you? So who am I working for?

GINA: Yourself.

FLIGHT: I never dream you were so wicked.

GINA: Wicked? What the hell you talking about?

THELMA: Look honestly, Stanley is in jail and I don't know what is happening.

GINA: Tell Thelma if you don't want to tell me. I don't care about your secrets any more.

FLIGHT: All right Thelma, what do you want to know.

THELMA: You know what I want to know.

FLIGHT: For God's sake leave me alone. I going mad to rass. Why didn't I listen to what Stanley have to tell me. I going to wash me face before I start balling the place down. Boy I feeling sad again to rass.

FLIGHT exits to back.

GINA: Stop calling yourself boy, you know you don't like it. Well at least we're getting somewhere Thelma.

THELMA: Yes, I think so.

GINA: He's cooling down. I bet he tell us everything tonight.

THELMA: Yes it will be a great relief.

Knock at door.

GINA: Who is that?

THELMA: Is not Stanley, he's in jail.

GINA: Flight.

FLIGHT: Yes.

GINA: Somebody at the door.

FLIGHT: We close, why they bothering me.

GINA: I don't know. Come and find out.

Knock at door.

FLIGHT: All right, all right I coming.

FLIGHT enters and opens door.

DALTON: Hello Brother Flight. I passing and I see the light was on and I want to talk to you.

FLIGHT: Yeh, all right, come in.

Enter DALTON with posters and leaflets.

DALTON: Hello Thelma. I hear your new man is in jail.

THELMA: It is not a joke.

DALTON: It is – why else would he thief Wally bicycle and then punch him on top of it?

THELMA: You know anything about him?

DALTON: No, but I hear him have money. You know, you women should stick to us local boys. You should know by now that all strange cowboys that comes to Brixton always hot up the place and then got to jail.

THELMA: Stanley's not a cowboy.

DALTON: What is he then when he hijack Wally bicycle with all his goods? Him is a bad cowboy. Him just ride the bicycle up and down on the front line like him mad. I never know you was so beautiful. Him jealous. It seems like you let him taste a little bit of love. Fucking sweet him.

GINA: Call yourself a poet with such a filthy mouth.

DALTON: No filth is in that, just facts. Anyway is not my business. Brother Flight, I putting on a little show in the Salt and Water club on Tuesday night, so can I leave a few hand-out on your table.

FLIGHT: Yes, man.

GINA: So why ask him and not me?

DALTON: What you mean?

GINA: Why is it that it is always men that is the boss of everything? And then always cause troubles out of hell hole on top of it. Listen Dalton, nobody's boss of me in here.

DALTON: Peace sister, lot of love. Yes Brother Flight, this show is going to be great.

He puts one leaflet on each table.

I going to pack the place out. The brothers them must get some culture from us the local artists. I hope to see you there Thelma.

THELMA: I don't like poetry. I don't undertstand it.

DALTON: You don't understand me?

THELMA: No.

DALTON: It seems like I will have to start taking care of you.

Police siren. Car driving past.

DALTON: Jack and his mates are busy again. It's not going to be just poets Thelma, some heavy music is going to fill the air, but still I feel you will like my poetry. Brother Flight, this is a dread poem. This is how the evening will start:

Takes poem out of his papers.

See the school children
Running up the front line
They are black school children
Running free
The white policeman truncheon
Shall not touch their heads
For Ja words
Is home for them
Younger than the youths
They are Ja schoolchildren
No violence shall touch them in
   Babylon Brixton
This is Ja ruling over all
His children
For peace and love is the wisdom
Of black school children
See them running up the front line
The black school children them.

This is where I get down into socomento rudiments with me poem them.

FLIGHT: Yes man I hear you.

DALTON: You like it?

FLIGHT: Yes.

GINA: It's getting late.

DALTON: Well I hope to see all of you at the Salt and Water next Tuesday night. So you are alone Thelma?

THELMA: Is what's wrong with you Dalton? I going home. Gina, see you tomorrow.

GINA: Yes. It seem like there is nothing more to be gain here tonight.

DALTON: Can I walk you home?

THELMA: Please yourself.

DALTON: Thanks Brother Flight – I see you.

FLIGHT: Yes man, all right.

GINA: Thelma take care luv.

THELMA: A feel cold and tired.

DALTON: Snuggle up in my arms.

DALTON *and* THELMA *exit.*

FLIGHT: Why you believe I don't love you?

GINA: You have too many secrets man.

FLIGHT: Gina, that Stanley is a bad man.

GINA: No he is a working man.

FLIGHT: Working man or not the carton box that you see him come in here with, it was full of ganja.

GINA: I can't stand that word. Ganja troubles upon troubles to rass. I don't want to know nothing more about it.

FLIGHT: I feel a little sorry for him, it's me who should have get the box of ganja and not Wally.

GINA: Shut your face. That only spell troubles. I thought it was jealousy over Thelma. Don't let him come back in the place or there will be murder.

FLIGHT: I can't bar a black man unless he cause trouble.

GINA: What more troubles you want? He fight you.

FLIGHT: That was different man. Let us see this thing out together.

GINA: I must tell Thelma my mind tomorrow.

FLIGHT: Listen man, I tired of quarrelling with you.

GINA: Me too, but promise me you will not get mixed up with my ganja business.

FLIGHT: Tell you truth, I don't want to lose you Gina.

GINA: I know you love me sometimes.

FLIGHT: No man, all the time.

GINA: I wish I could prove that. Life is only going to be hard for us if we don't make the right preparation. I don't want to break down in tears. Let us try and save the little money we making out of the caf.

FLIGHT: But if him have a lot of ganja we could make some good money in a short time.

GINA: No. He will kill Wally when he catch up with him.

FLIGHT: I feel Wally's going to disappear for a while.

GINA: Disappear what? He don't know anywhere else except Brixton.

FLIGHT: No man, him have money now, he can move into new ground.

GINA: I don't trust him. Why he thief the man ganja and then lock him up for his bicycle? That's when he should have disappeared.

FLIGHT: Yes, he's either wicked or stupid.

GINA: Both. I wonder if Jack know what is going on.

FLIGHT: I don't know, but don't tell him anything.

GINA: Don't be stupid, I am only going to talk to Thelma.

FLIGHT: Don't. You might cause more troubles. Make she find out herself. I will just keep on pretending that I know nothing.

GINA: All right, let's go to bed.

FLIGHT: Princess, I do love you.

GINA: I believe you.

FLIGHT: What do you say we lock up the caf for a week and go to the seaside? No I can't do that, I forget. I got an airport job tomorrow.

GINA: I don't mind. We probably can go the day after tomorrow. Come on, let's go to bed.

She holds his hand.

FLIGHT: Yeh.

He flicks light switch. Lights going down.

Scene Two
Lights up. Next day.
Late morning. Chairs on top of table. Cafe closed. FLIGHT sleeping at table.

GINA *and* CANDY *sitting at another table.*

GINA: No, it's not going to be long before we open again. We are just cooling it for a while.

CANDY: You mean they hot you up so quick?

GINA: That's life.

CANDY: We women should do something together. Men only cause trouble between the sheets.

GINA: I will do anything as long as it doesn't have anything to do with politics.

CANDY: What politics? Just a friendship that will benefit all of us. Look, I sorry about the caf, but I had to come and see you.

GINA: Yes of course, I would have done the same thing myself.

CANDY: You know when he didn't come by me last night I just know something was wrong. So as daylight I went to his house. His brother tells me he didn't come home.

GINA: Maybe he spend the night in the gambling house.

CANDY: I'm not having him back – she can have him forever.

GINA: Don't be so irrational, she's not like that.

CANDY: Oh yes she is. I hate her. She really gets up my nose. You remember our women's group, she fucks that up. We are friends, but she always seems to be the first one to get into trouble and look at this stranger that she take up with, he didn't know her for more than a few minutes before he was in jail.

GINA: Don't mention anything like that to her. She visit him every day while he's on remand.

CANDY: So what is she doing with my Dalton? Kissing and holding hands, when she knows everybody would tell me.

GINA: Maybe you should blame Dalton and not her.

CANDY: Come on Gina, she fell for his sweet talk as soon as my back was turned.

GINA: No man, she's not that type.

CANDY: I don't know, she's that type enough to take Dalton off me.

GINA: I don't think she would want to do that.

CANDY: I haven't seen Dalton for days.

GINA: Do you think he is with her?

CANDY: I don't know. I will find out when they get here together.

GINA: Listen man, you must cool it and take it easy when she gets here.

CANDY: All right. I will try.

GINA: How are you getting on with the show that you are putting on at the Salt and Water?

CANDY: I am beginning to think that Brixton people is not interested in anything like that.

GINA: Well I must admit that those sort of things have passed me by.

CANDY: That is wrong, it shouldn't.

GINA: Child, let me tell you something. Right now there is things that is much harder than poetry.

CANDY: All I hope is that all tadpoles will turn into frogs. Thelma really hurts me.

GINA: Candy, look at our cafe bar, we just opened and yet we closed already.

CANDY: I can't see what Dalton see in Thelma.

GINA: What a man can sleep like Flight.

CANDY: Yes, he's well away isn't he.

GINA: There is some dread troubles going on at the moment. (*Whispers.*) That Wally and Stanley business is very serious.

CANDY: Yeh – what you mean? I thought that Stanley was only mad with jealousy.

GINA: No man, ganja involved.

CANDY: Another ganja man? They are two for a penny these days.

GINA: But I don't think Thelma knows anything about it.

CANDY: What about Dalton?

GINA: What about him?

CANDY: Does he know about it – he's involved with Thelma?

GINA: No man, don't believe those things, but Dalton and Wally are friends.

CANDY: Yes they are friends. I wonder, I wonder.

GINA: Remember not a word to Thelma when she gets here.

CANDY: I feel as if I want to bad.

GINA: No you didn't mean that.

CANDY: She and her bloody one night stand.

GINA: Listen, I am not telling you nothing but I know Thelma. A don't feel she would do anything like that.

CANDY: You don't have to tell me nothing. As soon as I left Dalton house this morning people was telling me about last night.

GINA: Don't listen to them. Is only hearsay.

CANDY: This is a dread place. Everything always happen at the same time. Oh Dalton, why you hurt me so badly?

GINA: Maybe he haven't.

CANDY: But how could Thelma do it? All I am doing is trying to find my roots with the man that I love.

GINA: Cool yourself and watch the dice.

CANDY: All right, I will just give her a piece of my mind.

Enter JACK in police constable uniform.

JACK: What is this? No service? Chairs on the table. While Flight sleeps his lovely life away?

GINA: Boy oh boy, you is one for the gab. We hard up.

JACK: Look more like bankruptcy to me.

GINA: All roads in your head lead to the courthouse.

CANDY: So Jack, would you give evidence against black people in court?

JACK: What is a policeman job in court?

GINA: He gives evidence against everybody.

CANDY: I suppose Jack believes he's got a grand job.

JACK: I have got a job.

CANDY: A job to beat us youth into the ground.

JACK: It was only in recent years that I was a youth myself.

Police siren. Car driving past.

CANDY: Your bells are ringing.

JACK: Yes, back on the job. So when will you be doing business again Gina?

GINA: Soon.

JACK: Well, morning all.

Walking to door. Enter THELMA.

JACK: Hello Thelma.

THELMA: What kind of foolishness this about Stanley?

JACK: I don't know. I am not on the case anymore.

JACK *exits.*

THELMA: I am getting tired of men.

She puts her handbag on counter and leans on counter.

THELMA: I don't know what they do anymore. Morning Gina. You know, I feel Stanley's lying to me, but I can't prove it because he was so nice to me, but I can't take the pressure. So what's this? Why the chairs them on the table.

GINA: Flight didn't cook anything today. Have you seen Wally?

THELMA: Wally? If I see him, I wouldn't have seen him.

CANDY: But you have seen Dalton.

THELMA: Who are you talking to about men, Candy.

CANDY: You been sleeping with him?

GINA: Candy.

THELMA: I just come from Brixton prison to see one man, don't tell me about another man.

CANDY: Where is Dalton? You haven't jailed him have you?

THELMA: You little teenager bitch.

CANDY: Bloody whore.

GINA: Mice, mice, aah, aah, aah aah . . . . . . over there.

FLIGHT *wakes up.*

THELMA: Aah aah aah aah.

CANDY: Aah aah aah.

GINA: No, no, aah, get away from me.

GINA, THELMA, CANDY *holding each other.* FLIGHT *moves quickly, gets revolvers from gunbelts.*

FLIGHT: Where is he – where, where?

FLIGHT *running all over the cafe.*

GINA (*laughing*): You wake quick man.

FLIGHT *stops,* THELMA, GINA, CANDY *let go of each other.*

THELMA: You frighten me.

THELMA *leans on counter.*

CANDY: She shocked me.

GINA: So what were you going to do with the toy gun, Flight?

FLIGHT: I don't know. I just wake up.

CANDY, GINA, THELMA *laughing with each other.*

GINA: How can you sleep when the Lonely Cowboy is closed?

FLIGHT: I see. (*He puts revolver back in holster.*) So you don't have anything to do Gina. All right. I going to open the caf. I don't need no holiday.

GINA: Good.

FLIGHT *begins to take chairs off table.*

FLIGHT: Let the war begin. I don't care.

THELMA: So Candy, what were you talking about?

CANDY: Dalton.

THELMA: Child, listen to me. Dalton walked me home from here last night and I hold his arm because I was cold. I haven't seen him since.

CANDY: Did you sleep with him?

THELMA: No.

GINA: I told you there was nothing to worry about.

FLIGHT: All of you stop your rass noise in the caf. Gina, you not going to the shops?

GINA: Yes.

CANDY: I'm going to look for Dalton.

CANDY *is walking away.*

GINA: Wait for me.

GINA *exits to back.* CANDY *waits at door.*

FLIGHT: I don't care who get rich. All I want is the little that belongs to Gina and myself.

THELMA: So is who you dropping your word for?

CANDY: Gina.

GINA: I coming.

THELMA *lights a cigarette.*

FLIGHT: Me throw me corn. I man don't call no fowl.

Enter GINA, *wearing a short winter coat. She puts her hand on* THELMA's *shoulder.*

GINA: I see you later.

THELMA: Yes.

GINA *and* CANDY *exit.*

THELMA: You not just dropping words for me, you calling me fowl as well.

FLIGHT: I can't take other people's pressure with them bag of money.

THELMA: Everybody change since I met Stanley.

FLIGHT: And a lot have happened and a lot more is going to happen.

THELMA: I just met him by accident, but I like him. He likes you Flight.

FLIGHT *finishes putting chairs down on floor.*

FLIGHT: What for?

THELMA: I don't know, but I would really like to know.

FLIGHT: I don't know Stanley, but we know each other a long time.

THELMA: All Stanley will tell me is that it was a mistake to take Wally bicycle.

FLIGHT: He probably likes you.

THELMA: I know he does. He was nice to me for the few days I know him. I am sure he will get bail.

Police siren. Car driving past.

FLIGHT (*sitting very relaxed*): I know that nobody can take another person to heaven, no matter how much we love each other. After death you are on your own.

THELMA: Don't talk to me about death.

FLIGHT: Yes, but people die for all kind of reasons. Can you imagine when somebody die with love to find their love that was gone before and only to find out that they were two-timing each other. Yes, you only can get to heaven under your own steam.

THELMA: Are you going to give evidence for Stanley?

FLIGHT: No.

Enter WALLY *smartly dressed, mac, suit, tie, shoes.*

FLIGHT: I was closed a while ago, but I open again, but I don't have nothing to sell.

WALLY: I come to see you man. Thelma, no hard feelings. I tell you the truth, I'm not happy about it but I've got to protect me life. I really can't afford for anybody to kill me.

THELMA: You know, when I was a little girl I used to wish that I was a boy, but I don't wish that no more. You men give each other a hard time. Why should a man like Stanley take your bicycle, ride it up and down on the front line, then punch you in the police station?

WALLY: I don't know. I just got to protect myself. We're all cowboys and when you watch cowboys they win and lose a million every minute. So if a cowboy lose something he should take his pressure and don't threaten to kill people. Is right here me born. Right in the middle of Brixton and no stranger is going to come here and kill me.

THELMA: So what happened? Is scank you scank Stanley or what?

WALLY: No man. I just talking, but I was going away. Still I feel a shooter is much cheaper than going away.

FLIGHT: Wally's what the rass cloth you want to talk to me about?

WALLY: Cool it man. Peace. I is full of peace.

THELMA: All right, Wally. There is things going on that I don't know about, but I might just find out one day. I going home. Flight, tell Gina. I will see her after court tomorrow.

WALLY: I am not going to be there.

THELMA: Who cares.

FLIGHT: All right, I will tell her.

THELMA *exits.*

FLIGHT: I want a long rope to hang some people to rass clath. So is try you trying to kill me? From you rob the man ganja is the first time I see you. Wally, I really love me caf and I want to keep it for as long as I live. I don't see nothing else to do in this rass clath place that I was born and I don't expect to get rich quick. Have you prepare yourself to meet Stanley your maker? I just open my caf and you just walk in here and thief a ganja man box of ganja and then half run away and get nowhere and now you are back to wait for judgement between you and Stanley. So what you come to see me about?

WALLY: I come to give you some money.

FLIGHT: Every day that I get up I make a little profit from Lonely Cowboy and I would like it to continue that way.

WALLY: Man, I have made a nice little profit. I can afford to give you some of it.

FLIGHT: I must go and start cooking in a minute.

WALLY: So what you saying? You refusing my offer?

FLIGHT: Man, I want plenty more than what you got to offer me. How do you know is not my ganja you thief.

WALLY: Man, I am a born and bred Brixton man. I know everything.

FLIGHT: So is how long Gina expect to stay at the shop? Did you stop and think before you thief the man ganja? That plain clothes policeman was coming here and take my name to the police station.

WALLY: Perhaps they want to talk to me as well because news travel very fast in Brixton.

FLIGHT: But I haven't thief anything.

WALLY: First come, first serve.

FLIGHT: But what the rass this I am hearing. You cause plain clothes policeman to coming here to question me about your business, and now you come back in here to give me fuck re argument.

Enter DALTON.

DALTON: Yes, yes, it's cold outside but I just passing through. Nice, nice. So what happen Flight? The place feel real dead. You want to hear me read a poem?

FLIGHT: No man. So Wally I going to catch you later. Candy was looking for you.

DALTON: Thanks. So Wally, you walking up the road. Come on man, let's go on the line.

WALLY: Later. I want to say something to Flight.

DALTON: I came in with the breeze, but I'm going out with the wind.

DALTON *and* WALLY *clap right hands together and heavy handshake.*

WALLY: One love.

DALTON: Always.

DALTON *exits.*

WALLY: I feel say you is stupid to rass.

FLIGHT: You thief a man ganja and then come out with your pretty beautiful self to wait for the man who is going to come out of jail any day now to kill you. Yes of course I am stupid to refuse your money. You'd better leave Brixton for ever.

WALLY: Never. I will juk him rass first.

Enter GINA.

I'm not going nowhere.

FLIGHT: Gina is what kept you so long and your arms are empty.

GINA: I forget the money.

FLIGHT: So is what the men going to eat when they come out of the betting shop.

WALLY: All right, all right. I see you later Flight.

FLIGHT: Yeh.

WALLY *exits.*

GINA: So what have you done since I left? You not going to start cooking?

FLIGHT: Yes. Let me cool off for a minute.

VOICE OFF STAGE: We are police officers, what's your name?

WALLY OFF STAGE: Wally, you know my name is Wally.

Police siren. Car stops.

WALLY OFF STAGE: So what is this?

VOICE: We would like to search you.

WALLY OFF STAGE: No man.

VOICE: Would you like to come with us.

WALLY: Sure, I haven't done anything.

VOICE: O.K. Let's go.

Car drives off.

FLIGHT: Did you hear that?

GINA: Yeh.

FLIGHT: I suppose they only want to question him.

GINA: Please don't get involved with ganja.

FLIGHT: No I won't and I stop lending my money.

GINA: Thank God for that.

GINA *and* FLIGHT *hug each other. Lights going down.*

Scene Three
Lights up. Ten days later.
Midday. GINA *sitting at table with glass half filled with red wine, empty wine bottle.* FLIGHT *leaning on counter opening bottle of red wine. He fills his glass and* GINA's *glass. He sits at table with* GINA. FLIGHT *lights cigarette.*

FLIGHT: The dumpling them. (*Exits quickly to kitchen. Comes back with bowl of fried dumplings, puts them in glass case, sits, continues smoking cigarette.*)

So tell me something now spar, how comes you like Jack who's a policeman?

GINA: I don't see him as any policeman, I just see him as somebody I know for a long time. I can't help it, he was always nice to me.

FLIGHT: That was in the past.

GINA: There is no future without the past.

FLIGHT: The world is divided. Some people on one side, some on the other. When Jack joined the police him choose to be on the other side. The other side I mean is that when he joins the police he choose to lock up everybody including black people.

Police siren. Car driving past.

FLIGHT: And going to jail is not good for anybody.

GINA: But some people want to go to jail.

FLIGHT: And some of them want to go to work.

GINA: So how are you going to know who wants to go to work and who wants to go to jail, if it wasn't for the police.

FLIGHT: Then we want more social workers.

GINA: Brixton Babylon have more social workers than Fly have shit to smell.

FLIGHT: Are you saying every black man must join the police?

GINA: The name police is going to be alive when we are dead and gone.

FLIGHT: You see what I mean. Jack is on the other side.

GINA: Maybe you are right about the world is divided but if a so it go a so it go.

FLIGHT: Now you take our little Lonely Cowboy, if we are not careful the police will close the place and that is no good to us or anybody else.

GINA: And there's a lesson to be learned from that, yes everyday we all get a little more freedom because I know the police can't close Lonely Cowboy.

FLIGHT: What freedom? Only a few Black men that is walking up and down on the front line that haven't been to jail and is people like Jack who arrest them.

GINA: So if Jack didn't join the police force you don't think that the police would be still taking them off to jail one by one every day.

FLIGHT: Well as long as you know he's on the other side, it's all right.

FLIGHT *pours wine for* GINA *and himself.*

FLIGHT: So Stanley come up in court today?

GINA: He's going to get bail. Where is Wally?

FLIGHT: I don't know nothing about anybody.

GINA: More troubles, what are we going to do?

FLIGHT: What can we do.

GINA: So do you hate Jack?

FLIGHT: No, but I don't like the police.

GINA: I don't see the problem in your head.

FLIGHT: It's no problem. I going to look at the soup.

FLIGHT exits to kitchen. FLIGHT re-enters.

FLIGHT: It ready. It taste iree. So you pregnant?

GINA: What pregnant?

GINA kisses her teeth.

FLIGHT: Well you look a little fat.

GINA: It's your cooking.

FLIGHT: Well stop eating. I want to know when you're pregnant.

GINA: I don't know why we open so early. Nobody ever comes here until the pubs and the betting shop close.

FLIGHT: Yes, but we get the odd working men and strangers that come in sometimes.

GINA: Yes, but sometimes them never come.

FLIGHT: Well we must make sure that they come.

GINA: Stanley coming out of jail today, remember.

FLIGHT: Talk of the devil. See him outside a pay the taxi man, but if they want to kill us we will kill every one of them.

GINA: Yes, but no violence.

FLIGHT: Here he comes.

Black cab driving off.

THELMA: Hi.

GINA: Hello.

THELMA: I am just going to get a drink.

She kisses STANLEY and exits.

STANLEY: Well here we are again. I come to see you the minute I get bail.

FLIGHT: Would you like a glass of wine?

STANLEY: Yes, man.

GINA gets glass and STANLEY sits at table with FLIGHT. GINA sits at the same table. STANLEY pours himself wine.

STANLEY: Well, well, freedom again. But how can I forget. I suppose all of Brixton is laughing at me with my box of ganja. A sorry about our little differences. I did just come back. I was suffering from jet lag.

FLIGHT: So where is your car?

STANLEY: It was a hired car. I was suffering from everything. I am not used to driving on the left-hand side of the road. I was in the sky all the time, and now I am really down to earth. I am living no more double life. I going to tell Thelma everything.

FLIGHT: That's good man. When are you going back to court?

STANLEY: Next month. Well I was stupid enough to go and look for Wally to kill him. Anyway it did not work out that way.

GINA: So you're lucky you're not on a murder charge.

STANLEY: Wally think him is going to get away with my box of ganja because him think he's a bigger cowboy than me.

GINA: I don't like ganja.

STANLEY: I hardly ever smoke the stuff.

FLIGHT: Stanley, I am a peaceful man who is finished with cowboy life. When you come in here the other day I thought you was mad and come to kill me when you was talking about ganja like it was something you find on the street for nothing. Ganja is on the street, but you have to pay for it. But now I see that you are working on some big ideas.

STANLEY: Yes, my ship have come in and it takes a lot of men to drive a ship. The little box of ganja that I bring the other day was only a sample. I didn't know ganja was getting so expensive until I went into Brixton prison. Wally tried to fuck my head.

GINA: You realise that all this is putting a lot of pressure on Flight and myself. We are settled into our little cafe bar. We don't want no big time trouble.

STANLEY: You people don't understand how much you have been taken for a ride. You're only doing a little business because you want to do bigger business. I only ever talk about money or love for somebody like Thelma.

VOICE OFF STAGE: Flight, you dirty bombo cloth. You lock up Wally.

Brick comes crashing against door. FLIGHT *moves quickly.* GINA *screams.*

GINA: Don't go out there.

VOICE OFF STAGE: I going to bury your rass cloth in there today.

Brick crashes against door. Police siren. Footsteps running away. Police car drives past.

FLIGHT: I wonder if Wally pay someone to come and mash up me cafe bar.

STANLEY: This place is dangerous. It look like you going to need some protection.

Enter THELMA *with three bottles of wine.*

THELMA: So why is two brick outside the door?

FLIGHT: Is any police outside?

THELMA: No. Why?

FLIGHT: Somebody claim that me lock up Wally.

THELMA: I just see Wally going in the betting shop.

STANLEY: Which Wally are you talking about?

THELMA: The one that you punch.

STANLEY: Now that I am in Brixton I have no intention of leaving, so I must protect myself. Which betting shop you see him go into?

THELMA: Come on, this is your first day of freedom. Gina do you know what is going on around here, cos I don't.

GINA: Let us all have a drink and forget everything.

FLIGHT: I just don't want to start bad again, but if I have to I will. Everybody's gone mad. I have become an invalid since I open Lonely Cowboy.

STANLEY: And that is wrong. You should be living in luxury because it is a good business.

FLIGHT: All right Stanley, let us stop pretending.

GINA: I going to move the brick from the door.

THELMA: Listen, if you two want to talk privately, Gina and myself can find something else to do.

GINA: Well I suppose there is no harm in them talking. So Thelma you know, Stanley is a ganja man.

THELMA: I know now.

GINA: I don't mind saying it. I don't like ganja business. Whatever business you going to do, do it outside the Lonely Cowboy.

GINA *goes to door.* THELMA *gives wine to* STANLEY. STANLEY *opens wine.* GINA *comes back with two bricks.*

GINA: I will keep these in the kitchen to remind me of today.

FLIGHT: Did you notice that the guy who was throwing the brick was wearing a balaclava?

GINA: I never noticed because I don't want to know who throw the brick. (*She exits.*)

STANLEY: Well whosoever throw the brick doesn't have long to live.

THELMA: Are you going to kill somebody?

STANLEY: No, not unless I have to.

THELMA: You are more serious than I thought. I don't want to make a fool of myself, but I want to know what's going on. What kind of business you want to do with Flight?

STANLEY: Ganja business.

THELMA: I thought you was a hard-working business man.

STANLEY: There is no harder work than

ganja work.

FLIGHT: I feel sick again. I wish I did have guts enough to mash up the cafe bar. I can't take the pressure. I just don't know what to do since I opened the caf.

Enter GINA.

FLIGHT: All my power been taken away from me.

GINA: Stanley bring the rest of the world troubles with him when he comes to Brixton.

STANLEY: And I am not leaving it again, except for a few hours at a time to make my pick-up.

GINA: Give me the keys. I going for a drive. I have enough to drink.

FLIGHT: No man, stay here. I want you to know everything. I feel like judgment is only around the corner.

GINA: Look Stanley, your business is too big for us.

FLIGHT: Stanley, what exactly do you want from Lonely Cowboy?

STANLEY: Well the Lonely Cowboy to me is you and I would like you to help me sell some ganja because you know the place more than me.

FLIGHT: No, you're too hot.

THELMA: Why does every man that ever sleeps with me always lie to me?

STANLEY: I have never lied to you. So I am hot because that Wally thief my box of ganja.

GINA: What are you going to do about it?

STANLEY: Anything that I can do.

FLIGHT: I wonder who threw the brick, I getting angry now. I feel like killing one of them blood clathboy.

THELMA: I thought you came to take me away to paradise. Oh well, I might as well get pissed. I don't know what's going on. And I don't care.

FLIGHT: But what a rass cloth liberty all these people are taking with my bread and butter.

STANLEY: Listen old man, now that you know my business I expect all of you to keep your mouth shut. I am now just

another customer. I am heading for the top.

FLIGHT: These people start stoning me in the middle of the day. I going to do something about it.

STANLEY: You help me and I will help you.

GINA: No we don't need your help. All we want is peace in the Lonely Cowboy. We are only a young couple trying to pay VAT taxes like anybody else.

STANLEY: But you're going to need help.

He looks at watch.

STANLEY: Rass. It so, it late. I have got to meet a man in a few minutes. Do you want me to introduce him to you Flight? He could give you some protection.

FLIGHT: No Stanley. Right now I'm only thinking dread thoughts.

STANLEY: Well I going down the road. It won't take me more than a few minutes.

He kisses THELMA.

STANLEY: See you in a while. (STANLEY *exits.*)

THELMA: I wonder why the police pick up Wally. They probably know everything.

GINA: They always do.

FLIGHT: I have been through some strange things in Brixton, but this one is different.

THELMA: So I've got to finish with another man.

GINA: He's too much for you.

FLIGHT: Jesus Christ. We haven't had one customer today.

GINA: What do you expect if people is throwing bricks at the place.

THELMA: I will have to tell Stanley when he comes back.

GINA: Do you think he will hit you?

THELMA: If he does, I will split his fucking face. Any man hit me again I am going to kill them.

GINA: I don't blame you.

FLIGHT: I wonder if I should go and look for Wally.

GINA: What for? He have to turn up here sooner or later. You wait and see. Everything will soon be blown away.

THELMA: When is Mr Right going to turn up?

FLIGHT: You know that this brick business is very serious.

GINA: Yes I know. I wish those toy guns on the wall were real.

FLIGHT: What should we do? Lock up the café bar again?

GINA: No we can't do that everytime something goes wrong.

THELMA: And I am not going to do anything except get pissed. Finishing with somebody that you like is very difficult.

GINA: Since when are you interested in ganja people?

THELMA: Gina, I have no idea what is happening, everything is foggy.

Enter DALTON *and* CANDY, *holding hands, laughing and happy.*

CANDY: Hello everybody.

DALTON: Yes, hello everybody.

No response from GINA, THELMA *or* FLIGHT.

DALTON: So what happened? We can't participate?

FLIGHT: Yes man, have a drink.

CANDY *gets glasses,* DALTON *pours wine for* CANDY *and himself.*

DALTON: Everytime I get happy I just want to read my poems to black people.

CANDY: Yes, read the one you write last night.

FLIGHT: No man, somebody throw a brick at the Lonely Cowboy. You know who it is?

GINA: Somebody's trying to kill us to rass.

THELMA: No man, don't talk about that.

DALTON: Oh God. Let Ja spirit live. You not serious.

CANDY: I am very sorry to hear that. Come on, drink up, let's go.

DALTON: So it really happened?

FLIGHT: Yes man.

DALTON: All right, I see you later.

CANDY *and* DALTON *finish drink and exit.*

THELMA: Well, is back to my barmaid work from tomorrow.

GINA: I must admit I have got a terrible, terrible feeling. I just feel depressed and down. Why should this mash up our entire life? This is not pressure – this is death.

THELMA: Again she goes on about the undertakers.

Enter WALLY.

THELMA: Jesus Christ. Wally, keep away from the place. Stanley only come out of jail today.

FLIGHT: So Wally, how come people come throwing brick at my place and says me lock you up?

WALLY *leans on counter and lights cigarette.*

WALLY: Man is Stanley.

THELMA: Stop your foolishness. He was sitting down here when it happened.

WALLY: I get it on the news yesterday in the market and I check it out since then.

THELMA: He's only gone down the road to come back.

WALLY: Make him come back. He can listen to everything I have to say.

FLIGHT: Well talk and talk fast to rass man.

WALLY: Him come to set up everybody against everybody because he is really hot hot. Is hijack him and his mates, hijack a ton weight of ganja on the motorway. Me here say him take a whole caseload of ganja with him on the continent, sell it and then tour the world after that. A sure say him want to set up himself in the protection racket business. Because you understand that is London man them him rob so they will be still looking for him. Maybe that's why he was in such a hurry to go to Brixton jail.

THELMA *walks over to* WALLY.

Leans on counter.

THELMA: Tell me something, do you really know what you are talking about?

WALLY: The little ganja that I take off him was nothing. I was stupid. I should have waited and get more.

THELMA *lights cigarette.*

FLIGHT: So why does he want to pay people to mash up my café bar?

WALLY: Because him want to get into protection racket.

FLIGHT: Anyway, him soon come back.

GINA: You know, I don't think I will ever shed another tear, I will just band my belly and wait.

WALLY: Thelma, that Stanley's too big for you.

THELMA: How do you know what I want? (THELMA *walks to the window.*)

WALLY: Right, it's not my business, but I'm afraid of no strangers in Brixton.

GINA: So what did the police want with you?

WALLY: Well they say they were looking for drugs, but they did really want to take me to the police station to ask me about my bicycle and goods that they confiscated. I don't want to see no police station or courthouse for a long time. You can tell Stanley that from me Thelma.

THELMA: Tell him yourself. Here he comes.

FLIGHT: Now Wally, I don't want no trouble in the Lonely Cowboy.

STANLEY *enters, laughing. Sees WALLY – stops laughing.*

STANLEY: Wally, how nice to see you. Oh me, oh my. Let me see.

STANLEY'*s hand reaching into* WALLY'*s inside pocket, comes out with big wad of £20 notes. WALLY is shocked.*

STANLEY: Well let me see, the ganja that you thief from me was about six weights. I will take about two grand out of this and I will give you the change.

STANLEY *is counting money.* WALLY *takes a knife from his pocket*

and stabs STANLEY *in his left ribcage.*

FLIGHT: Wally.

GINA *and* FLIGHT *put their hands over their faces and scream.* STANLEY *holds his ribcage with the money.* WALLY *stabs at* STANLEY *and tries to snatch money.* THELMA *screams and hits* WALLY *with her handbag.* STANLEY *reaches in his waistband and brings out a revolver. He shoots* WALLY *in chest.* WALLY *drops knife.* FLIGHT *and* GINA *frozen.* WALLY *holds on to* THELMA. STANLEY *fires bullet, it hits* THELMA. GINA *tries to get to* STANLEY. FLIGHT *gets there before her.* STANLEY *looks up. Fires. Bullet hits* FLIGHT *in stomach.* WALLY *and* THELMA *dying together.* STANLEY *confused. Doesn't know why he shot* FLIGHT.

FLIGHT: Oh God. Take the Lonely Cowboy up to heaven.

FLIGHT *tries to reach gunbelt. He collapses.* STANLEY *doubled up.* GINA *snatches revolver from* STANLEY *and takes two steps backwards.* FLIGHT *dies.* STANLEY *moves towards* GINA. GINA *fires three bullets into* STANLEY – *he dies.* GINA *is frozen to the spot. Police siren.* JACK *enters. Police siren.* JACK *takes revolver from* GINA. GINA *remains frozen.* JACK *looks at bodies. Looks at* GINA *and starts crying. Police car stops.*

Blackout.

THE LOWER DEPTHS

– an East End Story –

an adaptation of the play by Maxim Gorky

TUNDE IKOLI was born in London's East End in 1955 to a Cornish mother and a Nigerian father. He left Secondary Modern School at 15 and spent the next two years as a trainee tailor's cutter. In 1973, with the help of an East End youth worker, Dan Jones, and film-maker Maggie Pinhorn, he wrote, co-directed and acted in *Tunde's Film* shown at the London, Edinburgh, Mannheim and San Francisco film festivals and nominated for the John Greirson Short Film Award. The film led to a job at the Royal Court Theatre as Assistant Director under Oscar Lewenstein. His productions included *Play Mas*, *Loot* and *The Tokyo Kid Brothers*. He then worked as a personal assistant to Lindsay Anderson on the film of David Storey's play *In Celebration*.

In 1974 the Royal Court performed his first professional play *Short Sleeves in Summer*. This was followed by *On the Out* (Bush Theatre, 1977), the first production in his long association with Foco Novo.

Since 1977 his work includes: *Scrape off the Black* (Riverside Theatre, 1977) and revived in 1985 by Temba Theatre Company; *Time for Celebration* (Theatre Royal, Stratford East); *Duckin' and Divin'* for the Bubble Theatre, and for Foco Novo: *Sink or Swim* (on tour and at the Tricycle Theatre), *Sleeping Policemen* (written with Howard Brenton, on tour and at the Royal Court), and *The Lower Depths*. Tunde Ikoli is currently working as Resident Dramatist with Foco Novo.

Author's Preface

When I first read *The Lower Depths*, it had a great influence on me. I saw in it a world I recognised and it made me realise that I could write about situations and people from backgrounds similar to my own. Up until then, I suppose I thought plays and films were like Hollywood movies – removed from my life.

The Lower Depths remained in my mind and when Roland Rees and Foco Novo encouraged me to adapt it and set it in the East End, London I was able to see that influence turn into a vehicle for the things I wanted to say.

Tunde Ikoli

The Lower Depths – an East End story – was commissioned and produced by Foco Novo Theatre Company in conjunction with Birmingham Repertory Theatre. It was first performed at the Birmingham Repertory Studio Theatre on 6 February 1986, and at the Tricycle Theatre, London on 9 April 1986. The cast was as follows:

ANNIE	Maria Charles
ERROL	Sylvester Williams
DOREEN, *wife of Mr Koli*	Joy Lemoine
RUTTER	Colin Tarrant
TEACHER	Robin Summers
CHIEF	Rudolph Walker
MELONIE	Tilly Vosburgh
MR KOLI	Rudolph Walker
NICOLA, *younger sister of Doreen*	Janet Palmer
TALKER	Ram John Holder

Directed by Roland Rees
Designed by Tanya McCallin

The action of the play takes place in the basement of Mr Koli's house and in the backyard. It is summer. Time present.

ACT ONE
Scene One

The basement of MR KOLI's *house. A dank and sombre place. What was once a large, roomy space, has now been divided up into makeshift, plywood partitioned cubicles, the doors of which face out towards the audience. Centre stage a table, chairs. An old, dirty and rusting gas cooker stands in one corner. On one side of the stage is a door off to the backyard, on the opposite of the stage, a door off to the upper part of the house. A window, through which a pavement grill can be seen.*

Early morning. A bird sings. A loud fit of coughing comes from one of the rooms. A woman's frail voice 'I'm sorry . . . I can't help it . . . I'm ill!'. Another fit of coughing. A man's voice from the same room: 'Bloody hell woman, keep it quiet. You want to get us thrown out of here?'. The woman manages to stifle a cough. Silence. One of the doors opens. ANNIE *comes out, with laundry bag in one hand, tray of uncooked patties in the other. She looks around, makes sure she is alone, she puts the bag onto the table and the tray of patties into the oven. After making sure the oven is lit, she quickly takes her bag and goes back into her room. Silence.*

ERROL *enters, he is carrying a holdall bag and smoking a spliff. He sits by the table and unzips the bag. He takes out various items of jewellery, cameras, Japanese antiques etc. He smiles to himself, then sighs. He hears steps off, he quickly puts the items back into the bag and shoves it under the table.* DOREEN *dressed in nighty and dressing gown enters.*

DOREEN: Wha' time you call dis?

ERROL (*sucks his teeth*): What are you? My mother?

DOREEN: Haven't you got anything to say?

ERROL: About what?

DOREEN: Twelve o'clock . . . Las' night . . . I was to wait for you, in your room. You remember?

ERROL: I forgot.

DOREEN: How the hell you forget?

ERROL: I was busy.

DOREEN: Busy doing what? (*He doesn't answer.*) I ask you a question. Busy

doing what? You been out dancing with some young slut . . . ?

ERROL: Leave it out. (*He stands up, takes his bag.*)

DOREEN: What you got in there?

ERROL: That's my business.

DOREEN: I've been waiting for you all night.

ERROL: Tough!

DOREEN: Don't mess with me boy.

ERROL: Who you callin' boy?

DOREEN: I could make trouble for you.

ERROL: Try.

DOREEN: I'm warning you.

ERROL: Don't threatin' me.

DOREEN: I've been waiting . . . Errol . . . what's the matter?

ERROL: Nothing.

He walks towards his room. She follows.

You got to be joking. It's nearly eight o'clock in the morning.

DOREEN: I never joke about sex.

ERROL: I've bin out all night. I'm tired.

DOREEN: Is that my fault? (*She grabs him and starts kissing him.*)

ERROL: Give it a rest will yer. Go upstairs and wake your husband up. I'm sure he'll oblige.

DOREEN: He couldn't even if I wanted him to. He's about as much use as an over ripe banana. Hey come on Errol, don't play games with me.

ERROL: Who's playing? I'm tired! (*He pushes her away.*)

DOREEN: You want to watch it you know, is no school girl you messin' with now. I know all about you. You fuck me about an' you could find yourself in trouble.

ERROL: Yeah. I know.

ERROL *goes into his room, slamming the door behind him.* DOREEN *is left livid. Another cough from one of the rooms.* DOREEN *goes over to the door and knocks.*

DOREEN: I hope you haven't bought no

disease into my house. This is a clean respectable place. You got a disease, go an live in the hospital.

MAN (*heard off*): It's just a cough.

DOREEN: Sound more like T.B. to me. You get her to a doctor.

MAN (*heard off*): Yes . . .

DOREEN *storms off. From the other side of the stage dressed in pyjamas* MR KOLI *comes on. He tip-toes over to* ERROL's *door and listens. The banging, thumping and drilling of workmen next door starts up. It makes* MR KOLI *jump, he tries to put his ear closer to* ERROL's *door. He then hears the sound of a door opening; he very quickly runs off stage.* RUTTER *is about to come out of his room, fully dressed. Heard, to his* WIFE: *'Thumpin' an' banging. A person can't sleep . . . let alone die in peace!' He quietly shuts the door. He has a tea bag and a cup in his hand. He lights the kettle on the cooker and then goes and sits by the table. He is about to put his head in his hands when the* TEACHER *comes out of his room. The* TEACHER *is just in his underpants, dishevelled, gaunt, obviously suffering from a hangover.*

TEACHER: Every morning, as regular as clockwork. Bang . . . Bang . . . Bang . . . Thump . . . Thump . . . Thump . . . Bzzz . . . Bzzz . . . Bzzz. Mirrors exactly what's going on in my head. Have they no pity for my delicate constitution? (*He takes a chair and goes over to the window. Climbs onto chair and yells at the very top of his voice:*) Shut your fucking row! That's better, a little consideration is all I ask.

The TEACHER *sits next to* RUTTER.

TEACHER (RUTTER *turns away*): How's the wife?

RUTTER: She's alright.

TEACHER: D'you have a spare tea bag?

RUTTER: No.

TEACHER: Perhaps I could share the one you have?

RUTTER: No.

TEACHER: No?

RUTTER: That's right. No!

TEACHER: But why?

RUTTER: Buy your own.

TEACHER: I would if I could but I can't.

RUTTER: So, what d'you want me to do about it?

TEACHER: A cup of tea, please?

RUTTER: No.

TEACHER: I see . . . What's happened to the fellowship of man, brotherly love?

The kettle screeches to a boil. RUTTER *takes his cup and goes over to it.*

RUTTER: I'm not your brother.

TEACHER: Anthropologically and religiously we are technically brothers.

RUTTER: I don't know about that. But I do know you're not getting one of my tea bags.

The CHIEF *yawning and stretching comes out of his room.*

CHIEF: Well . . . What . . . Hmmm . . . What's all this then?

TEACHER: Our brother is making a cup of tea.

CHIEF: Tea!!! Tea!!! At this time of the morning. A disgusting English ritual. (*Makes to retch.*)

TEACHER: You got any better ideas?

The CHIEF *takes a small bottle of whiskey from his pocket.*

TEACHER: Ah . . . Now you're talking. The elixir of life. (*To* RUTTER.) Now you'll see a bit of human co-operation. The fellowship of man, in action. Chief . . .?

CHIEF (*drinking from the bottle*): Yes?

TEACHER: A drop?

CHIEF (*tips the bottle upside down*): It's finished.

TEACHER: Yes . . . I can see.

CHIEF: Did you want some? You should have said. Now I'm hungry!

TEACHER: I can't eat on an empty stomach.

CHIEF (*sniffs the air*): I think the little woman has prepared breakfast.

He goes over to the oven, is just about to open it when ANNIE *comes out of her room.*

ANNIE: Don't you dare!

CHIEF: Ah . . . Annie my dear . . .

ANNIE: Don't you 'my dear' me. You get your thieving hands out of the oven!

CHIEF: I was just checking, making sure they were not over-done.

ANNIE: Oh yeah and my name's Annie Walton.

TEACHER: It is.

ANNIE: What?

TEACHER: Annie Walton. Your name. I've seen it on your social security book.

ANNIE: Yeah, well, what of it?

TEACHER: Rather renders your witty analogy pointless.

ANNIE: I don't care about that. You keep your nose out of my social security book and you (CHIEF.) leave my patties alone.

CHIEF: Just one?

ANNIE: Fifty p?

CHIEF: I am temporarily without funds.

ANNIE: Tough.

CHIEF: Annie, have a heart . . .

ANNIE: No money. No pattie.

CHIEF: A man has got to eat.

ANNIE: And I've got to make a living. Can't do that if you're gobbling up all my profits.

TEACHER (*wistfully*): It's gone . . . Disappeared without trace . . .

ANNIE: What are you babbling on about?

TEACHER: The milk of human kindness . . . There is, in this world, this country, this city, this house, a lack of passion . . . compassion for those – who through no fault of their own – find themselves less well off than others.

RUTTER: You're just as well off as the rest of us. You just waste what you've got on drink.

TEACHER: Not wasted my friend. Alcohol is essential to my very being.

It gives me strength, hope and happiness. It paints the world out there in less depressing colours. Without it . . . I'm dead.

RUTTER: You're talking nonsense man.

ANNIE: Take no notice of him. He doesn't know what he's talking about.

CHIEF: True . . . That's the truth.

TEACHER: What do you know about the truth?

CHIEF: Me and the truth are good companions. I love the truth, hearing it, speaking it; the truth is sacred . . .

ANNIE: Oh my gawd now, you've started him off.

CHIEF: You see, my love of the truth is partly responsible for my downfall in life. You see before you a man who has fallen from his destiny, a drinker and gambler. But the truth, now that's a different story. Never in the whole of my life have I ever told a lie!

TEACHER: That's a lie!

CHIEF: That's the truth!

RUTTER: You're both bloody mad!

TEACHER: Three hundred miles from home, without a job and living in this hovel. He calls us mad.

RUTTER: I'll find a job.

CHIEF: Pigs will fly.

RUTTER: I will, I'm telling you I will . . . I'm a skilled craftsman.

TEACHER: That's a positive disadvantage these days.

RUTTER: I can build . . . I can make things . . . With these two hands I can make some . . . (TEACHER *and* CHIEF *are laughing.*) What's so bloody funny?

CHIEF: Why don't you take those two hands of yours and make yourself a job out of thin air?

ANNIE: Leave the poor man alone.

RUTTER: I can look after myself, thank you very much.

RUTTER'S WIFE (*her frail voice heard off*): David , tha' tea ready yet?

RUTTER: give us a bloody chance woman. I've only one pair of hands.

ANNIE: Don't shout at her, she's sick.

RUTTER: She's my bloody wife!

RUTTER *goes into his room,
slamming the door.*

ANNIE: Charming fellow.

CHIEF: His wife will die before he finds
a job.

ANNIE: Don't say that . . .

TEACHER: The woman is very sick . . .

CHIEF: That's the truth.

MELONIE *wearing earphones and
reading a book, enters from door
leading to the upper part of the house.
She walks across and towards door to
backyard.*

CHIEF: Good morning my dear . . .

MELONIE *walks on as if she has not
heard.*

TEACHER: So alert, so aware, so
responsive . . .

MELONIE: Why don't you piss off!

TEACHER: It hears, it speaks, whatever
next?

MELONIE *sticks two fingers up as
she walks off.*

TEACHER: I think she likes me!

ANNIE *takes the patties out of the
oven, she wraps them in silver foil.*
CHIEF *eyes her patties, greedily.*

CHIEF: Early start this morning Annie?

ANNIE: I like to get to the workmen
before they have their first tea-break.
Most of them buy my patties you
know . . .

CHIEF: I think I'll take a walk with you.
It's a dangerous world out there. A
woman of your age . . . refinement
shouldn't walk the streets alone. I shall
be your guardian angel, your protector,
your black knight in shining armour . . .

ANNIE: Here, for gawd's sake, have one.
Anything to shut you up!

ANNIE *throws a pattie to the* CHIEF,
which he catches and starts eating.

CHIEF: Delicious . . . Someday you are
going to make some man a very good
wife . . .

MELONIE *comes back on.*

ANNIE: Oh no; not me, never again. Not
for the price of a million Jamaican
patties would I get married again!

MELONIE: Just because you've had one
bad marriage doesn't mean all marriages
have to be bad.

ANNIE: Who said anything about it being
bad, my girl? In fact it was the one and
only great love of my life . . . Na . . . I
just happen to think that one marriage
is all anybody can afford in one lifetime.

MELONIE: You find the right person and
one marriage is all you need.

ANNIE: I found the right person, he's
dead and that's that.

MELONIE: I wouldn't want to go into my
old age alone.

CHIEF: If I'd stayed in Nigeria, who
knows, I might have had four or five
wives at least . . .

TEACHER: Ah, but you're a
masochist . . .

CHIEF: Oh no; in Nigeria we know how
to treat women . . . hard with firm hand.

ANNIE: You'll get the back of my hand.

CHIEF: We make them know their places
from birth. Not like you namby pamby
Englishmen, who wet themselves if
their wives just look at them.

MELONIE: You can't love more than one
person at a time.

CHIEF: Love has got nothing to do with
marriage . . . it's business. The father of
the bride, if one is clever, will be a very
rich man, have plenty of money for
a dowry.

MELONIE: I wouldn't get married for
money . . .

TEACHER: When you get down to it,
marriage is all about sex and money . . .

MELONIE: It should be about love and
caring . . .

TEACHER (*laughing*): Is that what it
tells you in those silly books that you
read? And which particular literary gem
are we reading today.

He snatches the book.

MELONIE: I'm warning you.

TEACHER: Dear, oh dear. 'Visions of
Bliss'. Why do you read this rubbish?

ANNIE: If she wants to read it let her . . .

CHIEF: She's not harming you.

TEACHER: Think of the damage she's doing to herself. There was a time . . . when I taught a room full of squabbling brats. Nothing would have given me more pleasure than to see their noses stuck in some book, but this . . . Oh no, far better to remain totally ignorant than read this garbage; it rots the brain.

MELONIE: I want my book back!

TEACHER: Lend me a fiver?

MELONIE: Get lost!

TEACHER: Come on, I know you've got it. You are the only one here who does anything that remotely resembles paid employment. I've seen you in the post office putting your hard earned money into that blue book. We've all seen her haven't we?

ANNIE: Not me. I like to keep my nose out of other people's business.

TEACHER: What's the point of saving? Live for today, (*No response from* MELONIE. *If looks could kill* TEACHER *would be dead.*) Three pounds and I'll let you have your book back.

ANNIE *snatches the book from* TEACHER *and gives it to* MELONIE.

MELONIE: Thanks. (*To* TEACHER.) Cunt!

TEACHER: Tell me something, how is it possible for someone to read that rubbish and listen to music at the same time?

MELONIE: How is it possible for you to walk around in such a filthy pair of underpants without shame. You make me sick.

The TEACHER *looks down at his underpants and for the first time realises he has no trousers.*

TEACHER (*embarassed*): I think I'll go and get changed . . .

TEACHER *runs off into his room. The others laugh. After a pause.*

MELONIE: I don't believe he ever was a teacher. He's too bleedin' stupid.

CHIEF (*helping* ANNIE *on with her coat*): Shall we go?

ANNIE: You're not getting any more patties.

CHIEF: Is that all you think I'm interested in?

ANNIE: Don't you try to get round me! I know you of old. Something for nothing. There are no more free samples for any of you. What do you think I am? The Salvation Army.

ANNIE *and* CHIEF *about to go.* CHIEF *takes a broom and hands it to* MELONIE.

CHIEF: Tidy up while we're gone.

MELONIE: It's not my turn.

CHIEF: Someone's got to do it. Just for today.

MELONIE: No.

TEACHER (*popping his head around the door*): Somebody has stolen my clothes.

MELONIE: What would anyone want with your old rags?

CHIEF: That's how you came in last night.

TEACHER: Where had I been . . . What did I do? What am I going to do?

CHIEF: Don't ask me, I've got to catch up with Annie.

The CHIEF *goes off.*

TEACHER (*calling after them*): Chief old friend, lend me a pair of trousers. (*They have gone. In desperation he turns to* MELONIE.) I don't suppose?

MELONIE: Not a chance.

TEACHER: What am I going to do?

MELONIE *with a smile shrugs her shoulders.* TEACHER *goes back into his room, closing the door behind him.* RUTTER *comes out of his room. Not unpleased to see* MELONIE. *He is a little shy.*

RUTTER: Mornin' . . .

MELONIE: What?

RUTTER: 'Speck you can't hear me with they ear plugs on. (*Louder.*) Lovely day . . .

MELONIE: Is it?

RUTTER: The sun is shining . . .

MELONIE: Don't make any difference to me. It could be pissin' down, I don't care.

RUTTER: I see . . . Don't mind me askin'?

MELONIE: What?

MELONIE: Well . . . I don't know you really, not havin' been here that long . . . You don't seem like the others . . .

MELONIE: Don't I?

RUTTER: I took to wonderin' what a young maid like yourself was doing here . . .?

MELONIE: I'm just passing through. On my way to better things.

RUTTER: I thought so. And you're working?

MELONIE: You could say that . . .

RUTTER: Maybe, you could ask the people you work for, if they need someone like myself. I'm a skilled craftsman, but I don't mind, any job will do, I pride myself that I can turn my hands to most things. (MELONIE *laughs.*) What is it here? Anytime I mention work people laugh. Is being out of work such a joke to you big city people?

MELONIE: You could go up Piccadilly . . .

RUTTER: Oh yeah, they have work there?

MELONIE: Of a sort.

RUTTER: What do I do?

MELONIE: You just stand outside the men's toilet and wait . . .

RUTTER: For what?

MELONIE: You'll find out . . . (*She laughs again.*)

RUTTER: What's so funny?

MELONIE: Nothing. (*She hands him the broom.*) You've got to do the sweeping up.

RUTTER: I beg your pardon. I don't do housework . . .

MELONIE: And it's your fuckin' turn so get on with it.

She thrusts the broom into a shocked RUTTER's *hand.* TEACHER *tip-toes out of his room, still in his underpants.*

RUTTER: Did you see that . . .? Did you see the way she talked to me?

TEACHER: She can be a rough diamond . . .

RUTTER: A woman swearing . . . I've never heard such a thing . . .

TEACHER: You haven't heard much then have you.

RUTTER: And I liked her, I did . . .

TEACHER: You could've had her . . . you know . . . what with your wife being ill . . .

RUTTER: What are you talking about?

TEACHER: For a price, she would have been yours, well for fifteen minutes at least.

RUTTER: You mean she's a . . .?

TEACHER: That's right.

RUTTER (*shocked and alarmed*): Good Lord! And I'm living underneath . . . the same roof . . .

TEACHER: It's alright, it's not catching . . .

RUTTER: It's disgusting that's what it is. There's no need for it.

TEACHER (*sly*): . . . Yes . . . yes . . . I know . . . I say old friend . . . A favour.

RUTTER (*wary*): What d'you want from me?

TEACHER: A pair of trousers.

RUTTER: You don't have any trousers . . . You ought to be ashamed of yourself . . . A man has got to have trousers!

TEACHER: I agree . . . Perhaps you could lend me a pair?

RUTTER: I'm sorry but I don't have any trousers to spare. (*He tries to hand the broom to* TEACHER.) Here . . . it's your turn to sweep up.

TEACHER: You've got to be joking. I do the sweeping up every February the twenty ninth . . .

He hears footsteps and quickly runs into his room. MR KOLI *comes on, furtively looks around, then realises* RUTTER *is watching him.*

MR KOLI: I'm a fool to myself.

RUTTER (*confused*): Sorry?

MR KOLI: My wife is always telling me what a fool I am. By the way you haven't seen her have you?

RUTTER: Who?

MR KOLI: My wife. Maybe she went into one of these rooms.

RUTTER: No ... no, I don't think so. I haven't seen her.

MR KOLI: She's neither here nor there. A little joke ... And do you know why she calls me a fool? Because I charge such reasonable rents and she is right. 'You can't afford to be a philanthropist' she says. 'Throw them all out, we could turn this house into a hotel ... we could make money.' But what is money when you are doing a service? Helping people. London's a big and lonely place. I only wish that when I first arrived in this town, I had someone as kind as myself to rely on for a warm and comfortable room. I know what it's like to be down on your luck, without friends and family and home many miles away. That's why I always like to think there's a room in Koli's basement for the poor and unfortunates of this world. (*A pause as* KOLI *chokes back the tears.*) No, no it's alright. I'm just thinking of my poor dead mother back in Africa. She would never have dreamt that her son, Joshua Herbert Koli, an African man of such humble beginnings would perform such a service for humanity. (*Pause.*) How long have you been with us?

RUTTER: 'Bout three weeks ...

MR KOLI: Yes ... Good ... Good. I'm afraid there's been an error. A stupid error on my wife's behalf. She's been charging you five pound a week less than she should have ... Women huh, I expect you have the same problem with them in your part of the world ...

RUTTER: Five pounds!!!

MR KOLI: I'm reasonable. I'm aware of circumstances. You don't have to give it to me today, tomorrow will do.

RUTTER: Killing me, that's what you are ...

MR KOLI: You tell me where else in this large unfeeling city, you are going to find accommodation at such a reasonable price?

RUTTER (*mutters to himself*): If one's not begging from you the other's stealing ...

RUTTER *sits by the table, his head in his hands.* KOLI *goes over to* ERROL's *door and knocks.*

ERROL (*opens the door.* MR KOLI *tries to peer in*): Yes?

MR KOLI: I ... er ... What it is ... is this ... I er ...

ERROL: You got the money then?

MR KOLI: I want to talk to you about ...

ERROL: You got the money?

MR KOLI: Money, what are you talking about?

ERROL: Twenty five quid, for the camera, you got it?

MR KOLI: Oh I see, you mean the ...

ERROL: Don't fuck me about. I sold you a camera yesterday for twenty-five pound, you've given me ten, I want the other fifteen, now. You understand?

MR KOLI: Sssh Errol. The camera, was ... well you (*Almost a whisper.*) know stolen. I can't have stolen goods in this house. This is a respectable house.

ERROL (*grabs hold of* KOLI): Then why d'you come down here disturbing my sleep? What d'you want?

MR KOLI: Oh nothing really ... just a chat ... If you're busy I'll go.

ERROL: Fuck off then and get the money.

MR KOLI: No need to swear. Anybody would think this was your house ... (MR KOLI *exits.*)

TEACHER *pops his head around the door.*

TEACHER: What did he want?

ERROL: His wife ... Fuck his wife!

TEACHER: I've heard that you do. God I need a drink.

RUTTER: What you need is a pair of trousers. (*Laughs.*)

TEACHER (*comes out of his room, a sheet wrapped around his waist*): Hey Errol, how about lending me a tenner?

ERROL: Till when?

TEACHER: Thursday.

ERROL: Alright.

TEACHER: I promise, Thursday morning, as soon as my giro arrives. I'll go straight to the post office.

ERROL: I said alright . . .

TEACHER: You did? You did! Well thanks . . . While you're in such a generous mood, perhaps you could lend me a pair of trousers and a shirt . . .?

ERROL: You what?

TEACHER: Can't expect me to go out for a drink with no clothes on.

ERROL: Na, 'course I couldn't. Wait here. (*He goes into his room.*)

TEACHER: Fandabbydozy. You see how easy it was, I should've asked him for twenty.

RUTTER: Money comes easy to those that don't work for a living.

TEACHER: Who cares, I'm going out for a drink.

ERROL *comes out of his room, with a shirt and a pair of trousers which he throws at* TEACHER.

ERROL: Will those do?

TEACHER: Of course, they're fine. I'll let you have them back in a couple of days.

ERROL: That's alright. Keep 'em.

TEACHER: Are you sure?

ERROL: I said keep them.

TEACHER: Cheers mate. I'm going to get as pissed as a potholer.

TEACHER *rushes off to his room.*

ERROL: He could send those clothes to the cleaners a million times. I'd never wear them again after they'd been on his back.

RUTTER: Why d'you give them to him?

ERROL: Felt like it.

RUTTER: He's going to drink that money.

ERROL: What do I care. How's your wife?

RUTTER: She's getting no better.

ERROL: You know something, all that running about you do, looking for work, it's a waste of time.

RUTTER: Oh yeah and what would you suggest I do?

ERROL: Nothing.

RUTTER: Then how would I live?

ERROL: On the social, like everybody else here.

RUTTER: But I'm not like everybody else here.

ERROL: What . . . You a bit special are yer?

RUTTER: Turns my stomach just to look at them – ragbags, spongers, excuses for men. I'm not like them at all. My stay here is only temporary. I'll soon drag myself out of this hell hole. My wife'll get better. I'll get a job and the council will find me a flat, you'll see. I'll soon get out of here and leave all this scum behind.

ERROL: Who are you to talk about them like that. You're just the same, down on your luck.

RUTTER: Me the same. I would kill myself before I'd compare me to them. I'm an honest man.

ERROL: It's helped you a lot hasn't it. Honesty got you a job, honesty got you a decent place to live, honesty'll probably make your wife better. Honesty is for those that can afford it, not for the likes of us.

TEACHER *comes out of his room smartly dressed.*

ERROL: Hey Teacher, you an honest man?

TEACHER: Who me, honest, no. Honesty's the luxury of those who have got something to lose.

ERROL: You see, you've lost everything . . . you've got nothing left to lose.

RUTTER: Not me.

TEACHER: You'll soon learn. Well, I'm off. I'll see you all anon. (*He exits.*)

ERROL: You see you're no different from him.

RUTTER: I'm a working man.

ERROL: You're a fool.

NICOLA *followed by* TALKER, *who carries a small bag, enter.*

NICOLA: How would you know? You've never been in love with anyone but yourself.

ERROL: What's the matter with you.

NICOLA: Nothing, I'm fine. Everything all right Mr Talker?

TALKER (*heard off*): Everything is wonderful!

NICOLA: Mr Rutter, don't forget your wife.

RUTTER: How can I? (NICOLA *exits.*)

ERROL: She's a really nice girl.

RUTTER: The only decent person here.

ERROL: Don't know why she's always having goes at me . . . Bringing me down all the time. I like the girl. She deserves better than this.

RUTTER: Oh yeah and you're the person to give it to her, are you?

ERROL: I might be.

RUTTER: You want to watch her sister don't catch you making love eyes at her.

ERROL: I don't care about her sister. Fuck it! I'm never going to get back to sleep now. If I could sleep, time would just pass away. What am I going to do?

TALKER (*off singing*): 'In the bleak mid winter . . .'

RUTTER: Will you listen to that racket. I hope he's not like that at night.

ERROL: Oy . . . You!

TALKER (*coming out of his room*): Are you addressing me young man?

ERROL: That's right. Give it a rest.

TALKER: Give what a rest?

ERROL: The singing?

TALKER: You don't like my singing?

ERROL: No.

TALKER: I see. And there's me thinking, it's a lovely day, the sun is shining, I have somewhere to live, new friends to meet, this calls for a song. But if my singing annoys you, of course, I shall stop or perhaps you'd prefer another song?

ERROL (*laughing*): Another song?

TALKER: If you like.

ERROL: Not so much the song as your voice.

TALKER: Well, I can't change my voice, I was born with that.

ERROL: If only we could change what we are.

TALKER: What would you be?

ERROL: I wouldn't be bored.

The CHIEF *comes on in a huff.*

CHIEF: Huh!!! Well . . . You'll never guess what I think I've just seen . . . No it can't be true. It must have been a mirage.

TALKER: You have mirages in this part of the world?

CHIEF: It's my eyes . . . There must be something wrong with my eyes. I really must get myself a pair of spectacles.

ERROL: What is it you thought you saw . . . a ghost?

CHIEF: That might be it. In the off licence . . . it looked like Teacher, but it can't have been . . . this man was buying a full bottle of vodka and was dressed very oddly . . .

ERROL: How odd?

CHIEF: He was smart, clean, tidy. No it can't have been the Teacher . . . I left him here myself only twenty minutes ago. He was naked and looked a mess as usual.

ERROL: It was him.

CHIEF: No, you're joshing me. The booze hasn't worn away that much of my brain. What did he do, rob a bank or something.

ERROL: I gave him the money and the clothes.

CHIEF: You did . . . whatever for?

ERROL: Because he asked me.

TALKER: No better reason.

ERROL: Would you like me to give you some money for a bottle?

CHIEF: Well . . . er . . . actually . . . I wouldn't say no.

ERROL: I didn't think you would. Get up on the table and do an African rain dance.

CHIEF: Are you mad, are you crazy, who me?

ERROL: You want the money don't you?

CHIEF: Of course but . . .

ERROL: Come on then, make me laugh, make some rain. Don't be shy because you know you'll do it. For the price of a bottle, you'd do anything.

CHIEF: You know that, I know that . . . where's the fun in making me look a fool over something you know that I'll do. Making me do something I'd be ashamed of would be much more funny, don't you think.

TALKER: That's true.

ERROL: Well, kiss my feet Chief!

TALKER: Chief, did he say Chief?

CHIEF: That's what I was meant to be. I am the son of a Youruba Chief. I was born to be a Chief, that was my destiny.

TALKER: How many of us are lucky enough to arrive at our destinations.

CHIEF: Who the hell are you?

TALKER: Talker.

CHIEF: What kind of a stupid name is that?

TALKER: A name, it does its job as well as any. It's the first time I've met one of your kind. I've met a Red Indian Chief, I've even met a few lords and ladies in my time. Even a duke but never a Youruba Chieftain. How do I address you?

CHIEF: Of course I wasn't actually crowned.

TALKER: Isn't that always the way. I have to meet a chief who hasn't got a tribe, a bit like eggs without bacon.

ERROL: That's right. He is the Chief of the chickens.

CHIEF: Oh yes, very funny. There was a time I could have had you flogged for making a statement like that.

TALKER: We're lucky, times change.

CHIEF: Eggs, bacon, chicken, wine, anything I wanted, just with the snap of my fingers. I wasn't always as you find me, I was meant for much better things.

TALKER: You're still a human being all the same. No matter what journeys we make, whatever luck or misfortune comes our way, we always end up with what we are: Human Beings. Be thankful for that.

CHIEF: I can see why you are named Talker. You find it hard to keep your trap shut. Anyway, who are you with a useless name like that, where are you from?

TALKER: Around.

CHIEF: Around, where, the corner?

TALKER: Maybe, then again maybe not. There are many corners, the world is a big place.

CHIEF: You think I'm stupid. You think I don't know that. I have travelled you know.

TALKER: It broadens the mind don't you find.

CHIEF: Ah ha, you didn't answer my question. Where are you from?

TALKER: What are you a Policeman or a Social Security snooper perhaps . . .

CHIEF: No . . . no . . . not at all. I'm on the Social myself. Just curious, that's all.

ERROL: He had you going there for a minute didn't he.

CHIEF: A man can't be curious?

TALKER: It's his duty.

CHIEF: Exactly.

ERROL: Come on Chief, I'll take you for a drink. If I stay in this place, I'll go mad.

CHIEF: I'll keep you company. (*To* TALKER.) You, my friend, are a scoundrel.

TALKER: I could be.

ERROL: You coming or what? Before I change my mind.

CHIEF: Whatever you do, don't change you mind.

The CHIEF *and* ERROL *exit.*

TALKER: Nice people.

RUTTER: Liars, thieves, cheats . . .

TALKER: Not friends of yours?

RUTTER: You can say that again.

TALKER: What are you?

RUTTER: How'd'you mean?

TALKER: If they're liars, cheats and thieves, what are you?

RUTTER: You trying to be funny?

TALKER: Me ... I couldn't be funny if I tried. If I could, then perhaps I might have been a comedian but, as it is, I'm interested in people. What are you?

RUTTER: I'm a working man.

TALKER: Really ... That's good. What do you work at?

RUTTER: Beg your pardon?

TALKER: What kind of work do you do.

RUTTER: None at the moment. I'm a carpenter by trade. You give me a hammer, a saw and a couple of bits of wood and there's nothing I can't make ...

TALKER: That's a handy skill to have at one's fingertips.

RUTTER: Can't find work. I'm looking mind. Always looking. Factories, yards and workshops I've been into. Looked all over I have. Sometimes I think it's a bleedin' waste of time.

TALKER: No, I don't think so. A man like you, a skilled craftsman, you'll soon find work. There is always a need for craftsmen. And maybe the reason you haven't found work is because the right job has not come your way.

RUTTER: You really think so?

TALKER: I do, I do. Nothing remains the same. Time changes everything. This world and life are made up of opposites: good-bad, happy-sad, recessions-revivals. In my time I have experienced them all. Right now we are in the bowels of a recession but tomorrow, the day after, next month, next year, the law of opposites says: times have to get better and when they do, there'll be jobs for everyone. You're from Cornwall?

RUTTER: How d'you know that?

TALKER: Lovely place, Cornwall.

RUTTER: It can be. Know it then, do you, Cornwall?

TALKER: Oh yes ... Pennygwillm,

Dartfield Hall, the country seat of the Abercrombies. Spent many a happy day, as a guest at the hall ... standing on the lawn gazing out at the many fields of swaying corn ... Peaceful ... The Abercrombies, good friends of mine, do you know them?

RUTTER: Who me? Hell no!

TALKER: Next time you're in Cornwall, you must introduce yourself, tell them Talker sent you ...

RUTTER *completely non-plussed. MELONIE comes back on, with make-up bag and book.*

MELONIE (*to* RUTTER): You wanna get on with it, you do.

RUTTER (*still puzzled*): Wha's that?

MELONIE: The cleaning up!

RUTTER: I told you. It's not our turn.

MELONIE: You'll be for it, you will ...

TALKER: He'll be for what?

MELONIE: The high jump when Mrs Koli finds this place lookin' like a rubbish tip.

TALKER (*looking around*): It would be a very difficult job for anyone, no matter what their cleaning skills, to do anything about that.

MELONIE *has set her book on the table in such a way that she can read while she's applying her make-up.*

MELONIE: Oh yeah and who are you?

TALKER: A new tenant.

RUTTER: Are you staying long?

TALKER: Maybe, maybe not. Who knows ...

MELONIE: You should.

TALKER: I should. Why's that?

MELONIE: A person's got to know what they are going to do with their lives.

TALKER: And you know what you're going to do with yours?

MELONIE: Yes.

TALKER: What's that?

MELONIE: That's my business.

DOREEN *enters.*

DOREEN: Hey you, country boy ...

RUTTER: Who me?

DOREEN: That's right, I'm talking to you. Go upstairs an' get your wife out of my living room . . .

RUTTER: I was just on my way . . .

DOREEN: You want to be quick about it. You pay rent for down here not upstairs. I don't want your wife spreading her germs all over my furniture, she belongs down here!

RUTTER: Okay, okay. I'll get her.

DOREEN: Don't let me find her up there again. (RUTTER *goes off.*)

MELONIE: He's not here.

DOREEN: Who's not.

MELONIE: Errol.

DOREEN: Did I ask you for Errol. You hear me calling his name?

MELONIE: I thought . . .

DOREEN: Leave the thinking for those of us that have brains. Look at this place. It's like a pigsty. How people can live among such filth. I don't know how many times I got to tell you dirty people to keep this place clean. You may want to live like animals but I want my place kept clean. Why you don't pick up a broom an' sweep the floor?

MELONIE: It's not my turn.

DOREEN: You think I care whose turn it is. I jus' want to see it done. You don't pick up a broom and sweep the floor, it'll be your turn to find yourself out on the street without a room to live in.

MELONIE (*reluctantly gets up*): It's not fair.

TALKER: Life rarely is.

DOREEN: Who the hell are you?

TALKER: The new tenant.

DOREEN: Well you'd better learn to keep your mouth shut otherwise you might find yourself becoming the ex-tenant.

TALKER: Yes and I'm very pleased to meet you as well.

DOREEN: Has my sister been down here?

MELONIE: I don't know, I haven't seen her . . .

TALKER: I believe she was the kind young lady who showed me to my room.

DOREEN: Was he here?

TALKER: Who might that be?

DOREEN: Errol?

TALKER: There was someone here by that name.

DOREEN: Did they talk?

TALKER: They . . . (MELONIE *looks over at him and shakes her head.*) Didn't have much to say to each other.

DOREEN: Much . . .? What did they say?

TALKER: Nothing at all . . . really.

DOREEN: You're as much bloody use as the rest of them. (*To* MELONIE.) And you get this room swept now! (*She goes off.*)

TALKER: I wonder who filled her pants with bees.

MELONIE: I suppose I might be like that, if I was stuck with a man I didn't love. (*Sighs.*) I don't belong here . . .

TALKER: Where do you belong?

MELONIE: I wish I knew.

TALKER: You said you knew what you were going to do with your life.

MELONIE: You were listening?

TALKER: I always do.

MELONIE: I'm going to save up enough money to stop work and to give to my husband as a deposit for our house.

TALKER: You're married?

MELONIE: No, not yet. But I will be when the right man comes along and he will you know, one day. I just feel it in my bones.

TALKER: I'm sure he will and a very lucky man he will be.

MELONIE: The others think I'm crazy but what do they know.

TALKER: It's what you know that's important.

MELONIE: He'll take me away from all this . . .

She abruptly stops talking as TEACHER *holding his bottle staggers on.*

TEACHER: I have been engaged in heated discourse with our landlady. Seems she's not satisfied with the sanitary conditions in this rat hole. Come on, Melonie, get it tidied up, can't sit around reading books all day.

MELONIE: Piss off!

TEACHER: Old timer what brings you here?

TALKER: My feet.

TEACHER: Ha-ha that's a good one. I do like someone with a sense of humour. Are you going to be aboding here?

TALKER: For the time being.

TEACHER: Must be hard up to want to live in a place like this.

TALKER: I'm probably as hard up as yourself.

TEACHER: I don't think there's anyone in this world as hard up as myself. I'm the poorest man in the world. I had it all you see, a home, a family, a job . . . Then . . .

TALKER: One day you'll get it all back.

TEACHER: Yes, that's right, one day. Listen old timer, it's the first time we've met and I'm half cut, well on my way to being fully sliced. I like a drink . . .

TALKER: Nothing wrong with that . . .

TEACHER: My feelings exactly but I want you to know that I could give it up anytime I want. It's just that there's not much else for me to do . . .

TALKER: You don't have to explain . . .

TEACHER: Ah, but I do. Don't want to create the wrong impression . . . I could give it up just like that. (*He snaps his fingers.*)

TALKER: I'm sure you can and will.

TEACHER: Don't see the point right now. Will you have a glass with me?

MELONIE: I will, I'm going to get pissed.

TEACHER: Old timer?

TALKER: No thank you. (*He takes the broom.*) I think I'll tidy up.

Lights fade.

Scene Two
Actors ready on stage. Same set as scene one. Evening.
CHIEF, TEACHER *and* RUTTER *sit around the table playing cards. A game has just been completed.* TEACHER *smiles as he scoops the kitty into his pocket.* CHIEF *shakes his head and sighs, as he gathers up the cards.* ANNIE *stirs contents of pan on the cooker. She slices up onions putting them in the pan.* TALKER *watches, dabbing his eyes with a hanky.*

ANNIE: You alright?

TALKER: It's the onions. Always liable to bring a tear to one's eye . . .

ANNIE: I'm used to them by now . . .

CHIEF (*to* RUTTER): Haven't had much luck, have we?

RUTTER (*impatient*): Come on . . . Come on . . . We're supposed to be playing cards!

CHIEF: Give me a chance to shuffle . . .

RUTTER: You shuffle them cards anymore and you'll wear them out . . .

TEACHER: Patience old boy.

RUTTER: Don't take half hour to deal a pack of cards . . .

RUTTER'S WIFE (*heard off*): David . . . David . . .

RUTTER (*looks at his hand, then at his door. Irritated*): What's she want now?

As he turns to look at his door, the CHIEF *slips some cards from his pocket into his hand.*

TALKER: I think she wants you . . .

RUTTER'S WIFE (*heard off*): David . . . (*She coughs.*)

RUTTER: Can't she see I'm playing cards.

ANNIE: Thin as these walls are it's impossible to see through them.

RUTTER: I've got a good hand. I might win.

TEACHER: If you want to check on your wife, it's alright, we'll wait for you.

RUTTER: I'm not leaving this table.

Cough.

ANNIE: His wife's in there coughing her guts up and he won't leave a stupid game of cards.

TALKER: Ah, but he's got a chance of winning. How many times will he have that opportunity knocking at his door?

ANNIE: A game of cards.

TALKER: A game of cards . . . Life . . . what's the difference.

TALKER *goes over to* RUTTER's *door and looks in.*

TALKER: Ah, but you're looking much better. Even in this pale light, I can just about see a rosy glow coming into your cheeks. You'll soon be well.

RUTTER'S WIFE (*heard off*): You really think so?

TALKER: For sure. For sure. Let me prop up your pillows for you and then you can tell me your plans for when you are well. (*He goes into the room.*)

CHIEF: He's gone into your room . . .

RUTTER: So?

CHIEF: You let a stranger go into your wife's room and say nothing.

RUTTER: He's too old and she's too sick and anyway he's alright . . . better than you. (*Excited, lays his cards on the table.*) Three tens . . . king, queen, jack and ace flush. Beat that!

TEACHER (*lays his cards on the table*): I can't . . . It seems this is your hand . . .

RUTTER: Could be . . . Could well be . . . Well?

CHIEF (*while* RUTTER *and* TEACHER *were talking* CHIEF *has taken, unseen, an ace from* TEACHER's *hand*): Without a doubt, that is the best hand you've had all evening.

RUTTER: That's the truth.

CHIEF: But I'm afraid it's not good enough.

RUTTER: How's that?

CHIEF: Ace flush . . . Back hand!

RUTTER: That can't be . . .

CHIEF (*holding up the ace*): Here's the proof . . .

RUTTER (*pointing to* TEACHER): He had that in his hand. . .

CHIEF: That's a physical impossibility because it's in mine . . .

TEACHER: I think Rutter's getting mixed up with the game we had before. I had two aces . . . hearts and clubs . . .

CHIEF: That's right and I had the diamond . . .

RUTTER: I know what I saw . . .

TEACHER: Don't be such a bad loser.

RUTTER: Loser? I won . . .

CHIEF: My father always use to say to me, 'Don't count your chickens son'. I could never make out whether it was meant as a parable or a matter of fact. You see we had over a thousand chickens and to count them all would have been a thankless task.

TEACHER: A chicken a day, keeps the parables away.

CHIEF: Chickens coming out of our ears, goats too and cows. My father got three cows for his fifth wife.

TEACHER: No sheep?

CHIEF: Smelly animals.

TEACHER: But tasty.

RUTTER: Deal them bloody cards. We could've finished another game by now.

ANNIE: You shouldn't be in such a hurry to lose your money.

RUTTER: Who says I'm going to lose?

ANNIE: You haven't won all evening. Doesn't that tell you something?

RUTTER: I've been unlucky.

CHIEF: That's right and you never know when your luck might change. There's always the next game.

TEACHER: Or the game after that.

ANNIE: Until he's got no money left. They're only after your money.

RUTTER: I saw that.

CHIEF: What?

RUTTER: While you were talking, you dealt that card from the bottom of the pack.

CHIEF: You're mistaken.

RUTTER: I saw you do it. You cheating swines.

TEACHER: Steady on. A mistake.

CHIEF: Quite by accident. I can assure you.

RUTTER: Accident, my arse! I want my money back.

TEACHER: That's not very sporting of you.

CHIEF: We won it fair and square.

RUTTER: Like hell you did. You cheated me. They cheated me.

ANNIE: What did you expect?

RUTTER: But a game of cards. A friendly game of cards.

CHIEF: Nothing friendly about a game of cards played for money.

RUTTER: I'll never play again. You keep the blood money and when you drink it, I hope it chokes you!

RUTTER *storms off into his room.*

TEACHER: Now that's what I call a bad loser.

CHIEF: He couldn't take losing, he shouldn't have played.

TEACHER: Fancy dealing from the bottom of the pack. It's the oldest trick in the book . . .

CHIEF: It was Annie, her talking put me off.

ANNIE: Don't you bring me into your sordid little tricks. (*She goes into her room.*)

TEACHER: I suppose he had it coming.

CHIEF: Don't worry about him, let's go down to the pub. Spend our ill-gotten gains.

TEACHER (*sighs*): I don't know. I think I'll give the pub a miss tonight.

CHIEF: What's the matter, are you sick?

TEACHER: No. I've been thinking.

CHIEF: What about?

TEACHER: Drink . . . Drinking . . . Alcohol.

CHIEF: A subject very dear to my heart.

TEACHER: It's ruined my life . . . I was thinking that maybe it's about time I stopped.

CHIEF: Whatever for?

TEACHER: I . . . might . . . teach again . . .

CHIEF (*laughs*): Now I know you're sick, talking such nonsense. Why do you want to teach again? Wasn't it teaching that drove you to drink in the first place. No, you're just feeling a little hung over. What you need is a good stiff drink, that'll knock all that nonsense out of your head.

TEACHER: I could give it up you know . . .

CHIEF: And I could go back to Nigeria and claim my birthright but it's not likely. Come on, let's go to the pub. A pint of beer . . . a glass of vodka, it'll make you feel much better.

TEACHER: You're probably right.

TALKER *comes out of* RUTTER's *room.*

TALKER: Her husband came in there as if he'd seen a ghost.

CHIEF: He did – an 'Ace' materialised out of thin air.

TALKER: I take it he lost.

TEACHER: In more ways than one. We're going for a drink, would you like to come?

TALKER: No, I don't think so.

CHIEF: Come on Teacher, let's go.

TEACHER: I'll catch you up.

CHIEF: Be quick about it. Money doesn't last forever.

TALKER: Nothing last forever. (*The* CHIEF *goes off.*)

TEACHER: I was a teacher you know . . . most of them here don't believe me. They assume I got the name because of my fondness for a certain brand of whiskey. I was a teacher . . . I want you to know that.

TALKER: I believe you. And now?

TEACHER: I'm a drunk.

TALKER: Why don't you teach again?

TEACHER: I couldn't . . .

TALKER: There's nothing stopping you. You must have had qualifications. No matter what you've done to your mind. It's still the same one you started out with. You've got a little more experience now, that's all.

TEACHER: Oh I see. I just walk into any old school tomorrow morning and say 'give me a job'.

TALKER: Why not? They can only say no. Put on some clean clothes, a shave, a wash. Make yourself into a new man. Appearances can be deceptive but also helpful. And as for being a drunk, there are places you can go to for help. Alcoholism is a very popular disease. There's nothing to stop you except yourself.

TEACHER: Me . . . That's right . . . It's all up to me. That's the problem.

TALKER: I have faith in you.

TEACHER: You don't know me.

TALKER: I don't need to. I'm a good judge of character.

TEACHER: I could try, there's no harm in trying, is there? I wouldn't be harming anybody. Nobody else need know. You won't tell the others. I don't want them laughing at me.

TALKER: My lips are constantly sealed.

TEACHER: Thanks old man . . .

TALKER: Why thank me? You're the one who has decided.

TEACHER: That's right. I have, haven't I? A new life . . . I think I'll go and have a drink to celebrate.

TALKER: You could start straight away . . .

TEACHER: What's that?

TALKER *lifts his hand in the shape of a cup to his mouth.*

TEACHER: One for the road! (*About to go.*)

TALKER: There is a law against drinking and driving.

TEACHER: I like that. That's a good one. Drink and driving.

Laughing to himself TEACHER *goes off.* RUTTER *comes out of his room putting on his coat.*

TALKER: How's your wife?

RUTTER: She's asleep. I've got to get some fresh air. I've got to get out of here. (*He goes off.*)

ANNIE (*who has just come out of her room*): What's up with him?

TALKER: He needs some fresh air.

ANNIE: Don't blame him. It takes you a few years to get used to the stale air of this place.

TALKER: Stale air, fresh air, we breathe it all.

ERROL *comes on slightly stoned. Smoking a spliff.*

ANNIE: Here he comes polluting the air even more.

ERROL: You what?

ANNIE: That stuff. It'll do you no good.

ERROL: I've got no complaints.

ANNIE: Helped send my old man to his grave.

ERROL: I heard it was your patties.

ANNIE: You should have one then.

ERROL (*holding up the spliff*): This is the only food I need. You wanna lug old man?

TALKER: No thank you, I've got nothing against it, under the right circumstances it can be very soothing, but not now.

ANNIE: Right circumstances huh, my old man puffed on that like it was going out of fashion. Made him all silly.

MR KOLI *comes on.*

ERROL: She's not here.

MR KOLI: Who might that be?

ERROL: Your wife!

MR KOLI: I'm not looking for my wife. I've come to greet our new tenant.

ERROL (*to* TALKER): Keep your hands in your pockets.

MR KOLI: To find out if everything is to his satisfaction.

ANNIE: As if you care.

MR KOLI: Annie, my dear, in your heart you know I care for you all.

ANNIE: Only the money we pay at the end of each week.

MR KOLI (*a silly little laugh*): You see how well we get on, having a little laugh and a joke. One big happy family ... that's what we are. (ANNIE *laughs.*) So you are ... ?

TALKER: Pardon?

MR KOLI: The latest addition to our family.

TALKER: If you like.

MR KOLI: I do, I do. Mr Koli. (*Shakes hands.*) and your name is?

TALKER: Talker.

MR KOLI: Talker ... ?

ANNIE: As in talks a lot.

MR KOLI: I see. How amusing! Christian name or surname?

TALKER: Whichever.

MR KOLI: I have to know for your rent book you see. I mean if you are out of work and wish to claim supplementary benefit, they will want proof of the rent you pay and I offer a little service to my tenants, whereby I charge you a certain amount for rent but in your rent book I write that your rent is say ten or fifteen pounds more ... the Social Security pay and we split the difference.

TALKER: I don't need supplementary benefit.

MR KOLI (*shocked*): You don't ... really ... You have a job?

TALKER: Just plain Mr Talker will do.

MR KOLI: As you wish.

TALKER: Fine place you must've had here.

MR KOLI: Yes I like to think so.

ERROL: It's a dump.

MR KOLI: Nobody forces you to live here you know.

ERROL: Nowhere else to go.

MR KOLI: London's full of empty rooms.

TALKER: That nobody wants to let and yet people still live in cardboard boxes underneath railway arches. That's disgusting, wouldn't you agree?

MR KOLI: I do what I can ... my house is full, always full ... you've taken the last room.

TALKER: A nice little room.

MR KOLI: There are certain rules, my tenants have to ...

ANNIE: What rules, first I've heard of them?

MR KOLI: Annie, you've been here for such a long time you've probably forgotten.

ERROL: I don't know anything about rules.

MR KOLI: Would you have obeyed them?

ERROL: No.

MR KOLI: So why should I waste my breath?

TALKER: Rules are only for those who will abide by them.

MR KOLI: Exactly.

ERROL: Same way he'd cheat those who'd let him.

MR KOLI: You know sometimes Errol, you are very trying ...

ERROL: What are you going to do about it, throw me out?

MR KOLI (*sighs and shakes his head*): I like to think that the rules are for the benefit of the other tenants ... No visitors in your rooms – don't want to be accused of running a brothel do I? – No music after six o'clock ... the kitchen place is to be swept and mopped twice a day ... you provide your own sheets and blankets and rent is to be paid on Thursday morning prompt.

TALKER: Yes, I've got that.

MR KOLI: Good, any problems, difficulties you come to me ...

ERROL: If you're short of money and want a loan at seventy-five percent interest ...

ANNIE: Or want the use of an old and dangerous paraffin heater for an extra fiver a week.

MR KOLI: It will keep you warm.

ANNIE: If the fumes don't kill you first.

MR KOLI: I like to see my tenants ...

ERROL: Hung, drawn and quartered ...

MR KOLI: Comfortable. Any problems?

TALKER: None that I can think of. But I'll let you know.

MR KOLI: Well then, good, carry on. (*He makes to go.* ERROL *calls him to one side.*)

ERROL: I want to talk to you.

MR KOLI (*nervous*): I gave you the money. What about?

ERROL: How's Nicola, she alright?

MR KOLI: She's fine, why shouldn't she be?

ERROL: I heard she had a row with her sister.

MR KOLI: Begging your pardon but that is none of your business.

ERROL: I'm making it my business.

MR KOLI: It's a family matter. Nothing at all to do with you. (*About to go,* ERROL *pulls him back.*) Remove your hand from my person.

ERROL: You'd better warn your wife.

MR KOLI: I beg your pardon . . .

ERROL: If she touches Nicola again, I'll . . .

MR KOLI: Are you threatening me?

ERROL: I warning you and your wife.

MR KOLI: Who the hell do you think you are, eh? I don't have to take that kind of talk from you. Who are you to talk to me like that. You're just a thief, not a very good one at that. You start threatening me or my family, you will find the police involved very quick.

ERROL: The old bill might be very interested to find out who has been buying all the gear I've stolen.

MR KOLI: I never knew.

ERROL: Don't play the fool, I go down, you follow. I know all about you, the weed you imported to buy this house . . . you're no better than me . . . perhaps worse because you pretend to be something you are not. Call the police and we'll go down the drain together.

MR KOLI (*livid but frightened almost speechless*): You . . . You . . . I'm telling . . . you . . . If . . . this was Africa, I'd have your hands chopped off . . .

ERROL (*takes out a knife*): Here, go on, try it.

MR KOLI: No respect . . . This is my house . . . I will not have you acting as though it were yours . . . I want you out.

ERROL: Take the knife and make me get out. Come on, show me what you'd do in Africa. Come on.

MR KOLI: You are mad . . . Crazy.

ERROL: And you're nothing. Not worth. (ERROL *spits on the floor in front of* MR KOLI.) You're not worth that . . .

MR KOLI: I'll get you . . . I'll show you.

ERROL: I'll be waiting and don't forget to tell your wife, what I told you.

MR KOLI *storms off.*

ANNIE: You want to watch it Errol, those two'll tear your eyes out as soon as look at yer.

ERROL: Let 'em try.

ANNIE: I'm going down to the pub before there's anymore trouble.

ERROL: Trouble, what trouble?

ANNIE: You be careful. (*She goes.*)

TALKER: She has given you some good advice.

ERROL: I don't need anybody's advice.

TALKER: Whether you need it or not, I'm going to give you some. You'd be better off away from this place.

ERROL: Oh yeah and where would I go?

TALKER: Many places.

ERROL: Like where?

TALKER: Birmingham.

ERROL: What the fuck would I do in Birmingham?

TALKER: Start a new life.

ERROL: What would I do with a new life?

TALKER: Live it, enjoy it. Get away from everything that is causing you pain. Birmingham is a nice place, nice people . . . you could do well for yourself up there.

ERROL: I can't run away.

TALKER: You wouldn't have to run, you could walk at a leisurely pace.

ERROL: It wouldn't matter where I was, Birmingham, Manchester, Liverpool, I'd be what I am, Errol, the thief . . . It's all I know.

TALKER: You go off to Birmingham and when you come back, then you can tell me what a liar I am.

ERROL: I'll stay with what I know. Look, old man, I've taught myself not to expect too much out of life. I get by. Now you want to fill my head with all sorts of dreams that can never come true.

TALKER: What is a dream if it isn't a possibility?

ERROL: I don't deal in dreams, I deal in reality. I am a thief, and as that old cunt says, not a very successful one but I've been unlucky . . . maybe one day I'll get lucky . . . who knows? I'm not goin' to sweat about it. I can't change what I am.

TALKER: You have become what people say you are but it is within your power to be whatever you want. Don't let the world pigeon-hole you . . . break out, prove them wrong.

ERROL: What are you . . . ? A priest or something.

TALKER: I'm just a man like you.

ERROL: All this goodness and light. I don't get it.

TALKER: That's because you've never reached for it.

DOREEN *enters.*

TALKER: They say trouble comes in pairs.

DOREEN (*at* RUTTER's *door*): She's quiet, no wheezing or coughing. What's she dead?

TALKER: Sleeping. Best if she's left in peace.

DOREEN: You trying to tell me what to do in my own house.

TALKER: Wouldn't dream of it.

DOREEN: What are you hanging about for?

TALKER: Nothing in particular. I could go for a walk.

DOREEN: Then why don't you.

TALKER: Yes, I think I will. I need some fresh air.

TALKER *shrugs his shoulders and walks off.* DOREEN *turns and walks over to* ERROL. *As she turns,* TALKER *comes back on and rushes into* RUTTER's *room without being seen. As* DOREEN *moves closer to him,* ERROL *moves away.*

DOREEN: Stop playing games with me, Errol. I want to talk to you.

ERROL: What have we got to talk about?

DOREEN: Plenty. Come here . . .

ERROL: I can hear you from where you're standing.

DOREEN: Why are you doing this to me?

ERROL: Doing what?

DOREEN: Leading me on . . .

ERROL: I didn't come to your room, you came to mine . . .

DOREEN: What have I done to you?

ERROL: You haven't done anything. I'm fed up, that's all. Tired of all the aggravation.

DOREEN: Fed up with me?

ERROL: Yeah, you could say that.

DOREEN: Thank you.

ERROL: For what?

DOREEN: The truth. I wouldn't want to make a fool of myself. If you don't want to know, that's fair enough. Have someone else do you?

ERROL: That's my business.

DOREEN: I've got a right to know.

ERROL: You've got no rights as far as I'm concerned. If you want to talk about rights, see your husband, not me.

DOREEN: Okay, okay, why so angry? I don't like to see you like this. I'm the one who should be angry. You just come straight out and say you don't love me anymore.

ERROL: Love!!! When did I ever use that word? I didn't tell you that ever . . . never. I've never said that to anyone.

DOREEN: There were times when, you know, we were in bed, I took it for granted that you felt something for me.

ERROL: Yeah, well, I don't feel nothin' for you . . . right?

DOREEN: I know it was a bit silly of me . . .

ERROL: So what . . . Have you come to say goodbye?

DOREEN: If you like.

ERROL: Just like that. We part friends.

DOREEN: I don't think we were ever friends.

ERROL: It's been nice knowing you . . . see you about.

DOREEN: I've not finished yet.

ERROL: What, more is there? You're not going to cry are you?

DOREEN: Over you, some chance. No I was thinking. My sister . . . you like her, don't you?

ERROL: Do I?

DOREEN: I've seen those childish little looks and smiles . . . it's pathetic, but if that is what you want . . .

ERROL: That's why you're always having goes at her . . .

DOREEN: Is you make me do it. When I think of what you meant to me and she, with her horrible little English ways and manners, has taken you from me, I just see red. I don't know what I'm doing to the poor girl.

ERROL: Don't touch her again.

DOREEN: I know it's wrong but I can't help my feelings, can I?

ERROL: I'm warning you.

DOREEN: The girl has been a weight around my neck since the day she was born. She's the one who's had all the advantages . . . born here, school . . . while I had to go to work at fifteen. And now I'm a big woman, I'm still stuck with her . . . she haunts me . . . I can't stand the sight of the girl. Maybe I should just send her back home to join our parents.

ERROL: She's old enough to decide where she wants to live.

DOREEN: That's true. But where she's going to live? Who she going to live with? She has no job, no money . . . all she good for is to read books. Maybe

you would like to look after her. I could make that happen you know.

ERROL: What are you talking about?

DOREEN: I could give you money. More money than you could ever get with your pretty little thieving. I would give you money and my blessing.

ERROL: Let me get this right. You want to give me money to take your sister away.

DOREEN: That's right. Simple you see.

ERROL: D'you take me for a fucking idiot? You don't give nothing without expecting something in return.

DOREEN: Errol, I take you for what you are: a disappointment to me. When we were first together, I thought that you were going to be the man who would take me away from this rabbit hutch and rabbit of man I call my husband. You seemed so big and strong, you were supposed to free me.

ERROL: You got me all wrong.

DOREEN: Yes, I know. I've hitched myself to two dim stars . . . I won't make the same mistake a third time. Men have been a total disappointment to me . . . you all seem as weak and useless as each other. But we can help each other Errol. I've got plans . . . I'm going to turn this place into a hotel.

ERROL: Some chance, the top floors are uninhabitable.

DOREEN: I've been to the bank . . . they'll give a loan for repairs and refurbishments.

ERROL: You're as mad as your husband. What sort of people are gonna want to live in a place like this?

DOREEN: Homeless families. They are worth a fortune. I've read about it in the papers. No problems with arrears, because the council pay it all by cheque every three months or so. Since they stopped building council houses, they've got waiting lists as long as my husband's face. I wouldn't even have to live here, I could buy a house elsewhere and just live a life of luxury. No more bowing and begging any man.

ERROL: What's your husband got to say?

DOREEN: He don't like the idea . . . too

much work involved. He's useless, he couldn't cross a road without me. He just holds me back.

ERROL: But it's his house.

DOREEN: And I'm his wife. His next of kin.

ERROL: Fucking hell. I see what you want. Oh no, there's no chance of that, I'm not that stupid. That's really clever. Your husband gets topped and I go to prison, and you get to run the Savoy Hotel. No thank you!

DOREEN: You don't have to go to prison ... you don't even have to do it. You've got friends, desperate people, I know that, the life you lead. I read about these things in the papers all the time. These are hard times, you can find any number of people who will do anything for money.

ERROL: Go down to the dole office, ask for the section that deals with murderers ...

DOREEN: I'm serious.

ERROL: You are an' all.

DOREEN: My life is nothing to joke about anymore. Think about it, Errol ... you and Nicola could go off somewhere with money in your pocket and be happy. And I'd be free ... he's been sucking the life out of me for years. I shouldn't tell you this ... I didn't want to, but I shouldn't ... he beats Nicola ...

ERROL: Nice try Doreen, but it won't work. I might be a thief but I'm not a killer. (MR KOLI *creeps on.*) You'd better go.

DOREEN: Think about it. (*Turns and sees her husband.*) Been looking for me, dear?

MR KOLI: I've caught you ha! Together ... alone ... How could you do this to me, you whore ... I've been looking for you everywhere, the gas cooker won't light ... After all I've done for you ... I married you, I gave you my name ... I've been so good to you ... kind, considerate, understanding and this is how you repay me – with him. You lousy bitch!!!

DOREEN *turns and slowly walks off*

looking at ERROL. MR KOLI *stands rigid.*

ERROL: Why don't you join her?

MR KOLI (*screams*): This is my house. Do not tell me what to do. You common garden snail ...

ERROL: Watch it Koli.

MR KOLI: I'll put you in prison.

ERROL: An' I'll put you in hell.

He grabs hold of MR KOLI.

MR KOLI: Help ... Help ... Call the police, he's killing me to death.

ERROL *hears a bang. Lets* MR KOLI *go, he runs off stage.*

ERROL: Who is ... who's there ... ?

TALKER: It's only me. (*He comes out of* RUTTER's *room.*)

ERROL: What were you doing in there?

TALKER: There was nowhere else to go.

ERROL: You were listening?

TALKER: I tried hard not to.

ERROL: Why d'you start making all that noise?

TALKER: I got cramp bending down at the keyhole ... lucky for you I did, you could have quite accidently killed our dear landlord.

ERROL: I should have.

TALKER: Those sort of accidents happen all the time. You listen to me, take the sister and get away ... if she won't come go by yourself. Your life here is coming to an end ... it's time to move on and now!

ERROL: Don't worry, I'll be alright. I don't get why you care?

TALKER: There's nothing to get, it's natural.

ERROL: What d'you get out of it?

TALKER: I've got to check on the Cornishman's wife ... she was breathing a bit heavy just now.

He goes into the room and after a pause comes out with his head bowed.

ERROL: What's the matter, is she alright?

TALKER: She's passed on, hopefully to a better place.

ERROL: Oh fuck, she's dead?

TALKER: Yes, I'd better find her husband.

ERROL: I'll come with you, I don't like being around the dead.

TALKER: Afraid.

ERROL: No . . . no really, just don't like death.

They go off. The stage is silent. After a pause the TEACHER *staggers on, holding a book.*

TEACHER: Hey old man, I've found the book my pupils wrote. (*He looks around. Sits on the table, reads.*) 'Schools and teachers are like contraceptives . . . Bleedin' pointless.' (*He laughs.*) I'll make them write another book . . . that's what I'll do . . .

He gets up, about to go. NICOLA *comes on.*

TEACHER: Have you seen the old man?

NICOLA: No.

TEACHER: There's nobody here . . . this place is like a morgue. Well hello and goodbye.

NICOLA: You're in a hurry . . . Where are you off to?

TEACHER: I'm off on the road of recovery . . .

NICOLA: You're drunk, Teacher.

TEACHER: But not for much longer (NICOLA *goes into* RUTTER's *room*) I'm going to a meeting, AA, a marvellous place . . . they are going to cure me of this terrible malady. No more Teacher's whiskey but Paul David Douglas if you don't mind. I want you all to call me Paul – that's a strange name.

NICOLA (*coming out of the room*): She's dead . . .

TEACHER: Why?

NICOLA: She's not breathing.

TEACHER: Oh no.

NICOLA: What's the point of living, if you end up dying like that, with no one . . . no one, alone . . . it's so sad.

TEACHER: We're born, we live, we die. It's the same for us all. I'll get her husband.

He goes off. NICOLA *goes back to the room, looks in. Comes back to the table, sits and starts to cry.* RUTTER *rushes on, he goes straight to the room.* CHIEF, TALKER *and* ANNIE *follow.*

ANNIE: So she died. I didn't think she'd last much longer.

NICOLA (*still sobbing*): She must've had a terrible life.

ANNIE: Then she's probably better off dead.

CHIEF: I wonder if Cornish people have wakes.

ANNIE: Who knows.

CHIEF: The Irish do . . . they're not unlike we Africans in that respect. I once went to an Irish wake. I had a marvellous time, I got drunk as a skunk . . .

NICOLA (*angry*): She's dead and all you can think about is whether you are going to get a drink.

CHIEF: She's dead. I'm alive, I've got to live.

NICOLA: Haven't you got any feelings at all.

TALKER: Calm down, don't take on other people's worries. How can they feel for the dead when they can't feel for themselves.

RUTTER *comes out of the room in a daze.*

RUTTER: I'll have to bury her . . . I've got no money . . .

ANNIE: You'll have to go to the Social Security . . .

CHIEF: They'll give you a grant.

MELONIE *walks on.*

MELONIE: What's going on?

ANNIE: His wife died.

MELONIE: She won't be coughin' no more then.

RUTTER: What am I going to do now?

Nobody answers. Lights fade to black out.

ACT TWO

Scene One

Seven to eight days later. The backyard of MR KOLI's *house. A yard of concrete, which has cracked and split, overgrown weeds have sprouted from the cracks. There is a small patch of grass in the centre of the yard, where a small, twig-like tree has been planted. The yard is covered with all sorts of litter and useless objects: a wheel barrow, an old rusty mangle, an old tin bath etc. For sitting there is a park bench, two wooden creaky garden chairs. In one corner of the yard, a small shed (the outside toilet). Two doors lead onto the basement, one up from the basement, the other off to the street. Above the basement door a window looks out into the yard.*

A summer evening.

KOLI *can be seen peeping through the curtains of the window. He is, for the moment unseen by those in the yard.* RUTTER *sits/lies in the tin bath.* ANNIE *sits knitting on the park bench,* TALKER *sits next to her.* NICOLA *is tending (watering/pruning) the tree.* MELONIE *sits on the concrete, legs outstretched and crossed.*

MELONIE: ... And so the sun set behind the spires of St Pancras Station. We met underneath the clock. That's where we first met. I was in tears but I knew what I had to do. He ... He ... (*To* NICOLA.) Why do you bother with that twig ...

NICOLA: It's not a twig. It's a sapling. It's mine and I want to see it grow into a tree.

MELONIE: Some chance, it looks dead to me ...

NICOLA: It's alive. You haven't been here long enough to see how much it has grown. All it needs is a little care and attention ...

ANNIE: Don't we all ... (*Pause.*) Are you going to tell us the rest of that story?

MELONIE: It's not a story. It's the truth!

ANNIE: Sorry.

TALKER: Do carry on, it was most interesting ... you were saying you met underneath the clock ...

MELONIE: I know, I know ... So he said to me, 'My dearest dear, I have decided to leave my wife and four children ...'

NICOLA: He was willing to give up his family?

MELONIE: That's right ... He said he could no longer live the lie of being a family man, while loving me ...

ANNIE *caught sight of* KOLI *peering at the window.* KOLI *quickly moves out of sight.* ANNIE *chuckles.*

MELONIE: Then he kissed me, passionately, on the lips ...

ANNIE (*under her breath to* TALKER): He's always watching looking ... spying on his wife ... checking on us ...

MELONIE: ... 'I can't live without you' he said ...

TALKER: Us ... Why's he checking on us? What are we liable to do?

ANNIE: God knows. He'll wear his eyes out one day.

TALKER: Or see something he does not wish to see ...

MELONIE: Are you two interested or not?

TALKER: Of course we are ...

ANNIE: I want to know what happens ...

MELONIE: Right then but you've got to listen ...

TALKER: We are all ears.

MELONIE *prepares to carry on with the rest of her story. Half-way through the speech,* CHIEF *comes out of the toilet.*

MELONIE: All the time my will power was getting weaker and weaker ... If I don't act now, I wouldn't act at all. I pulled away from his embrace and said, 'you can't' and he said, 'I can't what?' and then I had to tell him, he couldn't live with me, much as I loved him I could not bear to think of those four fatherless little children. 'Phillip' ... I said ...

CHIEF: Phillip!!! Who's this Phillip? Last time I heard the story the man's name was Andrew! (*He laughs.*)

MELONIE: Shut up . . . you slimy little toad. How could you ever know what his name was.

CHIEF: If the others are to believe your story . . . I felt for the benefit of accuracy I had to interject.

MELONIE: It's not a story. It's the truth.

CHIEF: The truth . . . What would a common street-walker know of the truth?

MELONIE: About as much as a 'tramp' who passes himself off as an African prince.

CHIEF: I am what I am, I can't help what I was born . . .

MELONIE: You're full of shit!

TALKER: Hold on a minute . . .

NICOLA: Stop arguing you two . . .

MELONIE: It's not me. It's him. He should've stayed in the toilet, that's where he belongs . . .

CHIEF: And you my dear should not go around parading lies as the truth. First it's Andrew, then it's Phillip . . . Next time no doubt it will be Charles. Nothing more than a fairy tale!

TALKER: You really should not interrupt, it's not polite. We all make mistakes with names from time to time . . .

CHIEF: Not me, I've got a memory like an elephant.

MELONIE: You've got a face like one as well.

CHIEF: You believe this woman's tales?

ANNIE: Yes.

TALKER: Why should she lie?

CHIEF: Why should the sky be blue?

TALKER: That's no answer.

CHIEF: Nobody knows why, it just is. I mean look at the poor woman, she can't even be consistent with the names of her imaginary lovers . . .

MELONIE: He was real!

TALKER: Of course he was. Names are unimportant. It's the person that carries the name, we are interested in. Please carry on . . .

ANNIE: Yeah, go on. I'm dying to know the end.

MELONIE: Don't see why I should if he's going to take the piss.

ANNIE: Be like the world: take no notice of him.

NICOLA: He's only jealous . . .

CHIEF: Jealous! Me of her? I'll have you know . . .

ANNIE: Why don't you shut your trap! If you don't want to listen go back in the toilet. Just don't try and spoil it for others. Now carry on dear . . .

CHIEF (*mumbles to himself*): Can't take the truth . . . none of you . . . rather listen to lies . . . that's the bloody trouble with this country . . .

CHIEF *sits in garden chair away from main group. After suitably lengthy pause*, MELONIE *carries on with her story.*

ANNIE: Go on, Melonie, we're listening.

MELONIE: So I said to him, 'Phillip, I love you but I can't come and live with you. My husband has just come out of prison and I feel honour bound to go back to him'. To say Phillip was devastated would be an understatement. 'I can't live without you' he said. 'You'll have to', I said as I turned and walked away and left him standing there. I had to lie. I couldn't be happy knowing I had broken up a family. He really did love me. (*During the latter part of this speech, tears start rolling down* MELONIE's *face.*)

TALKER (*To* MELONIE): Don't cry, someone else will come along . . .

MELONIE: When?

TALKER: . . . Soon . . . a lovely looking woman like yourself.

MELONIE: You think so?

TALKER: I wouldn't say if I didn't. It won't take long.

CHIEF: Have you ever heard such twaddle? (*To* TALKER.) You don't believe all that do you?

TALKER: If she believes it, then it must be true.

CHIEF: It's all in those books she reads . . .

NICOLA: Why don't you shut up? Nobody asked for your opinion.

CHIEF: 'Undying Love' and such titles . . .

MELONIE (*still crying*): What d'you know, you fucking dirty bastard. You've never had a woman in all your life.

CHIEF: That's a lie. Slanderous.

MELONIE: You make me sick. I hate you. I'd like to stick a red hot poker right up your nose.

CHIEF: Seems Phillip was much safer without you.

MELONIE *makes a lunge for the* CHIEF, TALKER *manages to grab her just in time.*

MELONIE: I'll kill him . . .

TALKER: You can't go around killing people just because they don't believe what you say. You have to try to convince them of your truth and if they are not prepared or too stupid to listen, you ignore them. You must look at it as their loss and not your own. (*Takes her by the hand.*) That's better, be calm, come with me and wash your face.

MELONIE: On my life, it's true . . .

TALKER: I believe you.

MELONIE: It happened just the way he told it. He was an Insurance Agent. He drove around in a Ford Escort. And he loved me, he really did.

TALKER: I'm sure he did. And it was very noble of you, the way you thought of his family before your own happiness. There's not too much of that going on in the world today, I can tell you. (*They disappear down the stairs into the basement.*)

CHIEF: He's turning a liar into a hero.

NICOLA: Maybe her lies are the only way she can face the truth. Sometimes I . . .

CHIEF: Don't tell me you have a fondness for lies as well?

NICOLA: Well not lies actually. I sometimes imagine things.

ANNIE: Imagine what?

NICOLA: It's silly really . . .

CHIEF: Go on, you must tell us, you have whetted our appetites.

NICOLA: Well . . . I sometimes imagine

that something exciting will happen tomorrow, so there's something worth waiting for.

CHIEF: I've got nothing to wait for. Everything that can possibly happen to me has happened already. My life's over, done with . . .

ANNIE: You're just feeling sorry for yourself.

CHIEF: And so I should with the position I had in life. I sometimes think why me? How did I come to this? So low and to lead such a meaningless life. But . . . what will be will be . . . we can't change fate . . .

NICOLA: Why don't you go back to Nigeria?

CHIEF: I can't for shame. What have I achieved in this country that I could go back home with and show with pride. I started at the top and fell to the bottom. My fellow countrymen wouldn't find that very impressive . . .

NICOLA: Wouldn't your family be happy to see you?

CHIEF: What family . . . those that haven't been killed off in the various coups and civil wars, look upon me with great shame and resentment, they disowned me. I've failed them as well as myself. No I stay . . .

ANNIE: Worse luck . . .

CHIEF: I put up with England, now England has got to put up with me.

ANNIE: Tell me something; why is that you lot always seem to blame this country for all your troubles?

CHIEF: Us lot, which lot?

ANNIE: You, black people. My husband, he was a Jamaican. He was just the same, England this and England that . . .

CHIEF: England, my dear, is the root of all black peoples' problems. For such a small country to have wreaked such havoc on the world at large is nearly impossible to understand. They came into Africa without invitation, told us how to live, stole our natural resources to propel their own industrial revolution, made us second-class citizens in our own countries. They carved up Africa like it was a bit of cake and still they were not finished with us. They informed us that we should look upon England as the mother country and invited many of my West Indian brothers here after the war, to drive their buses, only to find out that they were not really welcome, given the dirtiest homes, spat at in the streets and still we smiled and danced and showed our teeth. But when jobs started becoming scarce, we were the ones to blame. Send us all back there's too many of us . . . You see our problem is somewhere along the line the English and the black races' history got intertwined; we can't get away from them, whether in the deepest jungle of Africa or the sunny beaches of the Caribbean, always at the back of our minds and the centre of our lives.

ANNIE: Have you finished?

CHIEF: I could go on . . .

ANNIE: No, I've heard enough . . . It's not that bad . . .

CHIEF: Really . . . look at the streets of Brixton, Liverpool and Birmingham. The townships of South Africa . . .

ANNIE: What's that got to do with you . . .

CHIEF: If only I was twenty years younger, you would, . . . but I'm not, I can't change anything. So I take what little pleasure I can, a drink . . .

ANNIE: And more drink . . .

CHIEF: That's right and why not? I have suffered . . .

NICOLA: Life isn't much fun.

ANNIE: You're a young girl, you've got the whole of your life in front of you.

NICOLA: What kind of life?

ANNIE: I don't know love, I'm not a fortune teller. You'll meet someone, won't she . . .

CHIEF: That's right . . . A good husband and you'll see . . .

NICOLA: If that's all there is to life, waiting for some man to come along and make it better, I'd rather not bother . . . (She sighs.)

CHIEF: You haven't lived long enough to make such a sour statement . . . leave

the moaning to those of us who are old enough to have earned it.

ANNIE: Haven't got much of a life, have she . . . that sister of hers gives you hell.

NICOLA: Who has got much of a life? From what I see it's the same for everyone.

RUTTER (sits bolt upright): Not everyone, that's the joke of this poxy life. If everyone was in the same boat, it wouldn't be so hard to bear . . . but there are them that sail about in yachts on the blue sea, drive around in cars with jobs. Some of them have homes with toilets that are bigger than my room. It's not bad for everyone . . . there are a few lucky ones and I'm not one of them. (He lies back down again.)

NICOLA: God he gave me a fright. Did you know he was there, lying in the bath tub like it was a coffin?

CHIEF: A bee must have stung him. I thought he was dead.

ANNIE: Might as well be for what he's doing to himself.

CHIEF: Yes, he'd probably be better off with his wife. They call some parts of Africa a jungle, but I say no man's been to a jungle until he's lived in London. And poor Rutter's an animal, not suited to this kind of uncivilised life. Perhaps he should be shot . . . kinder on the man.

NICOLA: Don't say that. While you're alive, there's hope.

CHIEF: You've got so much to learn my girl.

TALKER (coming back on): You really shouldn't chide the poor woman so. She only tells her stories to brighten up her dull life. What harm does it do you?

CHIEF: No harm. I just find it irritating.

TALKER: So that gives you the right to give her pain, to punish her?

CHIEF: No, of course not. You've made me feel thoroughly ashamed. Perhaps I should go and apologise.

TALKER: That's the spirit.

CHIEF: Yes, that's what I think I'll do. She's the only one here with any money, she might lend me the price of a pint. (*He goes.*) I'm sorry, so sorry ...

NICOLA: Why are you so nice to people?

TALKER: It doesn't hurt and it takes no effort. We all need a little kindness now and then and that's the truth.

RUTTER (*sits upright again*): Truth!!! Here's the bloody truth. (*Pulling at his worn clothes.*) This is the truth ... No work ... No money. No strength ... No hope. That's the bloody truth of the matter. (*Pause.*) What did I ever do that was so wrong ... all I wanted to be was a working man and it's just bloody impossible. That's the truth, the whole bloody truth.

ANNIE: He's really going off his cracker now.

TALKER: Listen my friend ...

RUTTER: I won't listen you. You just want to make everyone feel happy, when they've no reason to. What good did your words do my wife. That's right ... I might as well lay down and die, join her. I heard you. Well, that's maybe what I should do, but I want you all to know I hate you, the rotten lot of you. You understand that ... you'd better understand that. (*He runs off.*)

NICOLA: Poor man.

ANNIE: He's finally gone and lost his marbles. Well I've got patties to go and bake.

TALKER: Life goes on ...

ANNIE: Until you die.

ANNIE *wanders off leaving her knitting behind.*

NICOLA: Do you think Rutter's gone mad?

TALKER: Maybe, just a little bit ...

NICOLA: Why does life have to be so awful ...

TALKER: Because there's not enough people who know how to change it. They make the mistake, like Rutter of fighting themselves.

ERROL *and* TEACHER *enter.* TEACHER *nervous, shaky. It has* been some days since his last drink and the strain is beginning to tell.

ERROL: What's happening? Melonie's in the kitchen crying. Chief's on his knees begging and Rutter's running around as if someone has stuck a needle up his arse ... What is it here?

TEACHER: It's about par for the course in this house. You shouldn't be surprised.

ERROL: It's a bleeding mad house ...

TALKER: Life ... just life my friend ...

ERROL: Alright girl?

NICOLA: I'm fine, boy.

ERROL: Where's your family?

NICOLA: Bingo ...

ERROL: You're alone?

NICOLA: I'm with Talker.

TEACHER: Trying to show her the light?

TALKER: Just talking ...

ERROL: What about?

NICOLA: Not about you ...

TALKER (*to* TEACHER): How are you feeling?

TEACHER: Not too bad ...

ERROL: Not too bad! Look at him, he's shaking like a wet jelly and looks like death ...

TEACHER: I'm drying out. It's the alcohol that's still in my system ...

TALKER: Give it time. You'll look better and feel better. Get yourself some vitamin tablets, they'll perk you up.

TEACHER: Yes ... they told me at the meetings; also: Halt!

ERROL: You what?

RUTTER: H.A.L.T. Never get, Hungry, Angry, Lonely or Tired.

NICOLA: You should feel very proud of yourself ...

ERROL: All he's done is stop drinking.

TALKER: Don't underestimate the powers of alcohol; for some not drinking is the most difficult thing in the world.

ERROL: Do me a favour, if you don't wanna drink, you don't drink ...

TEACHER: I wish it was that easy ...

NICOLA: At least, he's trying.

ERROL: What's the big deal?

TALKER: If we put our mind to it, there's nothing stopping any of us improving our lives.

NICOLA: If we put our minds to it.

ERROL: Oh I get it, you think I should improve my life . . .

NICOLA: You're quick today.

ERROL: I've got all the weed I can smoke, all the clothes I can wear, all the money I need . . .

TALKER: And that's all . . .?

ERROL: I do alright.

NICOLA: And what happens when you get caught?

ERROL: You what?

NICOLA: You're a thief.

ERROL: That's right. What of it?

NICOLA: You are proud?

ERROL: I'm not ashamed. I'm a thief like some blokes are firemen, dustmen, you know . . .

NICOLA: D'you think I'm stupid? Fireman and dustmen don't go around taking other people's property . . .

ERROL: You wanna bet? Some of the best fiddles going being a fireman or dustman. Some house is burnin' down, an' a fireman sees a wallet full of money, he's not going to hand it in is he? Or a dustman rumagin' about in a dustbin finds some old dear's accidently thrown out the family silver, he's not going to knock on the door and say, 'Here's your silver Mam'. Everybody's at it, whereas most people do it part time, I do it full time.

NICOLA: But it's wrong . . .

TALKER: Who's to say what's right or wrong. We all have a living to make. We do what we know best . . .

NICOLA: You shouldn't be encouraging him . . .

TALKER: I don't encourage or discourage. I just state a fact. It takes all sorts to make the wheels turn. If there weren't any thieves, what would the police do?

TEACHER: Beat up pickets and anti-nuclear demonstrators.

NICOLA: It's not funny . . .

ERROL: You've got to laugh . . .

NICOLA: Oh yeah, why?

There is a pause. TEACHER, *uncomfortable, looks at his watch.*

TEACHER: I think I'll go for a walk . . . get some fresh air.

TALKER: Are you alright?

TEACHER: I'm fine . . . before I stopped drinking, I never realised how small and stuffy my room was. Free from that alcoholic haze, I have this unquenchable desire for fresh air and space.

TALKER: Now there's progress . . .

TEACHER: Yes. I'll see you later . . .

NICOLA: You've done very well . . .

TEACHER: Have I? . . . I have . . . Thank you. (*A pause. He then goes out of door to street.*)

ERROL: Poor bastard . . .

TALKER: He'll be alright.

TALKER *noticing the way* ERROL *and* NICOLA *are looking at each other. Sits on the park bench at the back of the stage and picks up the knitting* ANNIE *left behind and starts knitting.* ERROL *and* NICOLA *move to the front of the stage. After a pause.*

ERROL: I wanted to talk to you.

NICOLA: You did?

ERROL: Yeah (*Pause.*)

NICOLA: Well . . . ?

ERROL: Your tree is growing . . .

NICOLA: Yes it is. Is that what you wanted to talk about?

ERROL: No . . .

NICOLA: Well, what would you like to talk about, the weather?

ERROL: You make it really hard for me . . .

NICOLA: Do I? Why?

ERROL: I don't know, it's just the way you are . . . different . . .

NICOLA: In what way?

ERROL: I don't know . . . different . . . that's all . . . (*Pause. Then blurted out.*) Nicola let's get out of here . . .

NICOLA: Where? This backyard?

ERROL: This house . . . this life . . . (*Uncomfortable.*) I want you to come away with me . . .

NICOLA: You do. And where do you intend to take me, a tour round her majesty's prisons?

ERROL: Don't be funny . . .

NICOLA: That's what's in your future.

ERROL: I'll give all that up, thievin' an' that. I could get a job, any sort of job . . . I'm not fussy. The old man here told me about Birmingham.

NICOLA: Birmingham? It's just the same as London, perhaps worse and you want me to go there with you?

ERROL: Yes.

NICOLA: D'you know people there?

ERROL: No, that's the point. A fresh start. I'm sick of the life I lead. There's nothing to it . . . no future . . . you're right . . . prison and more prison . . . I can't face going inside again . . . maybe somewhere different will change all that . . . change me. I don't want you to think that I'm ashamed of anything that I've done or gone religious or something but I want to live better, get a bit of respect for myself . . .

TALKER (*to himself but meant to be heard by others*): A man has got to respect himself and that's the truth.

ERROL: I've been a thief since I was a kid. It's always been the same . . . living in fear of being pulled, arrested for some job I was careless enough to leave my fingerprints on. Living by night and sleeping by day . . . drugs to keep me awake . . . drugs to put me to sleep, that's my life . . . I want to be normal . . . You'd be good for me, I've watched you, you're straight, honest. I've come to like you a lot.

NICOLA: Oh you like me do you, what do you think of my sister?

ERROL: What's she got to do with it?

NICOLA: What's she got to do with you?

TALKER: If a man can't get gold he'll take brass.

ERROL: I thought your sister could have given me something that was missing out of my life. But it turned out she was after what I'm trying to get away from. We meant nothing to each other.

NICOLA: In time will you say that about me?

ERROL: You're different I told yer . . . Well . . . ? (*Pause.*)

TALKER: Go away with him girl. Take a leap at life. He's a good man, not at all bad as he's cracked up to be. All you need to do is to remind him of that, now and then. A kick up the backside, 'Errol, you know you're a good man' . . . that sort of thing.

NICOLA: I don't know why you have gone and confused me like this.

ERROL: Here, I've got something for you. (*He takes from his pocket a large gold chain and medallion.*) A present.

NICOLA: Errol . . .

ERROL: Go on take it, it's 22 carat . . .

NICOLA (*examining the medallion*): What is it?

ERROL: A sovereign . . .

NICOLA: No . . . it's not . . . It's a krugerrand . . .

ERROL: Well, whatever it is it's worth a lot of money.

NICOLA: It's South African.

ERROL: It's gold!

TALKER: Some of the best gold comes from South Africa . . .

ERROL: You see . . . Don't you like it?

NICOLA: It's not that. I don't want it . . .

ERROL: Pardon . . .

NICOLA: I can't take it.

ERROL: What are you talking about?

NICOLA: It's South African!

ERROL: That's right, South African gold.

NICOLA: Five more black people were shot in South Africa today. People the same age as you and me . . .

ERROL: It happens . . . Is it my fault?

What's that got to do with a gold chain?

NICOLA: It's not the chain, it's the coin.

ERROL: What?

NICOLA: People buying krugerrands and other South African goods are sustaining the white regime, enabling them to carry on killing black people. Do you think I could wear a coin round my neck that represented that?

ERROL: But it's worth a lot of money . . .

NICOLA: I don't care about bloody money. I don't want it.

TALKER: I think in the final analysis that it is wise to remember that it's the thought that counts.

NICOLA: I would say a lot of thought went into it, one black person giving another black person a krugerrand . . .

TALKER: Perhaps he didn't know what the coin represented.

NICOLA: He should've known . . .

ERROL: South Africa's thousands of miles away . . .

NICOLA: There's newspapers, televisions, radios. What are you, deaf, dumb and blind . . .

ERROL: I don't understand you. I give you a present and you act like I've stabbed you or something . . .

NICOLA: You have in a way . . . you just don't care . . .

TALKER: He cares about you . . .

NICOLA: That's not enough . . .

ERROL: I cannot go into the history of every single item, that passes through my hands. I didn't buy it, I stole it from a smashed shop window . . .

NICOLA: D'you think that makes it any better?

ERROL: What was I supposed to do? Leave it in the tray in the window with a note saying: in support of the struggle of my black brothers in South Africa, I refuse to steal this coin. That's really going to change the world, make people sit up and notice. The South African Prime Minister is going to say, 'Fuck me, Errol refused to steal a krugerrand. Things must be getting bad. I'd better

end apartheid now.' Do me a favour will you. You think anyone cares what people like us think . . .

NICOLA: It's what we think about ourselves that is important. Somewhere along the line, you have to make a stand. Fight for something you believe in . . .

ERROL: How can I fight for something that is happening thousands of miles away in Africa, the jungle, what's that got to do with me . . .

NICOLA: You're black.

ERROL: Yeah that's right and I've got my own problems right here.

NICOLA: That's a selfish attitude . . .

TALKER: I think what Errol is trying to say is, maybe it's better if one helps oneself before attempting to offer one's services to others . . .

ERROL (*after a pause*): So you don't want to come to Birmingham with me?

NICOLA: What . . . No . . . I don't know . . . I'm so confused. I want to do something with my life . . . get away from here . . . but my sister . . . I can't just run off and leave her . . .

TALKER: We've all got to live our own lives. We can't live other people's lives for them.

ERROL *moves closer to* NICOLA.

ERROL: Look I'm sorry about the coin . . . I'll throw it away . . .

NICOLA: Errol . . .

DOREEN *looks in from the window above.*

DOREEN: Well . . . well . . . well. Look at the two love birds, how sweet and charming. I think I'm going to throw up . . .

NICOLA *moves away from* ERROL *startled.*

ERROL: You haven't got anything to worry about. They better not hurt you now.

DOREEN: Eh . . . eh . . . tough words from the big man. He wasn't such a big tough man in bed. I can tell you, more like a little baby . . .

ERROL: Shut your mouth.

DOREEN: Now, don't get angry Errol. You don't want to give poor, sweet Nicola the wrong impression.

TALKER: Why should you want to do such terrible things to your own family . . .

DOREEN: You don't stick your nose into my business.

MR KOLI *strides on from upstairs.*

MR KOLI: Nicola what are you doing out here? I hope you are not complaining and telling lies about your family.

NICOLA: No.

MR KOLI: I come home for my dinner and it's not there. I mean you live here, rent free. I pay for your clothes, your food . . . I don't ask much in return.

NICOLA: I thought you'd gone to bingo.

MR KOLI: You shouldn't concern yourself with what you thought, rather with what you were told to do – your duties.

ERROL: She doesn't have to do what you say anymore. Nicola, you stay here with me.

NICOLA: It's a bit too early for you to start giving me orders.

MR KOLI: Nicola, you really should know better than to play with his sort . . . he's beneath you . . . he can only bring you down to his level and trouble.

NICOLA *turns and looks at* ERROL *as she goes.*

ERROL: Don't you ever talk to her like that again . . .

MR KOLI (*a sneer*): Really Errol, you shouldn't overreach yourself . . .

DOREEN: He's aimed for the sky and landed in the shit. Where he belongs. (*She laughs.*)

TALKER: Go on Errol, get away from here.

DOREEN: What could a hopeless thief offer my charming little sister? (*Laughs.*)

ERROL: Go on laugh . . . Laugh while you can . . .

DOREEN: I'm shaking in my boots Errol. I'm so frightened.

TALKER: Go Errol. Can't you see what she's trying to do?

ERROL (*pause*): I know (*To* DOREEN.) You won't get what you want from me.

DOREEN: And you won't get what you need either.

ERROL: We'll see about that. (*He walks off.*)

DOREEN (*calling after him*): Was it going to be a white wedding . . . I could have been a bridesmaid.

Now that ERROL *has gone,* MR KOLI *moves menacingly towards* TALKER.

MR KOLI: Well old man, what have you got to say for yourself?

TALKER: Nothing much, old man.

MR KOLI: I hear you're leaving?

TALKER: Soon . . . you have good ears . . .

MR KOLI: There's not much that goes on in my house that I don't know about. Where will you be going?

TALKER: Wherever I choose.

MR KOLI: So you think the world is your shellfish.

TALKER: A rolling stone.

MR KOLI: Can't stay in one place for too long eh?

TALKER: The world's a big place. I want to see it all.

MR KOLI: An honest man, with nothing to hide, has a home, a base . . . where he can be found if need be.

TALKER: I like to call the world my home, my base.

MR KOLI: Then you are a tramp, worthless good for nothing.

TALKER: If it pleases you then I'm a tramp.

MR KOLI: There! Thought as much. That was my guess the minute I set eyes on you. You have caused more trouble than you are worth. Filling my poor tenants' heads with all sorts of nonsense. They were all quite happy before you arrived, they knew their place in the scheme of things and now you seemed to have turned this house into a lunatic asylum.

DOREEN (*enters*): Herbert your dinner's ready . . .

TALKER: So you're a Herbert, I rather thought you looked like a Herbert.

MR KOLI: Don't push me . . . be warned . . .

TALKER: I mean no disrespect . . .

DOREEN: Old man, your mouth is too big for its own good. We don't want your sort here. You just turn up here with a kettle and a parcel and expect to take over everyone's life . . .

MR KOLI: We know nothing about you, not even your name.

TALKER: Talker . . . I gave it to you.

MR KOLI: What kind of fool name is that?

DOREEN: How do we know you're not some sort of pervert wanted by the police . . .

MR KOLI: Maybe I should phone the police, give them a general description, we'll soon find out what you've got to hide . . .

TALKER: Why should I have anything to hide?

DOREEN: Because you don't act like a normal human being . . .

TALKER: And how does a normal human being act . . .

MR KOLI: You are nice to everybody, that's not normal . . .

TALKER: Well you had better call the police, inform them how nice I am to everyone, they'll be around here in seconds, it's a very serious crime . . .

MR KOLI: This is no joking matter . . .

DOREEN: I've had enough of him . . . pack your bags and get out.

MR KOLI: One moment my dear . . .

He takes DOREEN *aside.* TALKER *carries on knitting.*

MR KOLI (*low whispers*): You see when we mentioned the police, he didn't bat an eyelid . . .

DOREEN: So?

MR KOLI: I'm thinking we made a mistake . . .

DOREEN: What mistake . . .

MR KOLI: Perhaps he is from the Social security, an investigator, investigating frauds . . .

DOREEN: What frauds?

MR KOLI: The rent books, maybe he's been sent here to spy on us, you know, they have squads, undercover agents, he could be one of those . . . they are after me I know . . . Think of the trouble we are in . . .

DOREEN: Well? It's your house, it's in your name . . .

MR KOLI: But we're married . . .

DOREEN: Don't be stupid . . .

MR KOLI: We went to a registry office . . .

DOREEN: Not that. I'm talking about the sly old dog over there. Look at him knitting. The man is sick in the head, throw him out.

MR KOLI: He's leaving soon . . .

DOREEN: Herbert, this is your house . . .

MR KOLI: Our house, my dear . . .

DOREEN: You are the man of the house, it is for you to decide, when people come and go . . .

MR KOLI (*pause*): Yes . . . I think you are right.

DOREEN: Poor Herbert, you try so hard to help people and this is the payment you get. Isn't it about time you thought of yourself . . . we should be here together, in this house, all alone, there's so many things we could do for each other.

MR KOLI: True, true . . . the strain of being a philanthropist is beginning to tell . . . I long for peace . . .

DOREEN: And we shall have it, first we get rid of this toad.

MR KOLI: Yes . . . yes . . . okay . . .

DOREEN *takes* MR KOLI *over to* TALKER.

MR KOLI: My wife and I have decided . . .

TALKER: It warms my heart to see

marriages . . . couples . . . who . . .

DOREEN: Will you shut up. I want you out of this house . . . today. You understand?

ANNIE (*enters*): Excuse me I forgot my knitting . . . who's being evicted?

DOREEN: None of your business . . .

TALKER: I am . . .

DOREEN (*To* MR KOLI): Come on, your dinner's getting cold.

ANNIE: You lucky man, you've found a decent place to live.

DOREEN: Watch it, Annie.

ANNIE: Oh I'm alright, you can't afford too many empty rooms.

DOREEN: Don't be too sure. Just because you're an old woman that means nothing to me. I've no pity for any of you.

TALKER: Enjoy your dinner.

DOREEN: Shut your mouth you swine. Come on, Herbert.

MR KOLI *and* DOREEN *exit.*

TALKER: Something tells me that woman does not like me.

ANNIE: She can make your life hell.

TALKER: She has already. I'll go tonight.

ANNIE: It's always best to go before you outstay your welcome.

TALKER: That's true. One should never be the last guest to leave a party and what a party it has been.

ANNIE: Some party.

TALKER: It hasn't been bad as life goes. I've met some good people.

ANNIE: I wish you had met my husband. You two would have got on . . .

TALKER: What was he like?

ANNIE (*pause*): My Gabriel . . . Well he was . . . (*Chuckles.*) . . . He was a lovely looking man . . . and different, different from any man I'd ever met . . . He loved to talk, you know, about everything, he'd seen so much, felt so much. Trouble was, the only person he had to talk to was me . . . Oh I didn't mind, loved it really, just him and me, in this little bedsit. That was our world,

all we needed. His family and friends were thousands of miles away. Mine had disowned me because of Gabriel. We loved each other with a single minded sort of madness . . . Five years . . . and then . . . Well all that's in the past . . . over . . . what's gone is gone . . .

TALKER: But not forgotten . . .

ANNIE: Oh not forgotten . . . Never forgotten (*Pause.*) . . . (*Draws a breath.*) . . . So you're leaving . . . Where will you go . . . ?

TALKER: Who knows, it's unimportant. What will you do?

ANNIE: Carry on, selling my patties as normal. Nothing else to do. It's funny, you give the whole of your life to someone and they go and die. You feel lost, you don't know what to do, but you carry on living in spite of that no matter what you feel . . . you don't know how you do it, life just goes on . . . and soon it's as if that person you gave those years to never existed and you begin to wonder if to live for someone else isn't just a waste of time.

TALKER: Time is never wasted.

ANNIE: I don't know about that. I've lost a few years along the way.

CHIEF *and* TEACHER *enter arguing.*

CHIEF: Look who I found pacing up and down outside the pub like an expectant father . . .

TEACHER: I was exercising . . . getting some fresh air . . .

CHIEF: If I hadn't have come along, you would have gone in for a drink if you hadn't had one already . . .

TEACHER: I haven't had a drop, no alcohol has passed my lips all day.

CHIEF: Rubbish. It's not possible.

TEACHER: Look. (*His hands shake.*) Would my hands be like this if I'd had a drink?

CHIEF: An optical illusion . . .

TEACHER: Here, here's a fact. (*He takes a five pound note out of his pocket.*) I went out with this, this morning and it's still here unspent. What do you say to that?

CHIEF: What a waste of money. You

give it to me and I'll drink it up for you.

TEACHER: No way. Just for today.

CHIEF: And what about tomorrow and the day after?

TEACHER: Just today.

CHIEF: It's very thirsty work staying sober.

ANNIE: Leave the man alone. He doesn't want a drink.

CHIEF: He's sick in the head.

TEACHER: Tell him old man, I'm going to be cured.

CHIEF: I'll believe it when I see it.

TALKER: Why are you trying so hard to put him wrong.

CHIEF: He's got to face the truth, reality.

TALKER: Yes. His truth. Not yours.

CHIEF: What do you think, you're some sort of witch doctor, with magic potions and cures for us all? Well he is what I am, a drunk, he should be proud.

TALKER: Is it that you're afraid?

CHIEF: Afraid . . . don't talk rot . . . of what?

TALKER: Of being alone?

CHIEF: Why should I. I've got friends all over London. I can drink with anyone. I might not have much but I do have personality.

TALKER: You're a lucky man.

CHIEF: Luck has nothing to do with it.

TALKER: I mean you bear up well. Poor Rutter was in here a minute ago, yelling, 'No work . . . no life, no nothing . . .'

CHIEF: He'll soon learn.

TALKER: Here he is again.

RUTTER *comes on looking downcast.*

ANNIE: Face as long as the River Thames. What's the matter with you then?

RUTTER: I'm just trying to think what to do. The funeral's over. I don't know what to do.

TEACHER: You wanna go and have a drink, mate.

ANNIE: Don't do anything. Perhaps you've done enough. All those years you say you've worked, you've earned a holiday.

RUTTER: But I'm a working man.

CHIEF: That's all in the past.

ANNIE: He's right. For once he's right. Don't worry about the work, it's all gone and forgotten. There's nothing to be ashamed of. Nobody cares from the highest to the lowest, they couldn't give a damn, so why should you go taking it on your shoulders . . . if they cared they wouldn't allow it to happen. Everyone should stop. Do nothing.

RUTTER: Then what would the world do.

ANNIE: Someone would have to do something.

CHIEF: Annie you're a Communist.

ANNIE: I'm nothing of the sort. I just think of myself.

TALKER: You try to be hard . . .

CHIEF: But her softness shines through like a light . . .

ANNIE: You're the one who's soft. Soft in the head.

CHIEF: That's better, that's the Annie I know. For a second I thought you had caught the old man's disease.

TALKER: So you think I'm a disease.

TEACHER: I'm the one with a disease. Alcoli . . . Alcoholism.

TALKER: And you're getting cured . . .

TEACHER: A day at a time.

CHIEF: What for?

TEACHER: What for what?

CHIEF: What are you going to do with this miracle when it happens?

TEACHER: That's too far in the future to think about.

CHIEF: So what's the point, it's no use having something if you don't know what you're going to do with it. I say again what's the point!

TEACHER: I get better . . .

CHIEF: They guarantee that?

TEACHER: No.

CHIEF: How much do they charge?

TEACHER: Nothing.

CHIEF: Then it definitely won't work. You know as well as I do, nobody gives anything away free these days.

TEACHER: Just today I've got to get over.

CHIEF: They're brainwashing you my friend.

TEACHER: No more than whiskey did. You should come along to a meeting, you could see.

CHIEF: Why should I go, there's nothing wrong with me.

ANNIE: Nothing right with you.

CHIEF: Annie, why don't we stop pretending and get married. You know you love me.

ANNIE: Like a cold grave.

From the window we hear a scream.

NICOLA: I haven't done anything . . .

Furious knocking on a door. The others in the yard stand shocked.

MELONIE (*heard off*): What are you doing to her . . . leave her alone . . .

DOREEN (*heard off*): Get away from my door (*More knocking.*) . . . this is none of your business.

From the window more screams, shouts etc. Noises of broken dishes and chair.

DOREEN (*heard off*): Bitch . . . (*Slaps.*) Good for nothing. (*Slaps.*) Herbert move, move your hand away from me . . . keep your damn African nose out of it . . . My sister's my business . . . You want this pot over you?

NICOLA: No! (*Screams.*)

MELONIE: Fuckin' leave her alone . . .

Pause followed by scream followed by silence. Then MELONIE's footsteps on stairs.
    MELONIE *enters.*

ANNIE: What's going on up there?

MELONIE: They're beating the shit out of that girl . . .

TALKER: Someone go and get Errol quickly . . .

CHIEF: I'll go (*He runs off.*)

MELONIE: No bloody time for Errol . . .

ANNIE: Leave the poor girl alone . . .

MELONIE: We've got to do something before they kill her.

TALKER: We shouldn't interfere . . . family business . . .

MELONIE: We've got to go up there, break the door down if we have to . . .

TEACHER: Should we go? . . . Should we help?

TALKER: We can't go around breaking other people's property . . .

MELONIE: It's alright for them to break her bones is it?

TEACHER: We can be witnesses . . .

TALKER: What use will I be as a witness, I'm leaving tonight.

MELONIE: What is the matter with you lot, they're going to kill her . . .

MELONIE *marches off into the house followed by* TEACHER, ANNIE *and a reluctant* TALKER. RUTTER *left alone. He sits rubbing his head very hard as if all the noise is distracting him.*

RUTTER: Well, that's that then. Got to pull myself together somehow. Nothing . . . all alone . . . that's what it's come to. No home . . . no nothing . . . she's left me to face the music on my own.

He walks off. There is an ominous silence. Then the commotion starts up again but now the noises are moving much closer to the backyard.

DOREEN (*heard off*): She's my sister, my responsibility. I can do what I like with her.

MELONIE (*heard off*): You've got no bloody right.

TALKER (*heard off*): You must stop this. You must stop this.

TALKER AND DOREEN (*heard off*): Move out of my way you useless bag of jelly.

TEACHER *and* MELONIE *are supporting a bedraggled* NICOLA. ANNIE *tries to keep* DOREEN *away from her sister.*

ANNIE: Keep away from her, haven't you done enough. If you don't stop you'll kill her.

DOREEN: You better watch it, if you want to have a place to sleep each evening. You'd better get out of my way.

ANNIE: You ought to be ashamed of yourself, move it, she's only a young girl.

DOREEN: She won't reach old age if I have anything to do with it.

ERROL *rushes on. He pushes his way through the crowd.*

MR KOLI: This is family business, none of your concern. Where are you goin'? (ERROL *grabs hold of him.*) You're going mad. I've warned you before.

ERROL: Get out of my way.

He pushes MR KOLI *backwards with a very forceful shove.* MR KOLI *falls backwards and off stage down the stairs to the basement.* ERROL *doesn't notice, he has rushed over to* NICOLA.

ERROL: Are you alright . . . what the . . .

MELONIE: The bastards have scalded her.

ANNIE: Tipped a saucepan over her as if she was a sink.

TEACHER: It might have been an accident. I mean we can't be sure, we didn't actually see.

ANNIE: Don't be so bloody stupid.

MELONIE: You had more sense when you were drinking.

NICOLA: Errol, take me away from here. Please. It hurts, it hurts so much.

ERROL: I'll kill them.

DOREEN (*by the balcony stairs*): Lord. Jesus Christ. Will you look at my husband. Somebody has murdered my husband in cold blood. Him the poor man who did nothing to no one.

ERROL *stil comforting* NICOLA. *The others rush over.* MELONIE *rushes back.* DOREEN *goes inside.*

MELONIE: Koli's dead.

ERROL (*as if he hasn't heard*): Go and phone an ambulance. She's got to go to hospital, then deal with them two.

MELONIE: Listen to what I'm saying, Koli's dead. (*The noise dies down.*)

TEACHER: It's true . . . he's dead . . .

DOREEN (*comes on*): He did it . . . him there, Errol Johnson, he's killed my husband. I saw him do it. I've called the police. This is my house now . . . you take orders from me.
   What have you got to say for yourself now, Errol?

ERROL *slowly walks over and looks down at the body.*

ERROL: So the old bastard's gone to meet his maker. Things have worked out well for you. (*Shrugs his shoulders.*) Might as well kill you while I'm at it. I ain't got nothing to lose.

He makes a lunge for DOREEN *who runs out of his reach.* TEACHER *and* ANNIE *attempt to hold* ERROL *back.*

ANNIE AND NICOLA: Use your head, Errol, one death is enough. Errol please no.

DOREEN: You'll get what's coming to you.

MELONIE: You could do a runner.

DOREEN: Where's he going to run to? They'll know who it was who murdered my husband.

MELONIE: No he didn't, it was an accident.

DOREEN: It was no accident. It was murder. You didn't see.

MELONIE: Neither did you.

DOREEN: You want to find yourself on the streets?

MELONIE: Don't worry me, I'm used to the streets, I've lived on them all my life. And if Errol gets caught, I'll tell them it was in self-defence, I saw just as much as you.

ERROL: I don't care if I get caught or how long I go down for, she'll be coming with me, that's what she wanted, what she planned. She tried to talk to me into killing her husband.

DOREEN: You disgusting filthy liar!!!

ERROL: And then, afterwards she wanted to turn this place into a hotel.

TEACHER: A hotel?

ANNIE: Who'd want to have a guest here by choice?

ERROL: Tell them about your plans, the money you offered me.

NICOLA (*in a state of shock*): Now I see ... it's all clear to me now ... Errol ... and my sister, they both did it ... together. Errol you lied to me ... all lies ... it was you, the two of you. I believed you ... I was in your way too ...

ERROL: What are you saying ... ?

MELONIE: What the hell is going on?

ERROL: What are you saying?

NICOLA: They did it, they killed him ...

MELONIE: You want to watch it, Errol, between the pair of them, they'll get you life for sure.

A police siren wails. Without being seen, DOREEN slips off.

ERROL: Nicola, you can't believe I would ... with her ...

NICOLA: It's the truth ...

Police siren. Brakes screech.

MELONIE: You'd better run.

ERROL: I've been running all my life, what's the point?

In the commotion, NICOLA's tree has been trampled to the ground. Slow fade to blackout.

ACT THREE

The same set as Act Three. Late evening. It is dark but light from the windows of the house illuminates the yard.

A table covered with the remnants of a party: a half-drunk bottle of vodka, patties, dirty dishes, glasses etc.

TEACHER asleep, lies flat on his back in the middle of the yard. RUTTER sits in the corner, screwdriver in hand, toying with the leg of a broken chair. ANNIE sits by the table, picks up one of her patties, is about to eat it, then decides not to. MELONIE sits next to ANNIE, her elbows on the table, her head resting in her hands, vacantly staring out in front of her. CHIEF, glass in hand, sits, slumped in an armchair.

CHIEF: Conspicuous by his absence ...

ANNIE: Who?

CHIEF: You know who. Him ... Old nosey joe ...

ANNIE: I didn't see him go ...

MELONIE: He didn't say goodbye ...

RUTTER: He must've slipped away while all that commotion was going on.

CHIEF: Melted into the night like an ice cube in the Sahara desert.

RUTTER: Must've been afraid of the police ...

MELONIE: Oh yeah and why's that?

RUTTER: Didn't see his arse for dust once they arrived.

CHIEF: And him the old fake, caring so much for us all. He couldn't even wait to see the outcome of his shennigans.

ANNIE: He was a strange old man alright.

MELONIE: There was nothing he didn't seem to know.

CHIEF: He didn't take me in with all that 'mystical nonsense'. He didn't fool me.

ANNIE: He didn't try to fool anyone.

RUTTER: He was alright he was.

CHIEF: If you ask me ... He was a ...

MELONIE: Nobody is asking you. The old man was a good bloke and you ... You're just a fool.

CHIEF struggles up from his chair. Walks menacingly over to MELONIE.

CHIEF: I'm not as gullible as some I could mention . . . I feel like dancing . . . (*He hums or sings a few bars of an African 'high life' song and does a couple of dance steps.*) Hup . . . Hup . . . Hup . . . Ha . . . Hup . . . High life! God bless me, since the day I've left Africa all I've known is the low-life . . . (*Does a few more dance steps.*) You know in Africa we know about dancing . . . singing . . . we know how to enjoy ourselves . . .

MELONIE: We're not in bleedin' Africa!

CHIEF: You're telling me. More's the pity. Annie you want to come and have a dance with me?

ANNIE: Gettaway . . .

CHIEF: Come on. Don't be shy.

ANNIE: There's no music.

CHIEF: We can make our own . . . (*He starts tapping the table with his hands.*) Drums . . . You see, music, as simple as that. Let's dance. I've got music in my head. Come on let your body go . . .

ANNIE: I wouldn't let my body go anywhere with you.

CHIEF (*looks up at the light blazing from the windows of the house*): While the mice are away the cats will play!

MELONIE: Daft sod. It's the other way round.

CHIEF: What is?

MELONIE: Never mind.

CHIEF: You sure you don't want to dance Annie?

ANNIE: No.

CHIEF (*pouring himself another drink*): You want a drink?

ANNIE: No. I've had enough and by the look of it, so have you.

CHIEF: I can never have enough.

MELONIE: That's because you are a greedy sod.

CHIEF: And you're a dreamy sod. Come on let's live!

RUTTER: We are.

CHIEF: I mean really live . . . Let's sing . . . dance . . . talk . . . argue . . . shout . . . for God's sake let's do something.

ANNIE: Why don't you sit down and give your legs and mouth a rest?

CHIEF: Tell me something, why is it, that the English are so damn boring? Can you tell me? (*Nobody answers.*) I give up . . . (*He slumps into his chair.*)

MELONIE: Thank God I won't have to go on living here with you lot anymore.

ANNIE: You don't really mean that . . .

MELONIE: Don't I . . .

CHIEF: You will miss us all . . .

MELONIE: Like I'd miss the pox . . .

CHIEF: Well I like living here among my friends.

MELONIE: That's because you've grown used to sponging off us . . .

ANNIE: Can you imagine . . . A whole flat to ourselves . . . Hot and cold running water . . . my own kitchen, bathroom and bedroom. I won't know what to do with so much space . . .

MELONIE: You'll soon get used to it . . .

ANNIE: If the old man did anything, he did that, got us all out of here and council flats into the bargain . . .

CHIEF: He had nothing to do with it. It was the newspapers and their heart-rendering stories of our plight, that got us council flats.

MELONIE: If the old man hadn't come here, none of it would have happened. You don't know how to be grateful.

CHIEF: I suppose if I went out onto the street tomorrow and found a fifty pound note, I'd have that old twit to thank would I . . . ? No, if I'm grateful to anyone, it would be the lady of the house, if she hadn't got Errol to kill her husband, the newspapers would have never been interested. And the council wouldn't have been shamed into providing us with accommodation. I drink a toast to Mrs Koli, may she have to sweep her prison cell out every day of the week!

ANNIE: Poor Errol's going to miss out on a council flat.

MELONIE: Errol was a fool . . . He should have run . . .

CHIEF: And where would he have run to?

MELONIE: Anywhere . . .

CHIEF: When you're black, it's very difficult to just blend into the background.

MELONIE: So what, you just give up . . . ?

CHIEF: No, you just get tired of bothering with it all.

ANNIE: Did you see Nicola tonight?

MELONIE: Yeah, she's still in a bad way . . .

RUTTER: I feel sorry for her . . .

CHIEF: When she comes out of hospital, she'll be all on her own.

MELONIE: She'll be better off.

CHIEF: Not in a big house like this. Perhaps she would like me to stay . . . keep her company . . .

ANNIE: Hasn't the poor girl been through enough, without you inflicting your company on her . . . ?

CHIEF: She'll be glad of a friendly face . . .

ANNIE: Your ugly mug . . . ?

RUTTER: Here then, don't you want your council flat?

CHIEF: What do I want with more than one room . . . All those floors to sweep . . . No it's not really my cup of tea . . . This has been my home for over thirty years. I can't leave it without a few tears.

MELONIE: They should knock it down. Smash it to the ground.

ANNIE: I can't say I'll be sorry to see the back of this place. At times it's been like a prison for me . . .

CHIEF: You see what that old twit has done to you all, he's made you forget the good times . . .

ANNIE: The good times . . . ? Huh . . . What good times?

CHIEF: All of us here together. We may have had our differences from time to time but we go on . . . like a family . . .

MELONIE: Don't talk stupid . . . We lived together because we had to. I wouldn't have stayed here if I had a choice in the matter . . .

ANNIE: Would any of us . . . ?

RUTTER: I'd have stayed in Cornwall . . .

CHIEF: That old man has turned and twisted your minds . . . We were happy before he arrived . . .

ANNIE: Happy, do me a favour. I can't remember the last time I felt happy. Come to think of it, I don't remember what happiness is.

CHIEF: He has tricked you all, made you see something that isn't there and left you walking around in the dark.

MELONIE: You don't know anything.

CHIEF: Don't I? Look here . . . (*Pointing at the* TEACHER.) Here's the proof, look what your old man has done to him.

MELONIE: What he's done, he's done to himself . . .

CHIEF: He was better off before, now look at him, his head is so full of nonsense, he doesn't know where he is.

CHIEF *shakes the* TEACHER.

ANNIE: Leave him in peace.

CHIEF: That's what the old man should have done.

TEACHER (*waking up very drunk*): Wha' . . . Wha's what is it?

CHIEF: Are you cured?

TEACHER: Am . . . I what?

CHIEF: Cured . . . ? Better?

TEACHER: Of course . . . I've had a slip . . . slipped that's all . . . Tomorrow I'll go to the hospital . . . Detox . . . get detoxicated. That's all . . . all that tomorrow . . .

CHIEF: What about today?

TEACHER (*angry*): Tomorrow . . . I said . . .

CHIEF: Tomorrow never comes . . .

ANNIE: Leave him alone, can't you see he's sick.

CHIEF: There's nothing wrong with him. He likes a drink that's all, where's the harm to that. It's what people put into his head that's harming him.

TEACHER: You don't understand.

CHIEF: What's there to understand.

TEACHER: The problem . . . It's all so complicated . . . so difficult to explain . . . but I know . . . what will be . . . will be and there's always the next day . . . you ask the old man, he'll tell you.

CHIEF: He went days ago.

TEACHER: Did he . . . Does not matter . . . I know all I need to know. I'm going to teach again, d'you hear . . . impart my knowledge . . . the benefits of my experience . . .

CHIEF: And who is going to benefit of the fruits of your experience?

TEACHER: The children . . .

CHIEF: God help them. As if they don't have problems enough these days, with sniffing glue and unemployment.

TEACHER: You don't believe I ever was a teacher . . . do you?

ANNIE: What does it matter what he believes . . . ?

TEACHER: None of you believe . . .

RUTTER: It's what you believe that's important . . .

CHIEF: Now I've heard it all . . .

TEACHER: I was a teacher . . . here, here's proof . . . (*He takes a crumpled book from one of his pockets.*) A book . . . A book, in fact by some of my more talented pupils. Printed by the local Arts Association. Poems and stories about their experiences in school and life. It caught the imagination of the public some years back. The fact that these poor, deprived, maladjusted delinquents could put more than two words together, was quite a shock to the powers that be, they were expecting prospective bank robbers, vandals muggers and murderers and not artists and poets. The local press got quite excited . . . headlines would read: 'SHOCK, HORROR, LOCAL CHILDREN CAN READ . . . AND WRITE'. Of course the local educational chiefs were none too pleased. If these kids could express themselves someone was not doing their job . . . namely myself. They tried to get the book banned and sacked me, which of course brought in the attention of the national media, tv, radio, I even spoke to a reporter from The Times Educational Supplement. For a while we were all celebrities . . . the kids . . . myself . . . we were going to change the whole educational system . . . I wrote this fiery article . . . demanding all sorts of innovations . . . making accusations of incompetence . . . It was never published . . . A week later and we were forgotten, yesterday's news . . . everything was as it always was . . . as it was always meant to be . . . the kids when back to beating up teachers and smashing windows . . . I remained sacked . . . Shame, really, for a while there . . . I . . . Some of that stuff was really powerful . . . (*He opens the book and reads.*) It's all a joke, this school, this life. No hope, no job, a pregnant wife, A council flat with one bedroom, The dole, the pub, I'm fucking doomed. A real book . . . real words . . . real people . . . real emotions . . .

CHIEF: That's the past . . . forget all that . . .

TEACHER: Forget. How can I bloody do that . . . I can't do that, it's a vocation. (*Shouts.*) I shall teach again. There's nothing to stop me.

CHIEF: Don't shout.

MELONIE: That's it you shout as much as you want.

CHIEF: What's the point?

MELONIE: Someone might listen.

CHIEF: To him . . . To you . . . That's funny that really is. That old man was an illusionist, all he gave you were mirages. Made you all believe you are something you are not. Nobody is interested in us . . . nobody gives a damn . . . what are they going to listen to us for? What have we got that anyone would want to know about? We are nothings . . . We are low lifes . . . that's all . . . He's made fools out of you all . . .

ANNIE: Shut up, you don't know what you're talking about. He was no magician, fake or anything like that, he was just a man, a kind man. What if he did tell a few lies, he lied for a good reason. He tried to make us feel better about ourselves. Where's the harm in that?

RUTTER: He did sort of feel sorry for us . . .

CHIEF: Sorry . . . What good is feeling sorry for someone?

RUTTER: Well . . . what I mean is . . . that way you know how not to hurt a person's feelings . . .

CHIEF: That's rubbish. You help someone by telling the truth.

ANNIE: When did you ever do anything to make someone else's life better?

CHIEF: Who me?

MELONIE: Never.

ANNIE: Well?

CHIEF: How can I make someone else's life any better if I can't do anything with my own?

ANNIE: Well then, you've got no right to talk badly about the old man. At least he tried to help.

CHIEF: I don't have the means to help anybody. If you talked to me thirty years ago. That was different, I had the means at my disposal . . . Come to think of it . . . I did help someone once . . . I gave my week's allowance to our house boy . . . one of my father's servants . . .

ANNIE: One good deed in thirty years . . . Somehow I don't think you'll be reaching the pearly gates . . .

MELONIE: You never had any servants.

CHIEF: I beg your pardon?

MELONIE: You never had any servants!

CHIEF: It's the truth . . . A house that size you needed them . . . well it wasn't a house, more of a mansion.

MELONIE: Liar.

CHIEF: We had servants . . . A car . . . A Bentley in fact.

MELONIE: All in the imagination of your bent up brain.

CHIEF: You'd better listen to me.

MELONIE: Why should I?

CHIEF: Because I'm telling the truth.

MELONIE: The truth . . . you wouldn't know the truth if it got up and smacked you in the face.

CHIEF: I don't get my life from books like some I could mention.

MELONIE: No you make it up as you go along. A Bentley . . . puh . . .

CHIEF: And a chauffeur.

MELONIE: There was no mansion, no servants, no Bentley and definitely no chauffeur. All lies.

CHIEF: You can't say that.

MELONIE: I can say what I like because I don't believe you.

CHIEF: Tell her Teacher . . .

TEACHER: Paul is my name thank you very much.

CHIEF: Tell her then, Paul. I've told you about my family. Tell her!

TEACHER: I don't know anything . . . It's all gone . . . It's the past.

MELONIE: All lies.

CHIEF (*to* ANNIE): You'd better warn her . . . You know what I am capable of . . . (ANNIE *is laughing.*) You laugh . . . What happen? You don't believe me?

ANNIE: What good are all those things to you now?

CHIEF: It makes me what I am.

MELONIE: Which is nothing!

CHIEF: Shut your mouth!

MELONIE: You shut it.

CHIEF: I will! Calling me a liar. In Africa, I could get you . . .

ANNIE: What does it matter?

CHIEF: Because I wasn't always like this . . . A drunk . . . a bum . . . living in a pigstye . . . I've known better, a lot better.

MELONIE: Jackanory . . .

ANNIE: Don't tease him.

CHIEF: You are getting very close to the edge of my patience.

MELONIE: What he's trying to say is that he's better than us.

CHIEF: So I once was.

MELONIE: Liar!!!

CHIEF: You need a damn good beating.

MELONIE (*picks up a bottle ready to hit him*): Try it, go on.

CHIEF: First she doesn't believe me . . . Now she wants to kill me.

ANNIE: Will you two stop it. Before somebody gets hurt.

MELONIE (*to* CHIEF): See what it's like when somebody doesn't believe you.

CHIEF (*nervous. Sits*): It's the truth. (*He forces a laugh.*)

MELONIE: That's it go on laugh . . . because you're the joke! (*She throws the bottle down.*) Me, I'm getting out of here, right now. (*She walks off.*)

CHIEF: You can't be upset with such stupid people.

ANNIE: She put you in your place . . .

TEACHER: We're all stupid people . . . all the education in the world hasn't changed that. None of us have learnt anything.

CHIEF: Have another drink?

TEACHER: No more drink. Time to go . . .

CHIEF: Go where?

TEACHER: Off . . . away . . . gone . . . (*He goes off.*)

ANNIE: The party's over . . . Time I was getting to bed.

CHIEF (*holds her arm*): Wait . . .

ANNIE: For what?

CHIEF: It's true . . . everything I have said . . . It's the honest truth. When I arrived in this country, it was for an education, preparation for my responsibilities at home. I came over on the same boat as the landlord . . . Koli . . . he was just a poor country boy. He looked up to me, he would've told you – I was meant to do something with my life.

ANNIE: You did. You wasted it.

CHIEF (*laughs*): That's the truth.

RUTTER: There!

CHIEF: What?

RUTTER: Fixed it . . . the chair!

CHIEF: Why'd you do that?

RUTTER (*shrugs his shoulders*): Something to do. (*Gets up and pours himself a drink.*) A night cap . . . I think I'll have a lay-in in the morning.

ANNIE: Not getting up at the crack of dawn to look for work?

RUTTER: Not much point really . . .

CHIEF: Ah ha, he's seen the light.

RUTTER: It'll be the same for us all . . .

CHIEF: That's it . . . That's it.

RUTTER: I haven't given up though . . . It's a sort of holiday.

ANNIE: Of course it is . . . an endless holiday!

MELONIE *shouts from the lighted window.*

MELONIE: Get in here quick . . . Quickly! The Teacher's slit his wrists . . .

Snap blackout.

BASIN

JACQUELINE RUDET was born in East London but grew up in Dominica. She began her career in the theatre as an actress (with Cast Theatre Company and Belt and Braces) before forming Imani-Faith, a theatre group founded to present theatre for and by black women, in 1983. Her plays include *Money to Live* (1984), *God's Second in Command* (1985), and *Basin* (1985).

Author's Preface

Basin took three years to write. It was my first attempt at putting pen to paper but the second play I finished. Between starting and finishing it I wrote *Money to Live*. *Basin* was previously called *With Friends Like You* and, along with some friends, I directed a production which we performed at assorted small venues.

Soon after, I became rather disillusioned with my writing, seeing its inadequacies but not knowing how to rectify them, so I went on holiday to Dominica to visit relatives I hadn't seen in a long while. I returned to England with a love for black woman. While out there, I'd suddenly realised how strong, how loving yet how abused and unappreciated black women are. I realised I had lost my love of black women through the general pressures and distractions of domestic life. Through a play, I wanted to show that all black women had much in common. This led me to much thought about the word 'zammie'.

Zammie was a word I'd forgotten about. It was a word my mother would use to describe a very close friend, but it had connotations of being more than friend and, in a strange way, it was a rude word that only grown-ups could use, as if 'zammie' meant lover. In *With Friends Like You*, I was writing a play about a friendship between two women but I hadn't been able to find a way or a word to describe that friendship.

The two 'zammies' in *Basin* become lovers but 'zammie' is not 'lesbian' in patois. The word refers more to the universality of friendship between black women; no matter what nationality, no matter what class, all black women have very important things in common. They're the last in line; there's no one below them to oppress. Whether they like it or not, every black woman is the 'zammie' of every other black woman. It's almost an obligatory thing. As one of the girls in *Basin* says, 'Who will love us?'

The basin symbolised the one article that all black women possess. Mothers always teach their daughters about cleanliness. If not dressed in smart, new clothes, at least clean. An important matter of pride. As a girl grows up, it's less a matter of pride, more a case of the women making herself smell fresh, just in case husband wants to relieve himself inside her.

Jacqueline Rudet

Basin was first presented by the Royal Court Theatre Upstairs on 29 October 1985, with the following cast:

MONA	Dona Croll
SUSAN	Beverley Hills
MICHELE	Susan Harper-Browne

Directed by Paulette Randall
Designed by Vanessa Clegg

ACT ONE

Scene One

MONA's *flat. She is clearing up after the previous night's party. She sings to herself.*

MONA: Honey, pepper, leaf green limes,
　　Pagan fruit whose names are rhymes,
　　Mangoes, breadfruit, ginger root,
　　Grandilliars, bamboo shoots,
　　Sugar cane, kola nuts,
　　Citrons, hairy coconuts,
　　Fish, tobacco, native hats,
　　Gold bananas, woven mats,
　　Plantains, wild thyme, pallid leaks,
　　Pigeons with their scarlet beaks,
　　Saffron, yams,
　　Baskets, ruby guava jams,
　　Fustles, goat skins, cinnamon, allspice,
　　Oh, island in the sun,
　　Gave to me by my father's hand,
　　La, la, la, la . . .

MONA hears a knock at the door.

Coming!

MONA goes to open the door.
SUSAN kisses her and comes in.

SUSAN: Mona, I've been knocking and knocking. Were you asleep?

MONA: Sorry, I was miles away. Back home, in fact. Thinking about all the good times.

So, you decided to come? Don't you think you're a little late?

SUSAN: Looks like you had a good time here!

MONA: Well, if you'd come, you'd've enjoyed yourself too.

SUSAN: What happened?

MONA: It was great! I mean! Pat and her new man business! The boy is so dry! He spent the whole night in that corner giving everybody cut eye! He's a joke. I don't know what she sees in him. I said, 'Pat, what do you see in this boy? He must have one big wood!' You could see Pat was shame. First, she kept making excuses that he wasn't feeling well, then, she couldn't take it anymore, just walked out and left him! It was really funny.

Everybody enjoyed themselves. And listen to this, nah! Herbert brought this box full of whisky. I don't know where he got it from because every minute him just a peep through the window to see if bull a come. So Michael plays this trick on him. He rushes in and says, 'Bull outside! Someone thief a box of whisky from the off licence!' Girl, I never see Herbert move so fast! When Herbert found out, him so vexed him fit to burst!

SUSAN: I would've liked to see that. Good! I can't stand him. And how was your Michael?

MONA: The boy makes me sick. The guy love woman! I'm serving drinks and the guy's got some piss an' tail gal in the corner a wind-up in front of me in my own fucking house! I'm fed-up with the guy. All he wants me for is jook, jook, jook.

SUSAN: I thought all you wanted was jook, jook, jook!

MONA: Michael's just taking the piss.

SUSAN: I've told you that too many times.

MONA: Never mind about me. Look at you! You look well miserable!

SUSAN tries to speak, but can't.

Come on, start at the beginning. I'll listen, no matter how boring.

SUSAN: Thank you!

MONA: Only joking! (*Pause.*) Come on!

SUSAN: Well . . . you remember when I was at drama school?

MONA: Back that far!

SUSAN: Are you interested?

MONA: All ears! Come on!

SUSAN (*pause*): I was the only black student. I felt really proud of myself. I was the only one of my friends to get somewhere and achieve something.

I was being kept back and not being given the chance to prove myself but, I knew I had the talent, so I just kept on going.

MONA: This isn't what's on your mind!

SUSAN: I'm getting to it. (*Pause.*) One month, I missed my period . . .

MONA: What's this got to do with drama school?

SUSAN: I'm jumping. Sorry. While I was at drama school, one month, I missed my period, took a test, found it was positive but, I felt so stupid, I couldn't bring myself to tell you. Anyway, I had an abortion, of course.

Pause.

MONA: Are we getting to it?

SUSAN: We're getting there.

MONA: This is all stuff to set the mood, is it?

SUSAN: I'm building up to it.

MONA: Is this why you didn't come to the party?

SUSAN: I would've liked to have come, but I had so much on my mind.

MONA: I organised the party so everyone could cast aside the troubles in their life and have a good time. Everyone said. 'Where's Susan?' I said, 'She's probably down Handsworth earning some pocket money.'

SUSAN: I was at home. I got to the top of your road and turned back.

MONA: There's this really cheap psychiatrist I can recommend.

SUSAN: I got to the top of your road and just turned back. I couldn't face it.

MONA: Face what?

SUSAN: Everyone.

MONA: Our friends?

SUSAN: The noise, the smoke, the chat-up lines, Michael . . .

MONA: You wouldn't have seen him anyway! He was tucked away in that corner getting all slippery with this little girl. I don't even know who invited her!

SUSAN: That's what I couldn't have stood! Michael: fucking around with another woman right under your nose!

MONA: What's new?

SUSAN: I would've said something.

MONA: We used to go out to parties. I'd go and get some drinks, or go to the toilet, and when I'd get back, where would he be? Pressing some girl up against a wall, supposedly dancing! Michael's a big slag, he always has been.

SUSAN: I've never understood this about you. You can't tell me you love him!

MONA: You've never been in love, have you? Michael was my first real man. He's been the only man in my life since I was 19. A man like that becomes part of your life. You don't 'go out' with him, it's not a 'love affair', he's just there. It's pathetic, I know, but I can't imagine life without him.

SUSAN: I can't bear the way he treats you.

MONA: And that's why you didn't come to the party?

SUSAN: You never rang me last night. You can't have been that bothered what had happened to me!

MONA: So, you need an invitation and then a call on the night to check you're coming? What's eating you, woman?

A knock on the door. MONA *opens the door.* MICHELE *walks in.*

Ah, now we come to the interesting part of the story!

MICHELE: What story? Hi, Sue, where were you?

MONA: Now we come to the *very* interesting part of the story!

MICHELE *helps* MONA *clean-up.*

MICHELE: What story?

MONA: Michele finds herself in the unenviable position of being in the same room as four of her ex-boyfriends.

SUSAN: Michele, you're good!

MICHELE: Where were you?

SUSAN: I didn't feel like it.

MICHELE: You missed one party!

MONA: What does Michele do?

SUSAN: Dunno.

MONA: She ignores all her ex-boyfriends and takes up with someone man!

SUSAN: Michele, you're good!

MICHELE: They're ex-boyfriends. Ex. You know, in the past.

SUSAN: So, who's the new one?

MICHELE: A guy called Steven. I don't know where he came from. Heaven, I'm sure!

MONA: Of course, Michele's looking so good, all of her man dem a eye-up her backside. So Michele's getting it on with number five while numbers one to four try their best, all night long, to get a dance.

SUSAN: Michele, you're a star!

MONA: Could it be charisma?

MICHELE: Leave it out!

MONA: Could it be the perfume she uses?

SUSAN: What perfume do you use?

MICHELE: Who'll make the tea?

MONA: She's just a regular girl really. See? She drinks tea like the rest of us.

SUSAN: Want a cup, Mona?

MONA: No thanks.

SUSAN *goes into the kitchen.*

MICHELE: Mona?

MONA: Yes.

MICHELE: Have you still got that nice red dress?

MONA: You want to borrow it?

MICHELE: Could I?

MONA: Whatever you want.

MICHELE: And do you still have those nice red shoes?

MONA: Take them too.

MICHELE: Thanks, Mona. I'm going out tonight but all my stuff needs mending or dry cleaning.

MONA: Aren't you tired?

MICHELE: Yeah, but I feel like going out. (*Beat.*) Mona, you did see that Steven boy, didn't you? Don't you think he's nice?

MONA: He bores me.

MICHELE: I could really check f'him!

SUSAN *enters and puts two cups of tea on the table.*

MONA: You're always talking about man and going out.

MICHELE: What should I talk about?

MONA: I tell you, you love man. Man fever, you have. It'll be a real problem in time to come.

MICHELE: How could it?

MONA: You rely too much on men. You think all a man thinks about is you? He's got lots of things on his mind; other women, for a start!

MICHELE: What can I do? I seem to get on better with guys. Girls really irritate me; they look at me and see where they can fault me.

Have you ever been to a party where women are just looking you up and down, checking you out to see which parts of them are more expensive than you. I've never been able to get into girls and what they talk about. All these girls at my school, all they ever talked about was marriage, kids and having big houses. I never wanted that. I always dreamt of having a little place of my own and doing what I wanted.

SUSAN: Your wish came true.

MICHELE: I'm working on it.

SUSAN: Sounds like you're overdoing it!

MICHELE: We all like being complimented, don't we? Where else am I going to get praise?

If you stick with a guy too long, the compliments dry up, so do the presents, so does the passion. That's why I keep checking new men. When you first get a guy, he takes real good care of you; takes you out, buys you things, tells you how good you look, and the loving is sweet! I like that.

SUSAN: You can't live on that.

MICHELE: I live on it. Believe me, I live on it.

MONA: Like I said, you rely too much on men. You've never been alone for two minutes. You don't even know who you are and what you're capable of.

MICHELE: Don't give me a hard time. All I came here to do was borrow the dress and some shoes.

MONA: The way you bring my things back sometimes, I might as well throw them away!

MICHELE: That's not true. I'll have the dress back, washed and ironed, by tomorrow night.

Mona, . . . I'm going out with Marcus tonight . . . and I've got to have money. Could you lend us a fiver?

MONA: You think I print money?

MICHELE: As soon as I get my cheque, I'll pay you back.

MONA: By Friday. No later.

MICHELE: Mona . . . (*Long pause.*) . . . you know that whisky?

MONA: Yes.

MICHELE: What did you do with it? Have you got any left?

MONA: Yes, lots, take a bottle.

MICHELE: You're an angel. (*To* SUSAN.) So, where were you? Having a little party of your own, were you?

SUSAN: I just didn't feel like it.

MICHELE (*to* MONA): If you can't find the red dress, I'll take the black one.

MONA (*wearily*): Take whatever you want, Michele.

MICHELE: Have you got Steve's number?

MONA (*looking in her bag for her address book*): What, are you going to go from Marcus to Steve tonight? Michele, your poom-poom must be well hot! (*She finds address book and shows* MICHELE *the number.*) You want Michael too? Michael's probably got some for you if you want it!

MICHELE (*copying the number on a piece of paper*): Thanks. No, I'm not going to Steve tonight. Tomorrow.

MONA: Go on, have another pickney! That's what you want, innit? You can't breed pickney like dog!

MICHELE: Everyone's allowed one mistake. I'm all equipped now, anyway, so it won't happen again. (*Beat.*) He's so nice though! How can I resist?

MONA: There are so many pretty boys, Michele.

MICHELE: I like pretty boys. Girl, I could eat him!

MONA (*to* MICHELE): Have you got any weed?

SUSAN (*to* MONA): You smoke too much weed.

MICHELE: No, she doesn't.

SUSAN: I wasn't talking to you!

MICHELE: There's nothing wrong with a smoke every now and then.

SUSAN: I don't like people who smoke a lot of weed. Everything's too cool with them. They haven't got a job, that's cool. They haven't paid the rent, that's cool. They just got pregnant, that's cool. Everyt'ing cool!

MONA: Have you?

MICHELE: Not with me.

MONA: I've got some, but just enough for one. I don't like not having any. Sometimes, you just fancy a spliff.

SUSAN *looks at her disapprovingly.* MONA *shrugs her shoulders.*

I don't know why you two bicker at each other.

SUSAN: We don't bicker.

MICHELE: No, you just dig at me.

SUSAN: I dig at you only when I have a reason. It just so happens that I find your manners a little lacking these days.

MICHELE: What have manners got to do with it?

MONA: Are you sure all this doesn't date back to Roland?

SUSAN: That was years back! I got over that years ago!

MONA: Are you sure?

SUSAN: Roland and I fell out, we split up, Michele was his next woman. I was glad to get rid of him.

MONA: That's not what you said at the time.

SUSAN: I was caught up in the heat of the moment.

MONA: You accused Michele of one set of crimes!

SUSAN: Mona, stop shit-stirring! I wasn't going to fall out with a friend over a man, a good friend at that.

MONA: So what is it between you two?

MICHELE: It's nothing.

SUSAN: It's not nothing, Michele. I don't like to see you abuse Mona.

MICHELE: Times are bad for me right now. I'm supporting myself. What I need to find is a rich man.

SUSAN: You won't find a rich man. You don't move in those circles.

MICHELE: I feel bad but I just haven't got any money. I'm feeding my baby rubbish. Things'll get better. I'll pay Mona back.

SUSAN: Things will get better?

MICHELE (*irritated; to* MONA): Can I just take those things and go?

MONA: Go look in the bedroom, you'll find them.

MICHELE: And where's the whisky?

MONA (*pointing*): Over there in the corner.

MICHELE: Mona . . . (*Long pause.*) . . . I know what Susan was just saying . . . but I haven't got any food in the flat. My dole comes on Friday. Is there anything left over from the party?

MONA: There's a tin of cheese biscuits on top of the fridge. I didn't even open them.

MICHELE: Are you sure that's all right?

MONA: You just sit there. I'll get it all together for you.

MONA *goes into the kitchen, then the bedroom, collecting things for* MICHELE *in some plastic bags. Uncomfortable silence between* SUSAN *and* MICHELE.

SUSAN: It's getting a bit bad these days, isn't it?

MICHELE: What?

SUSAN: The way people treat each other.

MICHELE *shrugs her shoulders, not understanding.*

SUSAN: The world is run by those who get the breaks. Some people are born into the breaks, others just strike lucky. Those who get the breaks – there's not many of them – they rule our lives; we; the mass; the majority. There's no such thing as an oppressed minority, most of us are part of the oppressed majority. What do we do, we minions, what do we do? We squabble amongst ourselves. They find that very funny.

MICHELE: Who?

SUSAN: Those in power; those who get the breaks. They laugh at us. As long as we run around in circles, they'll be all right.

MICHELE, *not really understanding, looks blankly at* SUSAN, *not sure what to say.*

I'm talking about us, Michele. We help you. You're meant to help us at some stage of the day.

MICHELE: I'm having it bad right now.

SUSAN: You're always having it bad!

MICHELE: It's not my fault, is it?

SUSAN: Whose fault is it? It takes two to make a baby. What, are you going to blame him for the pregnancy? Who spends all the money that comes into your hands? Someone else? No, you. It's your fault. You let men into your life. Try and give your fanny a rest and you might be able to save some money for yourself, and spend some time with your child.

MICHELE: All right, I feel bad. Happy?

SUSAN *looks mildly remorseful.*

Happy?

SUSAN: I'm sorry. You seem to upset me whenever I see you. You keep saying, 'Things will get better', but it's not 'things' that need to get better. It's you!

MONA *comes back in with several plastic bags, which she gives to* MICHELE, *who gets up and makes for the door.*

MICHELE (*to* MONA): So, when am I going to see you again?

MONA: When you want something.

MICHELE: Don't say that!

MONA: Michele, it doesn't really matter.

MICHELE (*to* SUSAN): I'll see you, madam.

SUSAN: Girl, just don't work it too hard tonight!

MICHELE: You jealous?

MICHELE *opens the door.*

See you both.

MICHELE *exits.* MONA *pulls a tobacco tin out from underneath a cushion, throws it to* SUSAN, *who rolls a spliff for her.*

SUSAN: Just this once.

MONA: Share it with me. Stay over?

SUSAN: You want me to stay?

MONA: It'll be good for you to relax and have a laugh. (*Beat.*) It used to be different when we were young. We were all living with our parents, money was something they had. We had nothing to give, nothing that could be borrowed.

SUSAN: It's like a blind spot with Michele. You've lent her more fivers than you can remember. She's forgotten about them all, that's for sure.

MONA: Maybe it gets to the point – that point where you can't feed your shrieking infant – when you don't really care what you're doing, you don't really care what you've become.

SUSAN: You can't say 'no', though. She needs all the support she can get.

MONA: You never did tell me what was bugging you.

SUSAN: It's not really distressing me. It's something that's rather pleasing me, actually. I'm not unhappy at all. I feel great.

MONA: Tell me about that.

SUSAN (*pause*): There's someone I like.

MONA: You must definitely tell me about that! Yes-I! News for me! Come on, tell me, who is it?

SUSAN: Well . . .

MONA: Having a quiet one on the sly, eh? Now tell your Auntie Mona.

SUSAN: What would you do if you liked someone but you weren't sure how they felt?

MONA: I'd tell them.

SUSAN: But what if it was someone you'd known a long time?

MONA: I'd tell them.

SUSAN: Mona, I'm really confused. I know little girls go through phases but I'm really not sure about some of the phases I'm going through!

MONA: There's nothing the matter with you. Everyone gets confused. That shows how normal you are. If you're caught up in some dilemma, you're at peak fitness. Whatever's going on in your head, it's not going to shock me, is it?

SUSAN *finishes rolling the spliff and lights it. She takes a few puffs and passes it on to* MONA.

MONA: Come on, girl. Before this makes us into a pair of idiots. What's your problem?

Pause.

SUSAN: I was walking down the road the other day, and I could see this young guy walking towards me. I could feel him looking at me and, as he got closer, I watched his eyes. He was obviously into tits 'cause he was staring at my chest. Then he moved down to my lower half; a few seconds on my crutch, a few seconds on my legs. Something seemed to please his eyes 'cause he then moved up to my face, seeing if I was good-looking. Not that that matters. Haven't you heard guys say that they don't need to look at the mantelpiece to stoke the fire?

Systematically, this guy checked me out. If he'd looked in my eyes, he wouldn't have seen something he liked, but my head didn't interest him. First he wanted to see if my implements for fucking were all in order. I really hate that, you know.

It's true, there are more female politicians, more businesswomen, more women in influential jobs, but that still hasn't improved men's outlook on women. I'm still, first and foremost, a fuck. I really can't stand that.

What I'm struggling to say is that I think I'm growing tired of that lovable, household pet known as the boyfriend.

SUSAN *kneels before* MONA, *opening her arms, asking to be held.* MONA *hugs her.* SUSAN *pulls back and tries to kiss* MONA. MONA *is shocked and stands up.*

MONA: Susan!

SUSAN (*embarrassed*): I'm sorry.

MONA: You're fed-up with boys and you want women instead?

SUSAN: Not really . . . I just . . . I just feel something for you. It's not really that I'm turned off men, it's not really that I'm turned-on by women, it's just ... well ... you're really special.

You're so patient with Michele, you're so patient with me, you're so patient with Michael ...

MONA: I don't know about that.

SUSAN: ... and that's the reason I didn't come to the party; I couldn't bear to see you in public with Michael. I couldn't bear to see him treat you with such disdain in public. He's disgusting. I don't know why you care for him, I don't know how you ever did. You're too maternal; I can't bear to see Michele and Michael take and take and give nothing in return.

You're really special ...

MONA (*embarrassed*): Cut it out!

SUSAN: Mona, seriously, you're just the best friend I'll ever have. I think you're really great ... and I just happen to fancy you as well.

MONA *passes the spliff to* SUSAN.

MONA: This is getting well out of order ...

SUSAN: ... stop and think about it ...

MONA: ... this is the spliff talking ...

SUSAN: ... when was the last time you felt loved?

MONA: Maybe there is something wrong with you!

SUSAN: There's nothing wrong with me!

MONA: This is one of the phases that little girls go through. Come on, girl, pass it, nah!

Playfully, SUSAN *moves away.*

SUSAN: Come and get it then.

MONA: Come on, pass it, before I give you two kick!

SUSAN *moves behind a chair.*

SUSAN: If you want it, come and get it.

MONA *comes towards* SUSAN *and tries to retrieve the spliff.* SUSAN *dodges out of her way.*

MONA: Look, I'm not joking, Susan, pass it!

MONA *tries to make a grab at the spliff and burns her hand.*

Ouch! Stupid!

SUSAN: Who tell you to put your hand on burning weed? (*Pause.*) Are you all right, Mona?

MONA: No, I'm not all right. Look what you've done! I'm scarred! Why can't you behave yourself? What's got into you today?

SUSAN *tries to look at* MONA's *hand but* MONA *moves away.*

Don't bother. I'm fed up with your foolishness.

MONA *exits.* SUSAN *raises her eyes to the ceiling, feeling regret, but picks up the tobacco tin and follows* MONA *out.*
  Blackout.

Scene Two
MONA's *flat. The morning after. She walks from the kitchen, dressed in dressing-gown and slippers, carrying a bowl of cornflakes and a cup of tea. She sits down and starts eating.* SUSAN *wanders in wearing similar attire.*

SUSAN (*cheerily*): Good morning!

No reply from MONA. SUSAN *goes into the kitchen – to put the kettle on – then comes back out again.*

Tea?

MONA: I've got some, thank you.

SUSAN: Sleep well?

MONA: Yes, thank you.

SUSAN: Feeling talkative? Feeling revived and refreshed, are we?

MONA *gets up, gets out her carpet cleaner and starts, aimlessly, pushing it up and down the floor.*

SUSAN: What's wrong, Mona? Are we still friends? Don't you feel well? I feel wonderful. I feel really happy. Don't you feel any kind of happiness? I knew this is how it would be, you know? I feel really different, don't you? Mona, please say something! Please! What's wrong?

MONA *continues hoovering.*

MONA: Look, it may be important to you but I don't intend to discuss last night.

SUSAN: But I really want to talk about it!

MONA: I know you do!

SUSAN: It's important to me, Mona, don't dismiss it.

MONA: I said I don't intend to discuss it!

SUSAN: Come on, Mona ...

MONA: Don't 'Come on, Mona' me! It's a bit of a shock to the system, you know. I've got a boyfriend, you know. It's a bit of a shock.

SUSAN: Can't we talk?

MONA: Stop it! In fact, I'm seeing Michael later on.

SUSAN: How can you!

MONA: He's my boyfriend and while I'm going out with him, you'd better relax.

SUSAN: Last night meant nothing to you, did it?

MONA: You're right, I'm too maternal, I'm too soft, I make sacrifices for everyone. You wanted me, I complied.

SUSAN: How can you say that!

MONA: People act funny when they're charged. I just let you do what you wanted.

SUSAN: That's really considerate of you. So, now you're off to Michael so he can do what he wants. You could run a little business, you know. Make people pay, Mona. Tell them they can do what they want, all they have to do is stick a coin in the slot!

MONA: Why don't you get hysterical! Why don't you insult me!

SUSAN: I just can't bear to see Michael use you. He doesn't need you, I do!

MONA: We go a long way back, you know. Michael and me talk. I like him – strange as it may seem – I like him. He was the first person that ever talked to me. He taught me a lot, he still does.

SUSAN: He just calls you when he want a jook!

MONA: Don't stop there, Susan, get really unpleasant!

SUSAN: Come on, Mona, admit it, you enjoyed last night. Don't let it bother you.

MONA: Get dressed and piss off, nah!

SUSAN: Don't be like that.

MONA: I don't want to talk!

Pause.

SUSAN: What are you doing tonight?

MONA: I'll probably end up staying at Michael's, won't I?

SUSAN: Okay. (*Pause.*) I'll see you tomorrow?

MONA: Don't start all that again. We made love. I don't know why. I don't know what's come over you. Maybe you were just upset.

SUSAN: Upset? I was happy! I'm really happy!

When we were back home, didn't we sleep together? As kids, didn't we kiss? Didn't we touch? Have you erased it from your memory?

MONA: Susan, we were kids. We didn't know what we were doing.

SUSAN: Didn't we?

MONA: Did you?

SUSAN: I did. You didn't know what you were doing? You didn't love me?

MONA: Susan, we were kids. This is now.

SUSAN: But you love me, don't you?

MONA: Of course I do.

SUSAN: In love?

MONA: In love? (*Dawning on her.*) Well, yes, I suppose I am. (*Pause.*) But we're talking being 'lovers'!

SUSAN: Not that much difference.

MONA: Of course not.

SUSAN: I'll come back here around tea-time. I'm auditioning for this small, touring production today. This left-wing group are dragging some radical piece all over Britain. They obviously feel they should have a black person in the group, so I'm going along to keep the side up.

MONA: You don't look happy at the prospect of work.

SUSAN: It'll carry me miles away from you.

MONA: Don't worry about me. I'll be here when you get back.

Blackout.

Scene Three

MONA's *flat. The morning after.*

MONA: Now that I think about it, who was always there for me? Susan. Where was Michael when I needed him? It doesn't bear thinking about!

What about when I couldn't find a job? Was I depressed! What miserable company I must've been! She was here, though. She stayed, she listened.

Who came up with the suggestion? She did. 'If you can't find a job,' she said, 'create yourself one.' So, I did. I started holding exercise classes at the local school. A few newspaper ads and I was away! She not only picked me up, she helped me find a way.

Maybe we've always been lovers? I'd never made love to her before, but maybe we've always been lovers? I always turn to her when I need comfort, I always turn to her when I need help. Maybe we've always been lovers.

The doorbell rings. MONA *opens the door,* SUSAN *stands there,* MONA *puts her arms round* SUSAN. *The two hold each other for a while.*

SUSAN: What a welcome!

MONA *pulls away and goes over to the sofa. Silence.*

(*With sarcasm.*) No, no, I won't be rushed. I know you're anxious to hear how the audition went but I won't be rushed.

Silence.

No, no, you'll have to control yourself. Let me make myself some tea first, then I'll tell you.

SUSAN *goes into the kitchen to put the kettle on, comes back out, sits down next to* MONA *and waits expectantly.*

MONA: Okay, what happened?

SUSAN (*calmly*): I got in. Starting Thursday, I'll be doing two weeks' rehearsals and a three-week tour with the Network Theatre Group.

MONA (*kissing her*): Well, congratulations.

SUSAN: Does that mean I can go and out and buy some vino?

MONA: Oh, yes, definitely!

SUSAN: Yes-I!

SUSAN *goes back into the kitchen to make her tea.*

MONA: What are this group about?

SUSAN: They're some political group but they don't seem too heavy.

MONA: What's the play about?

SUSAN: Unemployment, the dole, depressed school-leavers, you know the stuff.

SUSAN *comes back in with her tea.*

The people in the group seem rather nice. (*Beat.*) You look a bit down, girl.

Pause.

Don't tell me: another eventful night with Michael. He hasn't done the decent thing and killed himself, has he?

MONA *is not amused.*

If he's gone: good! Come on, Mona, what could be wrong? If he's gone: good! If he's gone, then it's a blessing!

MONA (*Pause*): He's gone.

SUSAN: Praise the lord! You're free!

MONA (*pause*): When I went to see Michael yesterday, I immediately felt there was something wrong. I knew he'd been with somebody because there was a stale smell of fuck in the air and the room felt different. I got the feeling I was intruding on something. I didn't want to say anything just in case I was wrong, but I felt really isolated, as if I was in an affair that Michael had left long ago. Michael's body was there but Michael was not there.

SUSAN: Mona, he was a poor specimen. You can do much better than him.

MONA: Anyway, we spend the night together but, when I wake up, Michael's gone and all that's left is a letter. Something about the relationship losing momentum and how he wants to end it because he doesn't think we've got any future.

SUSAN: Fairly standard.

MONA: So, that's it.

SUSAN: Good!

MONA: I don't really care.

SUSAN: A really poor specimen. You could easily find better.

MONA: Maybe.

SUSAN: You idolised him.

MONA: I know.

SUSAN: He saw that and took advantage of you.

MONA: True.

SUSAN: It was no basis for a relationship.

MONA (*pause*): Have you ever been in love, you know, like it is in those Mills & Boon books? Have you ever been really, pathetically sloppy?

SUSAN: Me? No, man!

MONA: You must have!

SUSAN: I can't really say I've felt that 'head over heels' feeling.

MONA: It's nice.

SUSAN: Is it?

MONA: You'll feel it one day.

SUSAN: I can't believe I'll feel that way about a man.

MONA: Remember what your mother taught you: you're not a woman unless you have a man to look after. Unless you have the love of a man, you're not a real woman.

SUSAN: It doesn't make sense to me at all. Don't you remember when we first came here? We were – what? – eleven or twelve? Boys were the last thing on our mind! We wanted to be film stars, didn't we? We didn't want those little boys trailing 'round after us anymore.

We'd just spent the first twelve years of our lives splashing around in a river. Then what did we do? We fell for those same lines. We fell for that same sweet-talk and climbed right back into the river!

Back home, we made these plans, didn't we? We were going to become rich, fly home, drive into town in our big cars and take care of our grandparents. Look at us! When did we last go home? When did we last send them money?

Things like Michael have been nothing but distraction. Distraction and destruction. He's kept you apart from your family, apart from your career and apart from me.

Women don't need men, I'm telling you. A man rapes a woman, so what? The judge is a man too! They think they can do whatever they want with a woman! Little girls as well! Sometimes I think the greatest mistake we women make is the breeding of more men!

MONA (*giggling*): Well you know what I was thinking about last night? While Michael was doing his stuff, you know what I was thinking about? The time I lost my virginity.

While Michael was doing his thing, I suddenly realised I didn't feel any different. He was no different to that first guy and I knew nothing more about sex.

When I was about fifteen, I used to know this guy. It was innocent. A peck on the cheek, holding hands on the way home. Then, all of a sudden, he put this proposition to me which was more like blackmail! He said that unless I went to bed with him, he wouldn't go out with me again.

SUSAN: So?

MONA: So I did! But for what? For nothing! It wasn't much cop!

SUSAN: I was so young – when I lost mine – that I can't really remember much about it. I was only about eight or nine.

MONA: How old!

SUSAN: They don't care how old you are in the West Indies! If you can say 'hello', you're no longer a child!

I remember I didn't bleed and, at first, I thought he hadn't done it, but he had. Nobody knew. I didn't tell anyone.

MONA: No pain?

SUSAN: Nothing. Nothing at all. I was numb all the way through.

MONA: Who was he?

SUSAN: I can't remember. It's part of the way of life over there, isn't it? It happens and everyone turns a blind eye.

Do you know what really hurts? The fact that I wasn't given a choice how I should experience my first fuck. Caribbean girls don't have the chance to enjoy childhood, we're catapulted into womanhood from an early age!

How can I help but feel a special warmth towards other black women. You see, not only do I love you but I know how it is to be how you are.

Sorry if I embarrass you but I love you. You're beautiful. Everything you do has beauty in it. You radiate! I know you haven't had it easy but still you've become strong and wise and independent. You inspire confidence.

I love you because you listen to everything I say, and you're always truthful. The love I feel for you is one I could never feel for a man.

Long pause.

MONA (*dumbly*): Okay.

SUSAN: Okay what?

MONA: Okay, I hear what you're saying. What do you want me to say?

SUSAN (*smiles*): No, there's nothing I want you to say. I just wanted to let it all come out . . .

MONA: That's cool.

SUSAN: . . . and to propose myself as an alternative to Michael.

MONA: That's not so cool.

SUSAN: You're so reserved, though. You've never been one for expressing emotions. I remember when we were kids, I remember telling you that you were my best friend, but you never told me I was yours.

MONA: Of course you were my best friend. You still are. Of course I love you. I always have and always will, but now we're talkin' somethin' else! You want to settle down and have a little family with me?

SUSAN: Why not? A few kids, an estate car, family holidays.

MONA (*shaking her head*): Back home, it's different. Two girls can walk along the street, arm in arm, and no one will bat an eyelid. You know that. We were intimate, yes. We loved each other, yes. But you didn't have to ask me to be your lover. It was the natural thing to do.

SUSAN: My point precisely!

MONA: Things haven't changed, and yet you're talking to me about some kind of marriage.

SUSAN: I'm grown-up. I want to live with you.

MONA: Michael's been part of me for a long time. It's going to take time to get that out of my system. (*Pause.*) I'm sure I can get over it.

Overjoyed. SUSAN *hugs and kisses* MONA.

SUSAN: Getting over a love affair is a traumatic time. You can come to me and cry on my shoulder.

MONA: And you'll start telling me about mortgages, insurance schemes, bulk-buying and home-improvement!

SUSAN: There's nothing wrong with being house-proud!

Pause.

MONA: Funny. I was remembering all the good times we had as kids. The fun we used to have at school. Those early morning smells: granny cooking bakes, the woman selling milk outside.

SUSAN: And the silly things we used to do!

MONA: Going to the most dangerous places just to pick fruit!

SUSAN: What was it called?

MONA: Washcase. (*Pron. 'Wash-kassay'.*)

SUSAN: The things I used to believe! Remember that time at Washcase I gashed my knee and my grandmother told me that if I let any boy see my knee something terrible would happen?

MONA: Mine told me that if I looked too long in the mirror, the devil's face would appear!

SUSAN: I liked the rainy season best. It was like having a shower in the open. We just ran around in the street, didn't we?

MONA: At seven o'clock, we used to gather around and listen to our grandparents telling stories or singing.

SUSAN: All the women would sit outside in the yard cooking, talking, putting out washing, feeding children and cursing the old drunk that hung around hoping to cadge a meal. Mal cochon! Mal chien! But he'd get his meal eventually.

MONA: My mother threw my father out once, after a drunken fight. But she took him back after a few days, only to discover that she had a few more step-sons and step-daughters.

SUSAN: Our mothers vowed to themselves that the men their daughters set up with would be different, but they never were.

MONA: It was for the woman to hold the family together. The men drifted in and out like irritating mosquitoes, and no matter how much the women swatted them, they still seemed to be there.

SUSAN: That's why Caribbean girls are instilled with a special sense of responsibility, a special type of strength. Men breed, men earn money, but where can a woman look for support and friendship?

MONA: My auntie brought up seven children by herself. She didn't even get his income. All on her own. Not a man in sight. She didn't need one, though.

SUSAN: After they got what they wanted, the men left like thieves in the night.

Blackout.

Scene Four
MONA's *flat. Evening.* MONA *exercises to a bouncy tune. A knock at the door.* MONA *stops her cassette machine to answer the door.* MICHELE *follows her into the room.* MONA *continues doing a few more bends and stretches.*

MICHELE: Wish I was as firm as you!

MONA: I bet parts of you are very fit!

MICHELE: Do you think I should exercise?

MONA: You probably don't need to. I'm sure all your limbs get stretched fairly regularly.

MICHELE: Well, it's a lot cheaper than aerobics classes.

MONA *picks up a towel and dries herself.* MICHELE *paces about uneasily.*

MONA: And to what do I owe the pleasure?

MICHELE: Well . . . I need a couple of favours, don't I?

MONA: Are Susan and I your only friends?

MICHELE: Well . . .

MONA: You know why? 'Cause you're a real pain in the perineum!

MICHELE: I don't want much.

MONA: Whatever you want, Michele.

MICHELE: You know that nice, blue, patterned dress you've got?

MONA: What about the last dress you took?

MICHELE: Have I still got that?

MONA: Somewhere!

MICHELE (*thinks*): Oh, yes, I know why I haven't brought it back. I haven't had time to wash it. Look, I'll bring both dresses back at the same time.

MONA: Going anywhere nice?

MICHELE: Just out.

MONA: Do you think if I had a baby I'd get asked out as much as you do?

MICHELE: I'm not going out with anyone, I'm just going out. If I had to stay in with my baby every night – as well as every day – I'd go loopy! I might even turn into a baby-batterer!

MONA: A very convincing argument. So, you're not going out with anyone but you are going out? (*Thinks.*) Gosh, isn't this fun? (*Thinks.*) I've got it! You're not going *out* with someone – you're going *to* someone!

MICHELE: Sort of. (*Pause.*) And there's something else.

MONA: Oh, yes, I forgot; a *couple* of favours.

MICHELE: Will you or Sue come over and babysit?

MONA: Well, I don't know.

MICHELE: Maybe I could bring him over?

MONA: How do you know Susan and I haven't planned a little candlelit dinner together?

MICHELE (*smiling*): Candlelit dinner! Come on, is it okay?

MONA: How do you know Susan and I don't want the evening to ourselves?

MICHELE: Look, if you want to get charged or drunk at my place, it's cool.

MONA: Susan's got a job on a touring production, she'll need time for the show, I probably won't see her until the end of the production.

MICHELE: Mona, I don't see what the problem is. You can both babysit together.

MONA: Maybe we'd like to spend tonight alone?

MICHELE: You can both babysit together! What do you mean you'd like to spend the evening 'alone'? You will be alone! You're not going to want to get into bed before midnight, are you?

MONA: We might.

MICHELE *stares at* MONA.

MICHELE: 'We'? (*Smiling.*) Don't wind me up!

MONA: Michele, I am not winding you up.

MICHELE: I think you're serious!

MONA: I am serious.

MICHELE (*pause*): You and Susan?

MONA: Me and Susan.

MICHELE *stares at* MONA *again.*

MICHELE: Stop fooling around, Mona. I know you don't want to babysit but, I promise, he won't make a sound. Put him to bed and you can do what you want!

MONA (*sighs*): Battered into submission! Bring him over later.

MICHELE, *relieved, kisses* MONA.

MICHELE: I don't know what I'd do without you. (*Pause.*) You weren't serious, were you, Mona? About you and Susan?

MONA: What if I was, Michele? Does that mean you'll stop borrowing my clothes?

MICHELE: Mona, tell me straight.

MONA: Yes, I'm serious.

MICHELE: Oh, come on, Mona. Truthfully?

MONA (*exasperated*): Michele, what do you want to do? Inspect the sheets?

MICHELE (*rambling*): But . . . Mona . . . but . . .

MONA: You're shocked?

MICHELE: Nah, man, you can't have!

MONA: What's so shocking about two women making love?

MICHELE: Mona, you haven't!

MONA: Oh, this is priceless! The liberated woman is going to tell me I can't sleep with another woman!

MICHELE: Mona . . .

MICHELE *pulls repulsed faces.*

. . . another woman?

MONA: Michele, take the dress and piss off! There's no way I'm going to listen to your thoughts on morality. You drag your fanny from bed to bed and you're going to tell me I'm perverse! Go away!

MICHELE (*pause*): Your mother would be heartbroken!

MONA: We don't intend taking my mother to bed with us!

MICHELE: She'll find out! Michael will find out! What's going to happen to him?

MONA: He'll be okay.

MICHELE: Does he know?

MONA: He'll find out soon enough!

MICHELE: That's no way to treat him!

MONA: Isn't it? Didn't I tell you? Michael's left me. Gone. I have been left.

He wrote me this heartfelt note in which he thanked my for opening my legs – without complaint – twice a week for the last five years. Twice on my birthday!

The note continued: he didn't think my pussy would hold an endless fascination for him and he was moving on to crutches new.

I think it's time for a little romance in my life. Susan says she loves me. It's a long time since I heard someone say that. Susan told me she loved me. I liked the sound of that.

MICHELE (*stunned*): It's sick!

MONA: Michele, take the dress and go away!

MICHELE: Forget about tonight!

Enter SUSAN.

MONA: Cutting yourself off from us, are you? Think we'll infect you and your child, do you?

MICHELE: I don't think it's right, that's all. I don't know how you can say all these things! I know you're not a lesbian.

MONA: How do you know?

MICHELE: Because I know you. I've known you from time, so I know you're not. Look, I can tell one.

MONA: How? Describe a lesbian to me.

MICHELE: I just know. You see enough of them down Moseley! Hair-cropped, looking like man in trousers, braces, big boots, badges there . . .

SUSAN (*to* MONA): Michele's shocked! You haven't had girlfriends, Michele? I thought you'd done it all!

MICHELE (*to* MONA): Look, I can tell a lesbian from a heterosexual! And I know you're not a lesbian. (*To* SUSAN.) I don't know about you!

MONA: Stop giving it names. This person says she loves me. We all need someone to love us.

MICHELE: But I went to school with you. I've been out with you.

MONA: That doesn't say anything!

MICHELE: 'Course it does!

MONA: What?

MICHELE: It says you weren't born that way. You have to be born a lesbian. It's a biological thing. You don't suddenly wake up and you're a lesbian!

SUSAN (*to* MONA): Has she got a degree in biology that I don't know about?

MICHELE (*to* SUSAN): Look, I'm not listening to you! You've obviously got a hormone deficiency!

SUSAN: So, you mean the way you carry on is okay? Having all those men –

apart from not helping your child – is very unhealthy. Disease, Michele, promiscuity carries disease.

MICHELE: I'm not talking to you! I know you don't like me!

MONA: Cut it out, you two. Michele, look, you'll just have to get used to it.

MICHELE: No man! No way! It's not normal! It's an abomination against man and God!

SUSAN: Michele, if you think we're such sinners, just go! You need never see us again.

MICHELE, *still trying to save* MONA, *takes her aside.*

MICHELE (*to* SUSAN): You keep out of it! (*To* MONA.) Do you know what lesbians do? Do you know what people think of lesbians?

SUSAN: What now!

MICHELE (*to* MONA): It's dirty! You can't make love to another woman! It's not natural!

SUSAN: There's more to it than that, but you're so bloody small-minded, you can't see it!

MICHELE: Yeah? I can see – just as plain as day – that you've poisoned Mona with this lesbian crap. Just because you're incapable of loving a man, that doesn't give you right to mess up other people's lives. I blame you for this. You're sick! It's your fault you fucking, filthy, dyke bitch!

SUSAN *walks over and slaps* MICHELE*'s face.* MICHELE *grabs her hair and the two begin to fight, rolling around on the ground.* MONA *dives in to separate them.*

MONA: Now just hold on there, girl! Michele, if you haven't understood what we've been saying, then you never will. So, just take your backside and go!

MICHELE: If that's the way you feel about it, Mona, I'll go, but you'll never see me again, that's for sure!

MICHELE *exits, slamming the door. A few seconds' pause while calm is restored.*

MONA: She wants us to babysit for her tonight. She'll be back.

Blackout.

Scene Five
MONA's flat. The morning before
SUSAN leaves for her tour. MONA and
SUSAN share out a breakfast of tea and
toast.

MONA: You're eating too fast.

SUSAN: I'm going to be late.

MONA: You really will be late if you throw up. Slow down, nah!

SUSAN: I'm sure I've forgotten something.

MONA: Everybody always does. There's no point worrying. Everybody forgets something when they pack.

SUSAN: So what have I forgotten?

MONA: Have you remembered a pen and some stationery?

SUSAN: What for?

MONA: What for! To write to me!

SUSAN: I'll write.

MONA: I bet you forget.

SUSAN: Three weeks, Mona! It's only three weeks! I bet you're glad to be rid of me!

MONA: On the contrary! I've got used to it and I think I like having you around.

SUSAN: Have I passed the audition?

MONA: I like your cooking.

SUSAN: Is that all?

MONA: I like having you around. It's been . . . interesting. (*Pause.*) Michael and I tried living together, remember?

SUSAN: I remember how bad-tempered you were.

MONA: It was hell, wasn't it? He expected me to clean up behind him, iron his shirts, be a wife. That took the romance out of things! Living with you is different, though. I feel secure. What have we done? Nothing. We just sat around, watched telly, got charged, but I really enjoy myself. You make me feel at home. I know it is my home, but I've never felt so at home. It feels right.

SUSAN *stares at* MONA, *half-moved, half-stunned.*

What's wrong with you?

SUSAN: I think I'm going to cry.

MONA: Don't take the piss!

SUSAN: I'm not! That was . . . really . . . touching. You . . . like me?

MONA: Of course I bloody like you! I think I'm used to it. We're lovers. If they don't like it, they can lump it.

SUSAN: You don't have to say 'lovers'. There's a Dominican word for it: 'zammie'. Tell people we're zammies.

I couldn't just take up with any woman tomorrow. She'd have to be someone who understands what I've been through. Someone who I'd known for a long time. It would have to be spiritual.

I can't hate Michele. She's the same as me. I'm not going to criticise any black woman, I know where she's coming from. We all share a spiritual bond. You and I have just taken it one step on.

SUSAN *looks at her watch.*

Look at the time! I knew I should've eaten fast!

MONA: Zammies.

SUSAN: Tell them we're zammies.

MONA: That's a word I haven't heard for a long time. I remember Mummy used to use that word when she was talking about an old friend of hers. Zammies! Yes-I!

SUSAN *gets up and begins packing things into bags.*

SUSAN: If they want to know about zammies, tell them about their basin. A1 black women know about their basin.

Some don't have hot water, some need the hot water to wash their kids, some don't have time to take a bath! We all know about boiling a pan of water and using a basin to wash ourself.

My mother gave me my own basin when I was about four. I think it was probably the first thing I possessed. Just before we went to bed, my mother would tell us, 'Go wash your kookalook!' That was when I first became conscious of being a woman and what it meant to be feminine. That was when I first began to think about my mother, and her mother.

MONA: At the end of another, long, unrewarding day, they'd wash themselves in preparation for the evening's ritual. No matter how tired they felt, they had to wash themselves in case their husbands wanted to make love.

SUSAN: Zammies. It's spiritual. Don't tell them about love, they'll never equate two women with love. Just tell them about their basin if they can't understand what's happened to us.

SUSAN has gathered together a suitcase and some holdalls, and has put on her coat.

Now, I have to go.

MONA gets up and hugs SUSAN.

MONA: You're really something! You will call me, won't you?

SUSAN: Three weeks will pass in no time. (*Pause.*) I feel really good. I'm working, and my love life has finally come together. (*Pause.*) I hope. (*Pause.*) Thanks.

MONA: You're thanking me?

SUSAN: I'm grateful. Thanks.

MONA kisses her.

SUSAN: My pleasure.

They embrace again.
Blackout.

ACT TWO

Scene One

MONA's *flat. Some days later.* MONA *reads a letter from* SUSAN.

MONA (*reading aloud*): 'My dearest Mona, I miss you very much and wish you were with me sharing the many wonderful moments we experience. Wherever we go, people are hospitable. Wherever we perform, audiences are generous. Because we're not playing in cities, we don't spend much time on boring motorways. Riding around the backroads of an area has proved fascinating. Performing in small village halls has meant winding our way through beautiful, country roads. This is my kind of touring. Instead of stopping at service stations and eating greasy food, we stop in scenic pubs and share fresh food and conversation with the locals.'

Well, I'm glad you're having fun!

(*Reading aloud.*) 'The members of the company have proved stimulating companions.'

I wonder which part of you they're stimulating?

(*Reading aloud.*) After every performance, we have long interrogations into the faults of that night's show. I've learnt so much.'

How fulfilling!

(*Reading aloud*) 'I've made numerous friends on this tour and when I come home I'll invite them over so you can meet them.'

I don't want to meet any of your fucking friends.

You don't need me.

MONA paces about, her body full of tension.

What does she take me for? Does she think I'll sit in here waiting for her to finish screwing the entire company?

MONA stops suddenly, taking stock of herself.

Oh God! What am I saying?

The door bell rings. MONA *goes to answer it.* MICHELE *stands at the door.*

MICHELE (*cheerfully*): Hi!

MONA: What are you doing here?

MICHELE *stands uncomfortably in the doorway trying to get in.*

MICHELE: Are you going to let me come in or what?

MONA: Girl, what are you doing on my doorstep?

Pause.

MICHELE: I've brought your dress and shoes back.

MONA *finally lets* MICHELE *in. The two women walk into the room.*

The dress has been dry cleaned.

MONA *looks at the dress in disbelief. (The dress hangs from a hanger, covered in a clear, plastic cover.)*

MONA: Is it my birthday?

MICHELE: So, Mon', how are you?

MONA: All right. (*Pause.*) No, that's a lie.

MICHELE: What's wrong?

MONA: You don't want to know.

MICHELE: I do.

MONA: You don't.

MICHELE: What, is it something to do with you and Susan?

MONA: I wouldn't want to shock you.

MICHELE: So what's wrong?

MONA: I miss her.

MICHELE (*embarrassed*): Oh.

MONA: I shocked you, anyway.

MICHELE: So? You miss her.

MONA: She's been gone ten days and, only this morning, I get a letter.

MICHELE: Ten days? So what? What's the matter, woman? Ten days? I thought she'd left you!

MONA (*thinks*): Yeah ... ten days ... so what? You don't want to listen to me. I get irrational when I fall in love.

MICHELE: You're serious about this thing you and Sue are having aren't you? Got anything to drink?

MONA: In the kitchen.

MICHELE: May I?

MONA: Of course.

MICHELE *lays the dress over the sofa and goes into the kitchen.*

MICHELE: So, how are you otherwise?

MONA (*thinks*): I'm wound-up. I'm irrational.

MICHELE *re-enters with a glass of orange juice.*

MICHELE: You're what?

MONA: Irrational.

MICHELE: Why?
You wouldn't know about it. It's all related to love. You're lucky, you don't suffer from such complaints, you just fuck.

I haven't seen you in a while. I wonder why?

MICHELE (*pause*): That whole thing about you and Susan ... it came as a bit of a surprise. I want to apologise for all that noise I made. It was just a bit of a shock to my system, telling me about it so directly.

MONA: You came here just to tell me that? You haven't come to borrow anything? You don't want me to do you a favour? What happened to you, woman?

MICHELE: I don't always come round when I want something.

MONA: But you do! Maybe we're not the only ones who have changed?

MICHELE: I just came here to bring the dress back, apologise and find out how you are. I haven't seen you for a while.

MONA: Yeah but I know what you've been doing! You've got a lot to answer for. I was appalled by your outburst last week and now I discover that the whole district knows about my business.

MICHELE: Mona, honest ... I only ... well, what did you expect me to do?

MONA: Michele, if you told one person, that's all it takes. If you say to someone, 'Now, you promise not to tell anyone else,' that person will run straight to someone else. You see, you shouldn't have told that first person.

MICHELE (*remorseful*): Mona, I'm

sorry . . . girl, I've known you for so long . . . and now you tell me you're getting into women . . .

MONA: Be sensible, Michele. I'm someone who's been honest, you probably know lots of people who're afraid to be honest. Think about it: there are probably cousins of yours that are gay but do you think they'd tell you! 'Course they wouldn't! Look at the fuss you're making!

MICHELE: It's just . . . I've known you for so long . . .

MONA: I don't like your attitude. I thought we were friends. You never have anything nice to say about people. Everybody's now talking about Susan and I. Not that I mind but you should have more respect for your friends.

I don't want an argument with you. We can't spend our whole lives fighting with one another. Tell me, what made you so uncaring? How come you hate so much? You make it so hard for people to understand you, you make it so hard for people to like you, no wonder you have so few friends!

Maybe you've forgotten what good friends Susan and I have been to you. We all understood each other, and that was special, and that's why I can't believe you can't understand Susan and I.

Michele, we're all in the same boat. We all have so much in common. Black woman have so much in common, so why are we arguing? Who will love us? White people? Black men? Who will love us if not other black women?

I'm the one who's always making an effort. I'm tired of caring for people, selfish people. You should make the best of a friendship like this.

MICHELE: I don't want to be your enemy. I do care about you and Susan. It's taken me a long time to understand how you and Susan had become lovers. I'd known you for so long. I had no idea you had those tendencies. Me? I like the love of man. I'd do anything for the love of a man!

Maybe you think I'm loose. You tell me I think about men too much. What am I supposed to do? I mean, what am I on this earth for? I don't know. To breed? Well, I've done that. I've done my bit. Now I want to enjoy myself. I'll be old soon. I'll be dead soon after that. I want to enjoy myself. You can understand that?

That's what I now realise. You're happy. You want to enjoy yourself, and you've found out how. You've told me how men will hurt me but, well, it's a physical thing. Men make me feel good.

Maybe I'm like my mother? No matter what my father did to her, she stuck with him. Sometimes the man would come home, fight with my mother and that used to hurt me so much because neither of us could control him.

MONA: Why didn't your mother leave?

MICHELE: She said she had nowhere to go. She said that my father was the only man she knew. Whenever they had problems, my mother used to say to me that we had to stick together because, back home, families stuck together. Back home, she'd been taught that blood was thicker than water.

Daddy was so possessive, so violent. He used to love us in a very primitive way. That's why I left. I couldn't bear to hear her cry anymore. The only way I could've left home and got a flat was to get myself pregnant. That's why I'm now imprisoned in my home.

MONA: That's why you should treat other black women as zammies. So many of them are imprisoned in their homes by their children. So many of them have to fight with their husbands at night.

MICHELE: Zammies? What are they?

MONA: It comes from 'ami'; French for friend. Only in Dominica, it's more than friendship. It's not only comfort, it's not only companionship, it's not only physical.

Zammies are friends, spiritual friends; zammies know about each other without knowing each other. Zammies are not necessarily lovers.

Black women know things that only black women know. They have so much in common. Susan and I won't preach to you about men, but you must consider us your zammies.

MICHELE: I know what you're saying.

MONA: Have you got a basin?

MICHELE: I used to have. Why did you ask that?

MONA: I just wondered.

MICHELE *gets up and makes to leave.*

MICHELE: Listen, I have to go. See? I didn't come to borrow anything or to ask any favours!

MICHELE *kisses* MONA.

I'll call you in a few days.

MONA: See ya.

Exit MICHELE.
MONA *thinks for a second then begins looking around to see where she discarded* SUSAN's *letter. She finds it and begins to straighten it out.*
The phone rings. MONA *looks at the phone.*

MONA: It can't be!

MONA *picks the phone up.*

MONA: Hello.

On the other side of the stage, SUSAN *talks into a pay phone.*

SUSAN: Hello, darling.

MONA: It can't be!

SUSAN: It's me, Susan.

MONA: I know who it is. After ten days I finally get a letter and a phone call. Wow! All in the same day! What, did you forget your own number?

SUSAN: Don't give me a hard time, we've been really busy.

MONA: What, interrogating each other? Having scholarly discussions after supper?

SUSAN: Mona, what's wrong?

MONA: What could be wrong? You've been away for ten days, not a word from you, I've been worried . . .

SUSAN: Ah, isn't that nice.

MONA: . . . then, this morning, a letter arrives. No, 'letter' would be dignifying the garbled note I received. Now, lo and behold, it's the first phone-call.

SUSAN: Mona, I've been busy.

MONA: I'm sure. Basking in the stimulating company and making friends? Have you made some nice friends?

SUSAN: I do believe you're jealous.

MONA: Me? You carry on! You can pass out your pussy amongst the cast. Don't worry about me.

SUSAN: What are you saying? What do you think I'm doing out here?

MONA: I don't know.

SUSAN: You think I'm screwing around!

MONA: You say you've been busy.

SUSAN: Woman, you're jealous! I don't believe it! Well, kiss me granny neck-back!

MONA: Don't be silly, Susan. I haven't heard from you in ten days, you could've called . . .

SUSAN: But I suppose if you're jealous, that must mean you've fallen for me too. That's nice to know.

MONA: I'm not jealous, I was just worried. I thought maybe something had happened, I thought they wouldn't know my number . . .

SUSAN: You've fallen for me too!

MONA: Come now, Susan . . .

SUSAN: So you care about me!

MONA: Course I bloody care! Come on, you'd be worried too.

SUSAN: And what's all this about me having all these affairs?

MONA: Keep me in contact, will you please? If you don't know how to use a phone box, ask a grown-up to help you.

SUSAN: What's all this flak for?

MONA: Just call me, please.

SUSAN: Do you miss me?

MONA: No way! I've had the entire West-Indian cricket team keep me company all week!

SUSAN: Mona, please!

MONA: Oh sorry, I don't want to distress you. I wouldn't want to affect tonight's performance.

SUSAN: Darling, I have to go. I'm phoning from a petrol station.

MONA: Go, go, don't worry about me.

SUSAN: I'll be home in a few days.

MONA: Now there's something to look forward to!

SUSAN: I love you.

MONA: Do you?

SUSAN: Yes, and I really miss you.

MONA: Then call me.

SUSAN: I will and I'll be home soon. Bye, Mona.

MONA: Bye, Princess.

MONA puts the phone down and looks down at her feet, disgusted at herself. She stalks around the room.

MONA: I mean, who needs Michael? Susan causes me just as much distress, what do I need Michael for?

Zammies, huh? If we're so zammie-zammie, how come you don't call me? You said you understood me. If you did, you'd call me.

Yeah, we're zammies, but I'm in love with you as well. That'll cause me the problems it always does.

Blackout.

Scene Two
MONA*'s flat. A Saturday afternoon.*
MONA *is curled up on the sofa with a book. The doorbell rings. She gets up to open the door.* MICHELE *stands in the doorway, beaming, a bottle of wine in her hand.*

MICHELE: You haven't got any plans for this afternoon, have you?

MICHELE *embraces* MONA, *hands her the wine and comes into the room.*

MONA: Look at you! Look at that smile on your face!

MICHELE: I feel good.

MONA: Really?

MICHELE: Here all alone?

MONA: Just me.

MICHELE: Good, that means we can sit down, drink this bottle of wine, chat and get merry.

MONA: What's the matter with you?

MICHELE: I got a job.

MONA *embraces* MICHELE.

MONA: That's great! Congratulations. Doing what?

MICHELE: General duties in that bingo hall on the high street.

MONA: You in a bingo hall? That's a joke!

Silence. Stony glare from MICHELE.

MONA: Really good news!

MICHELE: It's a start. It'll be boring and dirty, I'm sure, but I took your advice, I got a job. Now I won't have to keep borrowing so often.

MONA: It never bothered me. Look, we're friends and what are friends for?

MICHELE: Nah, you can't keep borrowing and scrounging all your life. Besides, I was getting lazy. You know, laying-in until midday, watching TV all day. My big arse was really beginning to spread out.

I was getting lazy and I was running out of people to go to. I went into my mother's to have some supper and she hardly had enough for two, let alone four! That was it! I thought, my God, my mother's run out, she's got nothing left to give me. That really hurt: my poor mother going without. I think it's about time I gave a little back to my old Mum.

MONA: That's really good. I'm glad you're getting yourself together.

MICHELE: I met this really nice girl at the bingo hall. I thought the place was going to be full of stuffy, white people but there's this black girl there, just a few years older than me. A really nice girl called Thelma. We got on right from the word go. Chat, chat, chat. We talked for hours!

She told me about this friend of hers. This is a really sad story. Thelma's just found out that this friend of hers is having an affair with her man. Thelma said she'd known the girl since they were in skirts and socks. One day, the girl breaks down in front of Thelma and tells her she's in love with Thelma's man. Thelma says to her, 'How does my man feel about this?' The girl says, 'I think he loves me too.' Thelma says, 'You can keep him!'

MONA: Damn right!

MICHELE: Is she?

MONA: If my man's in love with another woman, what use is he to me? I'd get over him. What's the point of staying with someone if their mind is on someone else? The girl's smart! Fuck him! She's better off without him.

MICHELE: You really wouldn't worry if it was happening to you?

MONA: No, not at all.

MICHELE: It wouldn't matter if the man you were in love with was having an affair with a friend of yours?

MONA: Good luck to them!

MICHELE *goes into the kitchen and brings out a corkscrew and two glasses. She pulls the cork out of bottle and pours the wine as the next lines are being said.*

MONA: So, you'll be all right, you've got this girl to talk to?

MICHELE: Yeah, she's nice.

MONA: And the money's okay?

MICHELE: It's not bad.

MONA: How many hours?

MICHELE: As many as I want.

MONA: And the baby?

MICHELE: Mum says she'll take care of him.

MONA: That's great.

MICHELE *takes a sip of her wine and sits back, almost looking as if the conversation has come to a complete end. Rather mystified, MONA reclines as well.*

MICHELE: Mona ...

Pause.

MONA: What's wrong?

MICHELE: I know about the letter.

MONA: What letter?

MICHELE: The letter from Michael.

MONA: His letter to me?

MICHELE: Yes. I know why he wrote it.

MONA: Did I tell you about that?

MICHELE: No, Michael did.

MONA: Oh, that's nice. Why is Michael telling everyone about my business?

MICHELE: I know what he wrote in the letter ... and I know why he wrote it ... and I know that he wrote a pack of lies.

MONA: You know more than me. Please, go on.

MICHELE (*pause*): This is really hard for me.

MONA: Don't worry about me, child. Michael's someone who I used to care for, you're not going to hurt anyone's feelings.

MICHELE: Are you sure?

MONA: Believe me. We haven't been broken up long but, in that short time, not only have I found someone who loves me but I've realised how little Michael cared. Just tell me, Michele.

MICHELE: He gave you all this crap about how it wouldn't work, how you weren't suited, how he wasn't ready to settle down ...

MONA: That was the jist of it. Well, what's the subtext?

MICHELE: ... he's in love with me.

Long pause.

MONA: Like I said, I'm better off without him.

MICHELE: Mona, I'm really sorry ...

MONA: What are you apologising for? You don't feel sorry, I'm sure he doesn't feel sorry ...

MICHELE: ... I would've told you sooner ...

MONA: You don't have to explain or excuse yourself, I truly mean what I say: what good is Michael to me if it's you he wants?

MICHELE: ... there was nothing I could do about it ...

MONA: I don't blame anyone, I'm really not that bothered ...

MICHELE: ... it sort of happened ...

MONA: . . . everything's fine . . .

MICHELE: . . . I feel really bad . . .

MONA: Why? Everything's fine, Michele.

MICHELE: . . . I hope it won't spoil our friendship . . .

MONA: MICHELE, EVERYTHING'S FINE!

Long pause.

MONA: How long has this been going on?

MICHELE: A few months.

MONA: He always fancied you. He knew about your infamous appetite, of course, and he always wondered what it was like making love to a really horny woman. You know, someone who was really into trying everything!

I guess I never really satisfied him. He wanted me to suck him off but I could never really do that, it didn't really turn me on. I guess you must be doing the job properly.

I just feel that there are certain things you should know about him and, because you're a friend, certain things I ought to warn you about.

MICHELE: Like what?

MONA: Oh, nothing drastic. It's not that he's got some disease he hasn't told you about. Nothing serious. Just some things you might be interested to know.

MONA *picks up the wine bottle and fills up their glasses. With* MICHELE *on the edge of her seat,* MONA *uses a few moments to further increase* MICHELE's *discomfort, then she begins.*

MONA: Michael's breath has a smell all of its own, doesn't it? I think it's because he puts so much salt and pepper on his food. Have you noticed that?

MICHELE: Yes. Why are you telling me about Michael's breath?

MONA: Plus the fact that everything is washed down with Lucozade. Salt, pepper and Lucozade. The combination makes for a very distinctive odour. Does it still smell like that?

MICHELE: I don't really know. He seems to drink a lot of Lucozade.

MONA: Does he bite your breasts?

MICHELE *looks slightly embarrassed.*

Does he?

MICHELE: Mona!

MONA: I used to like that. I like the way he bites, it's a harmless kind of bite. Does he still bite like that?

MICHELE *is silent.*

Does he?

MICHELE (*embarrassed*): Sort of.

MONA: He'd always make sure I was undressed first. As if he was scared that, having undressed himself, I'd run away! Crazy guy! Is he still like that?

MICHELE: Why are you asking me all of this?

MONA: So, most times, he'd undress me first, make sure I was there, in bed, waiting, and then he'd undress himself. Does he still do that?

MICHELE: Sometimes. Why are you asking me all of this?

MONA: His impulsiveness excited me, and he became excited for no reason at all; that made things unpredictable. I liked that. Just out of the blue, he'd want to make love, in unlikely places too! We did it in a car once, out in some dark car park. Is he still like that?

MICHELE: I don't know yet.

MONA: Is he still so impulsive?

MICHELE: He seems to be.

MONA: That's what I loved about him: we did it anywhere. He was such a slag but I suppose that's what I loved about him.

MICHELE: Is there a reason why you're asking all these questions? Why are you acting like this?

MONA: There are just a few things I think you ought to know about him . . . and I'm reminiscing.

You know, it's funny, Michael was only the second boy I'd been to bed with. The first time it'd been just a rushed and embarrassed fiasco which was more enjoyable for him than me, but Michael helped me enjoy making love. Michael was more experienced.

I like the way he's able to keep going.
Does he still retain his stamina,
Michele?

MICHELE *now looks embarrassed,
hurt and close to tears.*

Does he. Michele? Can he still pump
and pump and pump until you're sore?

Silence.

Can he, Michele?

MICHELE: Stop it, Mona.

MONA: Can he still fuck for so long,
Michele?

MICHELE (*angrily*): Yes, yes, yes!
Mona, stop it!

MONA: What's the matter? I'm not
embarrassing you, am I? Has he taken
you to Blackpool yet?

MICHELE *looks up, slightly
shocked.*

Have you spent the dirty weekend in
the hotel in Blackpool? Have you,
Michele?

MICHELE: Yes, yes.

MONA: We did that trip quite a few
times. We stayed in the same little
hotel, we took the same long walk
along the promenade, we spent the
same amount of time riding on the big
dipper and the big wheel. Did you do
that, Michele?

Silence.

Have you done all the things that I did?

MICHELE (*suppressing tears*): Okay,
Mona, that's enough . . .

MONA: Have you done the same things?
Of course you have. Michael's still the
same person. He's still the same. He's
doing the same things and going to the
same places.

MICHELE (*softly sobbing*): Mona,
please . . .

MONA: Ah, but, Michele – and here's his
pièce de résistance – has he told you
about this plot of land he's inherited in
Dominica? Has he told you about that?

Silence. MICHELE *cries to herself.*
MONA *fills up both glasses with wine.*

Has he told you that, in a few years
time, you'll go back to Dominica and

build a beautiful house on his plot of
land? Has he told you that? Has he?

MICHELE (*crying – angry*): Yes!

MONA: Well, that is one of the many lies
Michael will tell you. I met his aunt
when she was in London recently, and
I asked her about Michael's so-called
inheritance. When his grandparents die,
he'll inherit a broken-down shack, and
that's it! That's your dream home!

He tells lies Michele. He always did
and he always will because he'll never
change. Michele, that boy will make
love to you in the same way he did me,
he'll take you to the same places he
took me, and he'll probably love you
for as long as he loved me, at which
point, he'll climb in bed with another
girl.

Michele, you're just another month in
his calendar.

MICHELE, *weak from sobbing,
collapses into* MONA's *arms.
Blackout.*

Scene Three
MICHELE *asleep on* MONA's *couch.*
MONA *enters, crosses to the kitchen,
puts the kettle on, comes back out, tickles*
MICHELE's *feet.* MICHELE *wakes up
suddenly.*

MONA: Morning!

MICHELE: Mona!

MONA: Look at you! Didn't you sleep
well? You couldn't fall asleep, could
you? You were tossing and turning, and
then you came out here!

MICHELE: I snore. I didn't want to
disturb you.

MICHELE *gets up.*

I'll make some tea.

MONA: I've already put the kettle on.

MICHELE *stops dead in her tracks.*

Don't lie, Michele. You shouldn't be
afraid of sleeping with me just because
Susan and I have become lovers.

MICHELE: It's not that . . .

MONA: How many times we've slept
together! What did you think, I was
going to molest you?

MICHELE *looks ashamed.*

MICHELE: Kettle's boiling!

MICHELE *goes into the kitchen.*

MONA: No milk, no sugar.

MONA *folds up the blankets that were covering* MICHELE. MICHELE *re-enters with two cups of tea.*

MICHELE: I'm going for a wash. Can I borrow some underwear?

MONA: Oh, we're back to borrowing, are we?

MICHELE *looks guilty.*

Only joking, Michele.

Pause.

MICHELE: About last night. You made me realise a lot of things. I know Michael has his faults, I know men do, but I couldn't feel for a woman the way I feel for a man.

MONA: I wasn't trying to convert you!

MICHELE: I know. I still love and respect you and Susan, but you mustn't condemn me for loving Michael. Sometimes people find themselves unable to resist things that are bad for them.

MONA: I know how you feel girl. Believe me. I loved him once, didn't I?

MICHELE: Thank you for understanding. Even if I'd tried to stop myself falling for Michael, how long could I have stopped myself? How could I have stopped Michael falling for me? You know how he is!

MONA: I know what you love about him. I know precisely what you love about him. I won't condemn you for loving Michael.

MICHELE: I know how he is but I've grown used to men and their ways. I've accepted affection where it's been given. If someone wants to love me, I'm happy. Some people go through life waiting for a love that doesn't exist! There's no such thing as everlasting love, so I just get love where I can. I think Michael loves me, I don't know how long he'll love me for but I'm happy!

MONA: Sometimes you love someone and it's hard to explain to other people what you love about that person, but you just can't help yourself.

I'm not much better. Look what I've fallen in love with! It doesn't matter what sex you fall in love with. It's all too much hurt and worry.

Keys in the front door. SUSAN *bursts in.* MONA *and* SUSAN *embrace.* MICHELE *looks slightly embarrassed, and puts her shoes on.*

SUSAN: What, Michele, can't you say, 'Hello, Susan, did you have a nice time?'

MICHELE: Hello, Susan, did you have a nice time?

SUSAN: Yes, thank you.

MICHELE *gathers up her bag and makes to leave.*

MICHELE: I have to pick up Tony from my Mum's.

SUSAN: What's the hurry, Michele?

MICHELE: I'm sure you've got lots to talk about.

SUSAN: Don't you want to hear about it?

MICHELE: Must go, really. See you, Mona, Susan.

MICHELE *exits.*

SUSAN: She looked so embarrassed.

MONA *and* SUSAN *hug again.*

MONA: So, you decided to come home!

SUSAN: What was I going to do?

MONA: I thought you might have decided to shack up with somebody else!

SUSAN: Like who? What are you talking about?

MONA: One letter, one phone call. A bit low on your priority list, aren't I?

SUSAN: I don't believe this! Mona, it was really hectic! I'm sorry I didn't phone more often, I was just really caught up in things.

MONA: Make friends, did you?

SUSAN: Of course I did! (*Smiles.*) Come on, Mona, you're not giving me the whole suspicion-of-adultery routine.

MONA: Haven't you got an innocent face? I'm almost inclined to believe you, but I don't.

SUSAN (*half-angry/shocked*): I don't believe what I'm hearing! This is really taking me back to my youth. I used to give this whole number to my boyfriends. I used to do this whole offended and mistreated act.

I didn't know you were the jealous type.

MONA: It doesn't really matter what you've done. You've had fun, I've had fun.

SUSAN: You've actually gone to the extent of sleeping with someone just to spite me? I like your idea of a steady relationship. You're so childish. You think I've spent the entire tour fornicating my way down the credits in the programme? This is ridiculous!

Mona, is it always gonna be like this? I thought you understood what I meant by being 'zammies'!

MONA: You got me into this, you know. I was a peaceful, law-abiding heterosexual. True, I was co-habiting with a skunk, but at least he was male!

SUSAN: Maybe I should be flattered? Maybe I am. Mona, tell me, did you really fuck around?

MONA: 'Course I fucked around! What, did you expect me to wait in for your call? I went out, met someone, had a few drinks, back to their place. You know how it is. I enjoyed it, but it was nothing serious.

SUSAN: Oh yeah?

MONA: All right, then, you know that's a lie.

Yes, I am the jealous type. Just slightly. It's taken me a long time to realise but, yes, I am – and I always was – in love with you.

SUSAN: What!

MONA: You heard!

SUSAN: Girl, you're mad. Truly mad. So, you feel for me, do you?

MONA: No big deal.

   SUSAN *smiles. The two embrace.*

MONA: You'll never guess what!

SUSAN: What?

MONA: Michele's been having an affair with Michael for the last few months!

SUSAN: You lie!

MONA: She thinks they're in love!

SUSAN: Nah!

MONA: That's what she came to tell me last night. Where's me present?

SUSAN: Finish the story first.

MONA: Anyway . . .

Conversation continues and trails off, swamped by music. Lights fade.